Family Solutions
for Youth at Risk

Family Solutions
for Youth at Risk

Applications to
Juvenile Delinquency,
Truancy, and Behavior Problems

William H. Quinn, Ph.D.

Brunner-Routledge
Taylor & Francis Group

Published in 2004 by
Brunner-Routledge
270 Madison Avenue
New York, NY 10016
www.brunner-routledge.com

Published in Great Britain by
Brunner-Routledge
27 Church Road
Hove
East Sussex BN3 2FA
www.brunner-routledge.co.uk

Brunner-Routledge is an imprint of the Taylor & Francis Group.
Printed in the United States of America on acid-free paper.

Cover Design: Elise Weinger
Cover Image: © Getty Images

10 9 8 7 6 5 4 3 2 1

Library of Congress Cataloging-in-Publication Data

Quinn, William H.
Family solutions for youth at risk: applications to juvenile delinquency, truancy, and behavior problems/William H. Quinn.
    p. ; cm.
Includes bibliographical references and index.
ISBN 1–58391–039–5 (hardback: alk. paper)
1. Juvenile delinquents—Mental health services. 2. Community mental health services for teenagers. 3. Family psychotherapy. 4. Juvenile delinquents—Family relationships.
[DNLM: 1. Adolescent Health Services. 2. Community Mental Health Services. 3. Group Processes. 4. Professional-Family Relations. WA 330 Q7f 2004] I. Title.

RJ506.J88Q56 2004
616.89'156—dc22   2004006591

I would like to dedicate this book to my mother, Mary Elizabeth Walrath Quinn (1918–1990), who courageously responded to the death of her beloved husband at the age of 47, Leo Rebert Quinn, Jr. (1915–1962) and, at age 45, with three children to guide and support without a partner, demonstrated remarkable resolve to provide for, sacrifice for, encourage, defend, and patiently tolerate the resentment and misdeeds of her middle child, and rise above her illnesses and grief to exude love and affection beyond all else. I wish all youth who become separated from a parent in the growing up years could have the stability that I had with the reliable presence of a parent. I admire those youth who, despite long odds of reaching success or happiness as a result of the separation from a loving or unloving parent not of their own choosing, draw on their courage and quietly persevere without sufficient adult affirmation and guidance to achieve some measure of contentment.

Contents

Preface

Once a man driving in the scenic countryside became distracted with its beauty. Not paying close attention to the road, he missed seeing a dog rambling across the road until the very last second, and he had to swerve to avoid hitting the dog. He could not regain control of his vehicle in time to hold it on the highway, and settled in a ditch along the side of the road. Not being able to dislodge himself from the ditch, he looked around him and saw only a farmhouse about a quarter of a mile away. The driver walked to the farmer's house and knocked on the front door. The farmer's wife came to the door, and the driver explained his predicament. The farmer's wife said she would tell her husband, who was out behind the house, and told the driver that her husband would come down the road and help him. The driver thanked the woman and returned to his vehicle. Shortly thereafter, the driver noticed a farmer walking a mule down the shoulder of the highway toward him. The farmer walked his mule to the vehicle and tied the animal to the front bumper. The farmer and the driver walked to the rear of the vehicle to prepare to push. The farmer barked out to his mule, "OK, Nellie, pull!" The mule did not move. The farmer yelled again, "OK, Bessie, pull!" The mule remained motionless. Again, the farmer called, "OK, Buddy, pull!" The mule did not move an inch. Finally, the farmer yelled out, "Come on Buster, pull!" This time the mule jerked forward, the rope became taut, and the vehicle began to rock. Slowly, with the help of the farmer and driver pushing from the rear, the vehicle's tires became dislodged and the mule and the two men were able to get the vehicle up onto the shoulder of the road. The driver thanked the farmer; then the puzzled driver said, "But before I go, I must ask you a question. . . . Why do you call your mule by different names?" The farmer said, "Well, my mule is blind, and if he thought he was the only one pulling, he wouldn't even try!"

I have told this story many times to professionals, parents, and college students. It relates very well to the predicament that human service workers encounter in helping families. The challenge is formidable and the tasks are many, but resources to help families change are often limited. The story also relates well to parents who feel that societal forces neutralize their efforts to raise their children. The media counteracts parental attempts to be credible with their children. Television often characterizes parents as self-centered, goofy, or carefree. Schools and parents can be antagonistic towards each other, allowing the children to escape from responsibility. American culture, including the corporate sector, prioritizes materialistic gain. Even youth can feel this isolation. They can feel that their parents are too busy keeping a job, making money, or enjoying their own lives to care about them.

As a result, human service professionals and parents, as well as teachers, sometimes feel that no one else is working alongside them to advance the well-being of a child or family. Many think the burden falls to them alone, and if they don't succeed, it is their own fault. As each struggles to make a child's life slightly better, resentment creeps in that others are not accepting responsibility or doing their part. The parent wants to say to the teacher or counselor, "You fix him and let me know when he is better and I will pick him up"; the teacher or counselor wants to say, "If you could face your problems and admit your limitations or mistakes, we could move on and work together." Buster needed to know that other mules were helping; then he could sense that the task at hand could be accomplished. Otherwise, over time, a parent, a child, a human service professional, may begin to feel discouraged or frustrated and may eventually give up.

Often little credence is given to the notion that each person is connected to many others across varied social contexts. A parent may look for help, and a professional may slide into a "rescuing" mode. To use the story of the blind mule as an analogy, the man with the stuck automobile represents the youth, the mule represents the interventionist, and the farmer represents the administrator trying to pretend that one mule is enough if he (the farmer or the horse) believes in the fantasy that other mules are doing their part. Too often the mule has no help, and the "cargo" (a troubled or misguided youth, or a disorganized family under stress) being pulled is too "heavy" (too many problems) to get unstuck.

One blind spot of interventionists is the preoccupation with defining themselves as the agents of change. Just as the only force exerted to pull the vehicle from the ditch is isolated in Bessie, Nellie, Buddy, *or* Buster, but not all, so too do interventionists routinely define their role as one that blankets the needs of troubled individuals or families. This text is guided by the premise that professionals in human service delivery, such as child advocates, therapists, social workers, case managers, and administrators, need to shed the notion that their role is the most vital or essential to problem resolutions and instead explore collaborative relationships with youth and families in which the natural support systems and social environments contribute to problem resolution. This text tells the story of a multiple family group experience that is utilized to draw out resources (attitudes, beliefs, behaviors, and affect) of individuals and families that can be shared among participants.

The human service delivery system is steeped in traditions such as individual counseling or case management that fall short in reaching the social fabric in our culture that tears at the developmental processes of youth. Agency policy reimbursement requirements often stipulate either in written form or general unwritten agreement an adherence to individual sessions with youth. Decision-makers postulate this model because they, too, are immersed in traditions of training that conform to treatment units that circumscribe the individual client. The client, the youth advocate, the administrator, are all bound together with notions that keep the vehicle (youth) stuck. In this book, a case is made for the expansion of contextual factors in the lives of youth. *In particular, the central thesis is that the inclusion of the family is essential in intervention with at-risk youth, and that families participating in intervention with other families provide affirmation and the impetus for changing behavior and strengthening family relationships.*

This approach of family inclusion *illuminates the darkness that remains from the application of an individual lens to intervention.* The major tenet of this text is to specify the limitations of the individualistic model of human service delivery and to advance the notion that a relational and community lens for intervention is needed. What is offered in this book is a multiple family group approach that utilizes a wide range of shared experiences across families. Collectively, families interacting as a group create possibilities for resolving problematic behaviors and attitudes of youth.

The first chapter proposes that new ideas are needed to address serious and chronic problems of youth development. Youth crime and school statistics continue to indicate high rates of juvenile offenses and school failure that give rise to anxiety and in some cases fear and unemployment prospects in virtually every community. Attempts at school reform have not generated a higher school success rate or safer schools because they typically fail to include a consideration of legitimate family–school partnerships that require or actively foster parent involvement. As parents are often left out of the equation of equal partnerships with schools, so, too, have they been left out of intervention considerations when children have problems in school. A case is made for prevention and early intervention that requires parental involvement.

In chapter 2 a relational, family, and community perspective is taken to illuminate in an expanded way the necessity of social context in understanding and intervening with juvenile offenders, truant youth, and those with behavior problems. The individual model of youth intervention simply has not generated the results that justify the continued range of efforts constructed and implemented. The spotlight needs to be directed with higher intensity towards a broader context, including family and community. For instance, what are the outcomes of individual child counseling within schools or mental health environments that justify their continuation at current levels? Does a school counselor who provides encouragement and emotional support, such as a focus on self-esteem, generate change in a youth when that youth returns to a family environment that includes neglect, overreliance on punitive methods of parenting, alcohol abuse, domestic violence, chronic marital conflict, and the like? Families in particular need are those who often do not even request help. They may be exposed to a multitude of stressors such as economic deprivation or they may be unaware of the pervasiveness of their influence on their own children, such that their lives are not seen as intersections but rather as family members who travel in separate orbits. As such, a child problem is viewed as isolated and hence as requiring individual attention.

Reaching families who do not self-refer is emphasized in this book since human delivery systems have long been underorganized to reach these families who cannot afford services, feel hopeless, or possess distrust of such systems. Too often professionals fail to listen to the needs and experiences of their clientele. Professionals may try to solve a child's or family's problem instead of collaborating with them. My colleagues and I asked family members what their experiences in intervention were like. Chapter 2 delineates some of the descriptions, which we translated into themes of consumer/client experience. These themes can reveal to professionals the important elements of intervention that have sometimes been neglected.

In chapter 3 a family perspective is described in which we report what is known about the efficacy of family intervention. Arising from this, we are required to reexamine our assumptions about intervention approaches and how to reach families who do not self-refer, and more fully to explore the promise of multiple family group intervention as a unifying structure for intervention. The necessity of parental involvement is also discussed.

In chapter 4, the development of the Family Solutions Program (FSP) model is described as one framework for working with youth and families. This program has existed for over ten years and has demonstrated encouraging results, evaluated by rates of recidivism, family reports, and professional observations. The important role that parents play, the aims of the group program, and the assumptions underlying the model are also explained. The history, goals, and process of adjudication in the FSP process are described.

Chapter 5 details the program components of this multiple family group intervention model. The referral process is described in depth because it is so crucial to the success of the program. The emphasis in this chapter is on parent involvement and the collaboration of the FSP leaders, and juvenile courts and schools. Often parents do not understand why they should be expected or required to attend an intervention program since it was their child who was arrested, identified as truant, or viewed by the school as a behavior problem. Parents are confused and ambivalent about their role, and therefore deliberate interaction must occur between the court, the intervention program leaders (if different from the court) and the families. This is done during case review by the judge or officer in the court. For juvenile first offenders, the practice of a probation officer or a designated officer of the court is common. Additional contacts with the families are made prior to the inception of the program. The justification and nature of contacts are detailed in this chapter. The importance of the first session, major session topics and goals, and alternative session topics and goals is delineated to offer the reader an opportunity to translate the model into practice within his/her work environment. The Graduation phase is emphasized as a ritualistic experience that promotes a shift in attitude for families.

A fictional group of families will be presented to provide context and tell the story of a multiple family group experience. While the group is fictional, the events and group interactions that tell the story are "real," in that they actually occurred in 1 of over 250 FSP group cycles that have been completed. While Joan, Denise, Debra, Patti, Jackie, Mark, and Virginia (the parents), and Brittany, Robert, Sam, David, Brandon, Shay (the youth) are not their real names, the stories about them are real, and their attitudes, relationships with each other, and behaviors represent real events in the FSP.

Chapter 6 describes the central role that group process has in family intervention. Aims of group intervention are presented. Skills needed to facilitate group process are outlined. Scenarios of group processes as they have emerged in the FSP will be presented to provide tangible evidence that establishes the importance of group process.

New meanings of past events, perceived characteristics of youth and parents, and modifications of perceptions of oneself and one's future emerge in group process within and between families. Chapter 7 focuses on how group leaders create such an environment for these occurrences. The focus of this chapter is the delineation of ten group-leader skills offered to guide the reader to accomplish positive outcomes with families in groups.

Chapter 8 presents a profile of juvenile first-time offenders by reporting data on peer group affiliation, school status such as grades, suspensions, and absences, and family relationship data on communication, rituals, and family functioning. These data provide a rationale for inclusion of the family in intervention with youth and help to form the goals of the FSP (e.g., peer group changes, parent monitoring, school success, family cohesion, parent–child interaction, conflict resolution). Recidivism data are presented that demonstrate lower repeat-offense patterns for "graduates" of the FSP compared to noncompleters of the program, as well as a comparison group of juvenile first-time offenders placed on probation. These data are often crucial in conveying to juvenile court judges, youth service workers, school personnel such as teachers and administrators, and probation officers, as well as community level administrators, the value of a program of this kind. Qualitative data from families add context to these outcomes as they pertain to changes in families. Impressions from facilitators and group leaders are summarized to offer an additional vantage point from which to examine effectiveness and prevention.

Chapter 9 provides an account of the evolution of the FSP. The chapter addresses the challenges of institutional change that will permit, foster, and grow a multiple family group program in an agency, school, or juvenile court. The description outlines the institutional change from a program at its inception as an "experimental" program to one that currently serves as a "mainstream" intervention program within the juvenile court and schools. Challenges and obstacles of institutional change are identified. Recommendations for creating a similar family-based program in your own community are offered.

Finally, Chapter 10 examines the question: "What is the process of institutional change (e.g., juvenile court services, school intervention for truancy) necessary for change that incorporates the integration of family-based approaches?" This chapter explicates the identifiable facets of institutional change that occurred to take a family-based intervention, the Family Solutions Program, from an alternative "experimental" program viewed as a "trial for a few youth" to a program that became a mainstream and essential component of serving youth at risk. Growth vs. stagnation, evaluation, and an "early victory," were three such strategies to establish a family-based approach. It is the intention of this chapter to delineate the methodology utilized to inculcate a perspective that shifts the focus from serving youth to serving youth *and* their families to provide an optimal approach for altering the trajectory of youth development towards more functional and successful outcomes.

It is the hope of those involved in this program that you will establish a family-based program that warrants inclusion in the delivery of services for youth at risk in your community. Each community has unique features that require special attention. It is not expected that the FSP as offered here can be implemented hook, line, and sinker. In a way, each community does in fact have to "reinvent the wheel" so that those involved can be invested in it and so that the program is relevant for those who advocate for it or are the recipients of services. Yet this book can serve to provide guidelines in the development and implementation of a family-based model for youth who come to the attention of schools and communities.

The telling of the FSP story and the data provided may offer justification for the consideration of this model to those youth workers or community leaders who are skeptics and/or traditionalists and hold the view that such a program is too experimental, costly, or organizationally complex. I hope that the discussion of program effectiveness will provide assurance of its significant value and the cost-effectiveness outlined in the text will "speak the language" of policy-makers and administrative officers.

Acknowledgments

The Family Solutions Program (FSP) has benefited from the effort, compassion, and expertise of many people since its inception over a decade ago. FSP coordinators who have allowed for a successful collaboration with juvenile courts, schools, and agencies include Lauren Smith Reese, Shari Kaplan, Jennifer Dunn, and Alice Huff. These individuals have taken on many programming tasks, including FSP group leadership, supported the efforts of other FSP group leaders, provided information in response to inquiries from professionals around the country, and provided leadership to college student facilitators who participate in FSP sessions.

Research colleagues and staff who have helped identify relevant measures, gather data to evaluate the FSP, and prepare relevant substantive content for FSP sessions include Dr. David VanDyke, Dr. Marcia Michaels, James Barrow, Keith Bell, Sean Kurth, Dr. Richard Sutphen, Dr. Ed Risler, Dr. Jerry Gale, and Tricia Erwin. The FSP would not have been possible without the initial financial and professional support of Dr. Pete Colbensen and his colleagues at the Georgia Children and Youth Coordinating Council. The successful collaboration with the judicial system could not have occurred without the cooperation of juvenile court staff and probation officers, and particularly Judge James McDonald, Associate Judge Robin Shearer, Georgia Department of Juvenile Justice Administrator Kim Conkle, and Shari Fowler, who have been instrumental in this successful collaboration since the inception of the FSP in 1992. I am grateful to the probation officers and school teachers, counselors, and administrators who have been compassionate and courageous in reaching for something better for the children and youth they serve.

More than 200 graduate and undergraduate students enrolled at the University of Georgia have participated in each of over 250 cycles of the ten-week FSP since that time. Students have served as interns at the FSP, which has been their first professional experience in the field of family intervention. Some of these students have "found their calling" through this experience and pursued graduate education and professional training that incorporate a family perspective of human behavior problems. Their enthusiasm and commitment have contributed to the lives of many families and have bolstered the stability of Families 4 Change, Inc., the nonprofit organization that sponsors the FSP. The faculty and staff of the Department of Child and Family Development at the University of Georgia have encouraged these students to engage in service learning and provided opportunities for them to receive academic credit for their contributions to families and the FSP staff. Adult volunteers from churches, schools, and the business community have also taken part. The success of the FSP would not have been possible without all of these people.

Finally, I express my appreciation to all of the more than 1,200 families who have participated in the FSP. These families have accepted the responsibility not only to strengthen their own families, but to give much to other families who have traveled the same Family Solutions road.

CHAPTER 1

Family and Community Intervention for At-Risk Youth

Call it a clan, call it a network, call it a tribe, call it a family. Whatever you call it,
whoever you are, you need one.
—Jane Howard

Responding to an automobile accident, a woman passerby pulled her vehicle off the road and approached the driver, who was clearly hurt. As she approached, a man hurried past the woman and exclaimed, "Excuse me, I know first aid, let me through." The man with the knowledge of first aid made an attempt to help the hurt victim but was clearly overwhelmed by the situation. The injuries were beyond his training to treat. The woman passerby standing patiently noticed the man's confusion and said to him, "Let me know when you're ready to call for a doctor."

Why We Need Family Involvement

The family is an underutilized resource in human service delivery. Professionals are swayed by their academic training or orientation, as experts in helping, to initiate leadership, make judgments, and provide solutions. This text has a two-pronged approach. First, it presents a conceptualization and evidence that utilization of the family is an optimal approach to helping youth. Second, it delineates the benefits of bringing multiple families together to focus on their children to provide a context for locating alternative beliefs and solutions to behavior problems.

Often families are alienated in an attempt to mask difficulties they think they cannot risk acknowledging for one reason or another. They may be embarrassed by being associated with someone who is viewed as deviant. Or families may become disconnected from a larger community that is potentially a resource. For instance, schools may be seen by families as antagonistic to their needs. Resource elements such as neighborhood supports may be absent as more adults must work to support their families.

The prevailing attitude in our culture, unlike earlier times, is to avoid any perception of intrusion into the lives of other people. In previous generations, a child who spoke rudely to another adult in the neighborhood or crossed the line from mischief to malicious behavior was reprimanded by an adult in nearest proximity. Some say that when they were children, their parents would know their wrongful behavior before they returned home from the act. And the punishment might be more severe than what was doled out by the adult who observed the behavior. In school, for instance, unacceptable behavior was not only punished but was followed by more, sometimes more severe, punishment at home.

In the current culture, these same youth behaviors are met with a look-the-other-way attitude by adults for fear of being accused of meddling or being confronted by an unknown adult who might be aggressive in defense of his or her own child. School discipline might be met by a parental response in which the school is accused of mishandling the situation. As a result, children get suspended in a game of both sides against the middle in which the school and family blame each other, while the youth becomes a bystander not responsible for his or her own bad judgment or problem behavior.

The following excerpt is from a recent local newspaper's sports section (July 10, 2002) in which the local American Legion baseball team is in jeopardy of losing its playoff series. Part of the problem is that the team has a less-than-complete roster of players because some parents have encouraged their children to quit. The following quote is offered by the coach:

> We had a couple of kids quit because they couldn't accept their roles on this team. You know, some kids just aren't great baseball players, but they go home and have parents who tell them they're great and expect them to play every inning of every game and just generally think their kids are a lot better than they really are. I'll tell you, it's just a shame. These parents have to understand that this is real baseball. This isn't Dixie Youth anymore. You've got to come out and earn your spot on the field. But no, some of these parents want to coddle their kids and tell them they're great when they're not.

The article goes on to report that some of these players have opted to participate in optional football team workouts to prepare for the football season because they are not getting enough playing time on the baseball team. The coach believes that the football program, and the football coaches subtly, puts pressure on the youth to attend workouts if they expect to play. The baseball coach states: "I hope the football team has a great season, I honestly do. . . . I would never take a kid away from a football game to come to my baseball practice during football season. It's not right, and it's not fair to the kids."

So much for teaching loyalty and commitment to youth! The youth are left with the lasting impression that it is acceptable to withdraw from a commitment if it does not meet your expectations, regardless of the effect the withdrawal has on the group, in this case, the baseball team. One rule of a successful family group program is that the families must attend all the sessions, giving them a sense of accomplishment that they have completed something difficult or not of their own choosing.

A multiple family group model possesses a structure that permits and even encourages resource expansion as families learn about each other's lives and share common experiences and challenges in enhancing their children's development. Children learn from other adults besides their parents, which expands the child's perspective on the world and his or her place in it. This context provides opportunities for these other adults to validate the child in ways that parents cannot, either because their credibility is lacking with their own children or they view their own child with such disdain as a result of repeated conflicts or disapproval that their encouragement of their own child has been extinguished.

Some children have limited opportunities to learn from adults who might help them. Their social networks are limited, their housing may preclude their involvement with adults, extended family members may be geographically distant or influential in negative ways (data presented in the text demonstrate a relationship between juvenile crime and family members who have been involved in crime).

In a local high school, a parent meeting was organized by the school and parent leaders to discuss recent events of great concern to these adults. Recent reports of unsupervised parties on the weekends at students' homes, alcohol consumed by minors, drinking and driving worries, and suspected sexual behavior among some students generated parent resolve that led to the parent meeting at school. Parents broke up into small groups at the school to gather ideas about how to curb these risky behaviors of their children. A professional discussed the strategies that parents must incorporate to lessen the chances of these unsupervised parties from occurring in the future. A father made a remark in the discussion that sharpened the focus for the group He said: "We have a student directory at this school. I propose that as the directory for next year is prepared, the school has my permission to put an asterisk next to my daughter's name, and the asterisk means that anyone who suspects my daughter is engaging in unacceptable or risky behavior has my permission to intervene with my daughter and notify me or my wife. I will express my appreciation to you if that unfortunate event ever occurs." Immediately, many of the parents attending that meeting eagerly gave their permission for an asterisk to be placed in front of their child's name listed in the directory for the next school year. This tactic was beneficial for reasons far beyond the literal plan to place asterisks in the directory. First, the tactic was a vehicle to engage all parents and increase their commitment to help protect all students at the school. Second, the level of commitment reached at that meeting generated further actions to help reduce student risk. For instance, parents were more willing to call the homes of students where there were reported plans to have social gatherings, to make sure that parents would be in attendance. No longer could the children assume that if a friend's parents were out of town for the weekend they could have an unsupervised party.

A major change that has occurred in our culture has resulted in social isolation of families from one another and youth from parents (National Research Council, 1993). Working parents are precariously functioning without social support (Hewlett & West, 1998), and their social isolation reduces the likelihood of their readiness to resolve problems of their children in the early stages. Family group intervention provides a method to overcome this cultural malady.

More formal structures have developed to harness parental concern and shape this commitment into parental support systems. Parent education and multiple family group programs have formed not only to provide information to parents to help strengthen family units but to provide each family a support network to render encouragement and hope as well as to be available to facilitate the challenges of parenthood. The Family Solutions Program (FSP) is intended for just this purpose and will be the cornerstone of this text. This program is intended to provide early intervention to youth already identified as at risk because of a first juvenile offense, truancy at school, or exhibiting behavior problems in the presence of parents, teachers, or professionals.

Another model of engaging parents in a group program to foster support between families, one that targets younger children, is the Families and Schools Together (FAST) program (McDonald & Frey, 1999). The program is built upon referrals by elementary school teachers who have behavioral or developmental concerns about particular students. The family group format builds a "social capital," a network of relationship resources, to foster child well-being and healthy development. According to McDonald and Frey, the initial idea of social capital was to build a network of four or five parents for each parent of an at-risk child identified at school. The notion was that a youth who is stealing, fighting, or carrying a weapon at school would become known by another parent who would share this information with the parent group. This monitoring activity, it was believed, would increase the chances of this behavior being known by the school or the parent of the behavior-problem child. Action could then be taken to preserve the safety of all school children as well as to serve as a catalyst for engaging professional resources to aid the targeted child.

A family program that builds on this notion of interfamily support is the Strengthening Families program (Kumpfer & Tait, 2000). In each session parents and children meet together for social time, and then parents and children break into separate groups. Parents learn about child development, effective discipline and communication, and drug and alcohol threats. The children are identified as high risk and engage in sessions to learn social skills and peer resistance skills. Parents and children then have time together to provide more family cohesion and apply their learning in an interactional context. In both of these programs for high-risk elementary-age youth, there is a sensitivity to the precarious nature of parenting circumstances that compromise the well-being of children and a commitment to utilizing multiple family groups to overcome the isolated predicaments of many parents.

In a book called *Puppies for Sale,* Dan Clark tells the story of John MacMaster. As a star basketball player, John was All-Conference and All-State for three years in high school. In his final season he was Most Valuable Player of the league. John's mother never missed a game—home or away—regardless of the travel distance or bad weather. This despite the fact that his mother was blind! She was always in the bleachers cheering on her son. The author asks, "What's the message in this story?" The answer: Although John's mother could not see her son, John could see her! This is the way it is for children—they are comforted by the presence of something stable in their lives, and often the source of that stability is parents.

Parents must be in the lives of their children, whether they are directly influencing their behavior or simply present to observe, cheer on, or be available. The simple presence of parents conveys to the children that they are important and cared for and that expectations for their behavior are operating in the present. In the multiple family group program, this is stated by the group leader on the very first night to parents something like this:

> You might not believe this, parents, but your children are glad, or will be glad in time, that you are here. They won't tell you because at their age they are trying to prove their independence to you and to themselves. They don't want to appear as if they need you—it wouldn't be cool to their friends and it wouldn't help them get more freedom. But believe me, one of the best things that will come out of this program is that your children will believe you care about them simply by the mere fact of your being here, sacrificing your time for them, making them your priority; and if you enjoy the time with them, they will be convinced that they have value to you.

The cost of employing professionals in the way proposed in this text might well be counterbalanced by the delegation of resocialization functions away from the probation officer to families and groups of families, or a *community of families.* In our current social services, families, or communities of families, are often not sufficiently utilized. Regarding juvenile delinquency, as Geismar and Wood (1986) stated, the family is unquestionably the most underutilized resource in the corrections field, despite the fact that it has the greatest involvement in the well-being of its young: "The predominant service pattern of, at best, leaving the initiative for involvement up to the parents, or, at worst, keeping the family entirely isolated from treatment, has done little to encourage family participation or to harness and mobilize its potential for re-socialization of the offender" (p. 215). Despite the fact that this was stated over 15 years ago, most human service providers would be hard-pressed to argue a contrary position that much has changed. Although there have been, in this past decade, a few initiatives to address this problem, very little has been accomplished overall in most communities to harness the involvement of parents and families to address the problems of at-risk youth.

My collaborators and I have found in working with families that parents often display an ambivalence to participating and accepting the offer to get more involved in the lives of their children. Parents readily accept offers to help their children access resources. Some might want professionals to connect their children to summer camps, after-school programs, athletic teams, or mentors. These offers include Big Brother/Big Sister programs, college athletes as role models, adult volunteers who want to be mentors, tutorial services, consulting with teachers, and locating after–school activities. Unfortunately, if parents are involved, most of these occur more often with young children than with adolescents. Some parents do not view their role as an instrument of any one of these roles or purposes—counselor, mentor, tutor, or participant in after-school activities. How many parents initiate interaction with their children in the context of active pursuits such as school functions, sports, or artistic expression? Specifically, how many enjoy their children as coparticipants on the tennis court, in the community theater or school function, or in the simple parallel activity of silent reading at home? This, or course, requires energy, time, and priority-making. As such, parents must be expected to examine their attitudes and behaviors and expand their competencies and openness to play or involvement in the same way youth are expected to increase their life skills.

The Need for Community

A well-known philosopher and educator who was a colleague of mine, Ernst von Glasersfeld, told me once about a time in his life as a young man during World War II when he felt compelled to flee his homeland for political reasons. He fled to a city in another country, resulting in separation from his family. Over time he met a few others in this city who were in similar circumstances and who shared interests in philosophy, government, and world affairs. This small group of individuals organized themselves into a study group, read literature together, and discussed it in a social atmosphere at cafes or homes. What he realized later but not at the time was the extent to which these newfound friends served as a support system for him at a time that was difficult for him. He said that in a way, this group of "strangers" was what might be considered today as odd, and that persons in similar circumstances estranged from their families and homeland might seek counseling or psychotherapy. But psychotherapy as a resource did not exist then; if it had, it surely would not have been a resource for him as a person with little money or health benefits. He wondered aloud to me about the pervasive nature of counseling services in society currently. "Could it be," he asked, "that the common practice of psychotherapy today has artificially replaced the community in a world in which social ties are weakened and fragmented? Is it now one of the few places where our loneliness and confusion get recognized?"

Therapy itself has tended to fence off the community and its institutions (Doherty, 1995). Sometimes it has erroneously done so to repel the toxins of the culture. Therapy was often conducted under the guise of freeing the individual from family pathology. As the world of psychotherapy has pursued this track, there has been virtually complete silence on the issue of clients' responsibilities for and obligations to their communities (Doherty, 1995, 2000). In an ironic twist—but maybe with some willfulness—the more the community deteriorates, the more business the therapist has generated.

A few years ago, I read a news report of the town of "new Katonah," New York. Katonah was celebrating its 100th year of its move with a parade, art show, and tour. The town was known as the "town that wouldn't drown" because it actually moved a half mile from its original site after the city of New York condemned the land in "old Katonah" and planned to dam the river to create a reservoir for drinking water. Many of the townspeople decided the town should leave with them so they could remain together. They helped each other literally move their homes a half-mile, dragging them with wooden beams greased with laundry soap and tied to a capstan hundreds of feet away. Horses turned the capstan, winding the rope. While each home owner received a stipend from the city for his or her house, there was an unspoken agreement among the people that if an owner wanted to buy back the house, nobody would bid against that person. Said one current resident serving as historian, "these were people who fairly early on decided that they could and would control their lives." The 19th-century inhabitants spent seven years dragging their town onto new foundations. The land would change, but the community could not be extinguished.

In multiple family group intervention, the attempt is made to acknowledge the private world of the individual, which may include suffering, alienation, and oppression, while simultaneously making an effort to help repair the fragmentation in the individual's own community. Concurrently, each participant is viewed as a resource. A weakened sense of community is a product of both the culture's power to exert influence in the realms of government and market politics, in which achievements and rewards are seen as individual accomplishments, and the individual's effort to secure a "fair share" of these rewards.

Rates of depression, for instance, in the last 50 years have grown increasingly troublesome as the world becomes more urbanized and fragmented. It is likely that this is more a product of cultural change than evolutionary changes in biology. Everything is happening faster and people are cut off from the human connections that ground them in their own personhood. Many workers feel that they are expected to do more in less time, they have fewer coworkers to form a team to complete the expected tasks, and the incessant barrage of messages from computers and television reduces stimuli to sound bites. Relationships become reduced to fleeting moments of subtle connection.

The other side of the coin is when the individual, as client, is encouraged to explore methods of becoming integrated in the social web of the culture to discover fulfillment in altruistic experiences. This aim has not been privileged in the world of psychotherapy (Hillman & Ventura, 1992). This is elaborated upon in Hillman and Ventura's treatise, *One Hundred Years of Psychotherapy and the World is Getting Worse*, in which the current culture prioritizes individualistic experience such as materialism, personal wealth, self-esteem, and personal fulfillment. These priorities give minimal credence to the value of community because the goals for success are grounded in personal prosperity and contentment. What gets lost in this cultural bias is each human being's contributions to the well-being of other persons, which generate purpose and a sense of value.

In the FSP described in this book, an emphasis on volunteerism is a staple of the youth experience. The purpose is to help youth overcome their own self-perception that they have little value to others or to their community; instead, they view themselves as a "drain" on their family, school, and community, without a sense of the potential contribution they can make to the well-being of others. The absence of commitment and connection to their communities can be evidenced by their retreat into confined places in their homes where they have televisions, stereos, and video games, and where *time* becomes not an instrument of human striving and relatedness but a burden and an impediment to joy and pleasure. To youth, "having time on your hands" means the threat of boredom and an impending demand to acknowledge aloneness—warts and all. Youth view time as the absence of pleasure. The result is insecurity and self-doubt. As my own grandmother would remark, "idle hands are the devil's workshop."

The prevalence of single-parent families shrinks the sense of community for many families. A single parent may have less opportunity to consult with another adult about decisions pertaining to a child. Establishing a balance between structure and freedom for a child may become hazy without a partner to consult. Parents in marriages in conflict may have little capacity to discuss and hence clarify their expectations for their children or establish a consistent pattern of parenting that prioritizes clearly for children the values and expectations of one another. A parent can have work demands that reduce time spent with a child. This makes the management of daily tasks formidable, and to fit in "quality" time—the notion that conversation and shared play or leisure activities are healthy and necessary—becomes a challenge. The proportion of children living in two-parent homes declined from 85% to 68% from 1970 to 1997, according to the 1999 National Report of Juvenile Offenders and Victims (Snyder Sickmund, 1999). Never-married parents are becoming more common, with a five-fold increase from 1970 to 1997. Only 35% of African-American children live in two-parent homes. Single parents may have difficulty keeping their stress from contaminating their parenting practices (Sheeran, Marvin, & Pianta, 1997). Locating adult support can be a challenge. While the children have schoolmates and teammates, parents may be isolated and withdrawn from the social arena due to a sense of futility or worthlessness, or the stress of managing life.

A "community of families" can be an antidote to this personal stress and sense of futility. In the multiple family group model there are two ways to consider the concept of "community." One is the way each group member interacts with the culture. Methods can be developed to encourage greater interaction between the group member and his or her social world. This can be done through exploring social network processes such as relationships with neighbors and friends and connections to institutions such as school, church, and civic organizations. Our assessment of youth, for instance, suggests that fewer of the youth who repeat-offend are involved in school and out-of-school clubs and organizations than those youth who do not reoffend. In our own research on over 1,000 juvenile first-time offenders, involvement in school activities influences even the likelihood that a family completes the FSP (VanDyke, 2000). Youth who are not involved in school activities have odds of dropping out of family intervention 2.7 times greater than those who do participate in school activities.

This failure to comply with intervention might be a proxy for their failure to complete other life tasks or responsibilities. They are more likely to have parents who have few family organization skills such as making scheduled appointments, being punctual, completing household tasks, and coordinating the family activities of their family members, including transportation and availability. Hence youth who are not embedded in a network of social relations may be the same youth who will not participate in intervention programs either. Program leaders and administrators who have a grasp of this may be in a better position to construct interventions that ensure participation in intervention programs. School and community involvement (athletics, clubs, church, and the like) helps youth establish connections to their own community that help them have a sense that they are part of their community rather than outside it.

If youth feel outside the community, they have less responsibility for its welfare. They may then develop a hostility to being excluded. Part of the group aim in a multiple family group intervention context is to encourage youth to greater interactions beyond their own family members who can engage them with congenial and supportive influences. In this way, a stronger sense of self and a brighter view of their future can emerge. At the final session of the FSP, youth and parents share their experiences of what the program has meant to them. One youth, wearing a white shirt and tie for graduation night, rose and walked to the front of the room. He looked at the group and with great sincerity remarked, "I want to thank all of you for being my friend in this program, and I hope I never see any of you again!" Of course, what he meant was not that he didn't want to be friends anymore, but that he expected a future without committing delinquent behavior.

Parents may also be found to be without significant social connections. They may have justifiable reasons, such as a heavy workload or parenting demands. They may be parenting several children without adult help, and they may have health problems. However, we also find that some possess feelings of isolation that they long to escape. It is common that at the completion of a multiple family group experience, many parents and youth feel a genuine sadness that relationships developed in the program will end. We have acknowledged this disappointment and longing for more support by instituting booster sessions and "reunions" for them to continue to have the opportunity to attend. These booster sessions can take the form of weekly or bimonthly parent support group meetings. And these may be the same parents who enter the program possessing hostility or disdain for being required to attend. Many times these same parents not only express their appreciation to other families and group leaders for their support and guidance but also apologize to the group members for their hostility at the beginning of the program. We also observe families exchanging phone numbers and making plans to meet in some other way. While these connections may be lasting or they may be fleeting, the desire that these families have for extended interactions beyond the termination of the multiple family group experience is evidence that these relationships fill a gap in their social networks and provide comfort and validation that they have not previously experienced.

If youth are included at this stage of work, it is important in planning and implementing any activities for youth that adult leadership and supervision are available at all times. This is crucial to counter the potential negative, or *iatrogenic*, effects of delinquent peer groups—*deviance training*—that can occur when youth are unsupervised for substantial periods of time (Dishion, McCord, & Ponlin 1999). When adult supervision or active leadership from responsible adults is absent, it may be best to not plan youth activities simultaneously with an ongoing parent support group. For instance, it might be inadvisable to plan a bowling night or putt-putt for youth who are all identified as behavior problems or juvenile offenders. Even the presence of an adult volunteer, college intern, or group leader may not be sufficient to offset the deviance training that these youth receive from each other during these social events or prolonged interactions. These youth might model unacceptable behavior for each other at these social events and begin to make plans for future involvement together that is unsupervised by adults and leads to shoplifting, stealing, criminal trespassing, and other delinquent acts. The challenge of buffering negative peer influences in intervention is discussed further in chapter 2.

Reunions can serve as a mechanism for reminding parents and youth of their obligations and commitments built during the FSP. Parents are often interested in seeing other adults with whom they have entrusted their concerns and struggles. They have invested in each others' lives in a manner that engenders warmth and interest. Hence a spirit of concern and caring is felt by parents that motivates continued effort in resolving the difficulties and conflicts they experience with their children. Furthermore, such support experienced through interaction provides them with motivation to protect the positive changes that have occurred, such as increased time together in play or conversation, and richer positive affect, such as humor, appropriate physical contact and affection, encouragement ("You should try it, it worked/was fun for us"), and acceptance. The group leader of the FSP routinely advises parents and youth at graduation that they should plan to reserve for family night the same time each week that they have previously carved out to attend FSP sessions. When graduating, the families are reminded by the group leader that by attending the program regularly, they have proven they can reserve time for their families. This time could be used to play games, make decisions such as family vacations, weekend planning, or school-related matters, or for sports and artistic activities.

We also invite family members to call if we can be of help to them at any time. The sadness that some family members have at program completion is to some extent natural when friendships develop. But for some, the ending of the group experience suggests a return to a more isolated life experience, which brings on a feeling of loss. The other dimension to promoting a community sense of belonging is to help group members (both parents and youth) accept a legitimate and reasonable share of obligation to the personal well-being of others and to initiate more social connections in their natural world. For example, for the youth a group requirement in the program, described in this book, is that they must participate in a community volunteer activity. These have taken the form of visits to senior centers or nursing homes, where they play bingo with older persons and bring prizes for the winners, upgrading a primary school playground, a cleanup of an area of a city or town park, and preparing meals at a local homeless shelter. Often the families themselves are encouraged to select the volunteer activity so that they can "own" the activity and have a greater investment in the quality of its contribution. In a recent FSP, the family group built, with the permission of the park service, a bridge over a small creek at a local park.

Youth can be asked to write a letter of apology to, for example, a merchant whose property was vandalized (this must be done carefully so as not to be used as evidence of guilt), or to a parent who was humiliated or saddened by a child's offending behavior. This activity can allow a closure around the mistake to occur so that the youth has taken responsibility for breaking a community and legal sanction, but can experience the satisfaction that can be derived from now being deemed as acceptable to others.

Another way of encouraging a community identity in the group is to encourage group members to help each other solve transportation problems in attending an intervention program. The first reaction for most professionals is that it is incumbent upon them to provide transportation or locate a transportation source for their clients. Instead, it is more beneficial to encourage the families who meet together to help each other solve this dilemma. The leader can ask the group: "Is there anyone who lives near the Johnson family who could pick them up on their way here each week?" or, "Is there anyone that would be willing to be contacted by the Staples family at the last minute if their car doesn't start?" In this way, the message to the families is: "You are expected to help each other and contribute to making this experience a successful or satisfying one for each other."

Throughout group work, participants are encouraged to provide suggestions to other members and are assigned to small groups to help each other do problem-solving. An example of this interfamily collaboration is the Family Pledge, an activity in which each family during parent–youth contracting must negotiate a resolution to a problem and commit to changing behavior by signing a document denoting such commitment.

A second family can be paired with the first so that the family of focus can benefit from the input of another family in negotiation and contracting. In addition, the obligation to commit to the pledge grows stronger as each family is aware that the family they are paired with (as well as the entire group of families) is aware of their pledge. This "public" knowledge makes their obligation to succeed greater as the pressure of "quitting or giving up" on the pledge expands. This pressure on a family can be utilized to "push beyond" the impediments to meeting their pledge to each other.

In a multiple family group model, the members experience a "community" that provides an opportunity to secure a support system but also one in which the opportunity exists to contribute to the well-being of others. The group experience widens their "horizon of significance" (Taylor, 1990). Taylor states, "only if I exist in a world in which history, or the demands of nature, or the needs of my fellow human beings, or the duties of citizenship, or the call of God, or something else of this order matters crucially, can I define an identity of myself that is not trivial" (pp. 40–41). It may be that at least some group members, parents and youth alike, struggle with a sense of their own triviality. And only when they have searched for and accepted opportunities to "tie their wagon to something important" do they become more accepting of themselves. It is then that they sense a purpose in their aliveness and a significance to their lives. The group experience provides the opportunity to translate one's sense of isolation and vague sense of purpose to an interactional experience with others who strive for similar changes.

During graduation night in the multiple family group program, a time is offered for members to share their group experience with others. Recently, one male youth stood up and stated with great conviction, "thanks for letting me be part of the group and giving me a chance to contribute something." This particular youth had an appealing sense of humor that was enjoyed by the entire group, as well as a flair for leadership among his peers. He could be relied upon by the group leader to rally his peers to complete a group activity such as a role play or the "Ideal Parent" activity. To some extent, this striving beyond triviality for youth is a developmental demand for all. But those who have little success in school, experience a high level of criticality from parents, or experience daily life that is full of boredom or neglect become desperate for a sense of significance. Too often, they find a pseudo-significance in gangs, in brazenly engaging in behaviors that would impress their peers, or in desperately searching for "someone to love" them. This culminates in unhealthy outcomes that obstruct a life path leading to success, such as teen pregnancy, incarceration, or dropping out of school.

The View of Youth, Families, and Leaders in the Family Solutions Program

A multitude of approaches have been used to address problems of youth crime, drug abuse, and delinquency. Recently, punitive and correctional measures have led to increases in incarceration. Alternative schools, youth detention centers, and in some cases boot camps have become popular. Part of this momentum is due to the inability of youth services administrators and staff or school personnel to locate and offer intervention approaches that mean anything to community leaders and politicians. There is a dearth of programs that have evidence that will sway these leaders and administrators to consider intervention programs in some cases rather than placements that in theory are worthy because they protect the public. Placements in confined settings with constant supervision (e.g., alternative schools, detention centers) are partly the consequence of demonstrating few alternatives that are effective or offer evidence of good outcomes that deter future juvenile crime, drug use, or social disturbances in school.

Individual psychotherapy has been attempted without great results. Part of the problem is that too often a universal or generally accepted approach is thought to have potential for some newly devised theoretical conceptualization in vogue. Another part is because of ongoing tension between punitive strategies and rehabilitative models. When a poor outcome occurs, such as a second crime, subsequent to one of these categories of rehabilitative intervention, sweeping generalizations are made and a conclusion is drawn that such a model is not worthy of continued use.

Too much time, energy, and bias are devoted to "the magic pill" or the "one true light," the intervention that works for all youth. While there are those who suggest that nothing works—incarceration, probation, individual psychotherapy, group psychotherapy, behavior modification (Martinson, 1974; Kassenbaum, Ward, & Wilner, 1972)—others propose that everything works, but only for certain youngsters (Goldstein, Sprafkin, Gershaw, & Klein, 1980).

A current impetus appears to be one of focusing on selective treatments for specific problems. Preliminary data suggest that there are characteristics that provide indications of which parents may be amenable to which interventions. Yet two problems remain that currently make these matches unrealistic as they pertain to youth offenders. First, traditional youth intervention facilities and juvenile courts do not have the expertise or staff to determine these matches even if they existed. Individual assessments are too costly and have too little support for their utility to justify their expenditure. Second, personality, temperament, early learning, social context, and developmental interruptions offer very complex challenges to determining with confidence matching arrangements between youth and intervention. Goldstein et al. (1980) stated that "the task, therefore, is to develop and continuously refine an array of treatment and training programs to engage in research that enables us to make even better matches of practitioners, youngsters, and treatment approaches." In the past two decades since very little progress has been made on that front.

This volume is a description of an intervention model that has successfully integrated at-risk, acting-out youth with family and community resources. This is not a model that is currently widely applied. Therefore *this book offers both a theoretical foundation and documented evidence of the model's value and hence its potential as a more responsible and cost-effective approach to reaching at-risk youth.* While further elaboration of the specific target population for treatment and the conceptual approach and intervention skills of professionals that are needed is interspersed throughout the text, a brief overview is provided here.

The attempt to integrate youth, families, practitioners, community partners, and treatment is approached in this text in the following way.

Youth

This volume describes a definitive youth population, *youth first offenders.* This is an important declaration, because too often interventions are aimed at youth in general without regard to age, problem behavior, or developmental trajectory. It is the view expressed in this book that youth who are first offenders are often at a critical juncture of their developmental trajectory. They may be "adolescent-limited" or "life course persistent" antisocial youth (Moffitt, 1994). An adolescent-limited youth might be one of whom the first offense is the one and only incident of offending behavior. In this circumstance a youth is affected by the offense and possesses personal and family characteristics that preclude an additional offense. For instance, in one multiple family group setting that included youth who were referred to the program for shoplifting behavior, a representative of a national chain of department stores stated to the families that he could tell which children would likely shoplift again based on the result of a telephone call to the family. He said if one of the following conditions existed, it probably suggested that the youth would shoplift in the future: (1) he could not find the parent at home after several attempts; (2) the parent would not return his phone call even after the purpose of the call was explained; or (3) the parent answered the phone and either defensively or aggressively responded, such as "my kid wouldn't do that," "you must have the wrong kid," "what proof do you have?" or "that's not my problem." If the response of the parent was more like "I will be right in to see you," "I am very disappointed in him if this is true," or "what do I need to do?" the indication of parental acceptance of shared responsibility for the act or for implementing an appropriate consequence was more likely to resolve the shoplifting incident in a manner that would prevent a further incident.

> One referral to the FSP was a 14-year-old girl, Veronica, who had just moved from Mississippi to Georgia after her mother remarried. Veronica was referred because she had set a fire in her home. Veronica poured gasoline on the kitchen floor while her mother was taking a nap. She went one step further in her destructive strategy by secretly locking her mother in her room and then went back to the kitchen and lit the match. Fire-setting is considered a major offense, and the referral to the FSP instead of a youth home or incarcerated setting required courage on the part of the caseworker. Veronica secretly wanted to be sent back to Mississippi because she missed her friends and did not like her mother's new husband. She admitted she would rather live with her cruel biological father and be with her friends than feel alone and live with her stepfather, who "took my mother away from me." The FSP was a real antidote for Veronica because she was accompanied by her mother and stepfather to the sessions and they had an opportunity to resolve the problems that derive from triangular relationships in which competition, jealousy, and resentment stir up the interactional life of the threesome. While Veronica and her family used the sessions to resolve interpersonal conflict and confirm her mother's concern and affection for her, she was able to begin making friends in her new surroundings, and the pull toward her peers back in Mississippi waned. While the fire-setting was a dangerous and desperate act from a lonely and resentful young girl, the act was socially based and required an intervention that allowed for Veronica's emotional pain and lack of social stability and trust to be resolved. The FSP provided a foundation for family healing. To place Veronica in an incarcerated setting would have separated her more from her mother and fostered increased resentment and loneliness. At FSP graduation Veronica stood before the group and thanked the group for helping her and her family and expressed bewilderment at how she could have done such a crazy thing as starting a fire. It is very unlikely that Veronica will commit a second offense now that she has friends and easy access to her mother and has expressed her remorse for trying to hurt the one she loves the most.

A life-course-persistent youth is one whom the first offense may serve as a precursor of future offenses, often of a more serious nature. The current research literature has not as yet provided data that would confidently substantiate effective results in which differential interventions can be applied to these two groups. What is known from the statistical reports on juvenile crime is that a first offense in at least half the first-offender cases leads to a subsequent offense. Hence the question is: Why are there not more interventions for this group of youth to deter this pattern? In our way of thinking, a first offense is an expression of a problem of a youth and family—an expression that society claims is unacceptable behavior. Youth, in effect, are caught in the net cast out by the legal system to protect communities and citizens from harm. A secondary aim of this net is to identify youth who are in need of help so that intervention can provide opportunities to these youth for resolution of family conflict and despair in a way that fosters acceptable behavior and future success. Hence the multiple family group intervention model is intended to provide a means to advance more acceptable behavior that excludes juvenile crime and that would allow youth to achieve well-being and prepare for a successful life.

In this manner, the model described is a secondary prevention model. It is secondary in that it must be acknowledged that a youth has already exhibited a problem behavior that has come to the attention of a community, but that a pattern of illegal behavior has *not yet* been established. Hence the data presented on these youth, their families, and intervention outcomes are intended to be interpreted as they apply to *first*-offender youth and not those who have already established a "life-course-persistent" path that includes multiple offenses. Given that the family intervention model focuses on first-time juvenile offenders, there is a relevant and timely research opportunity to examine the effectiveness of this model, since curbing reoffenses is a major goal of any youth services or juvenile justice organization. *In an examination of ten years of data on the family intervention program, it is clear that a youth who completes a multiple family group intervention has a much greater chance of avoiding a reoffense than a youth who is assigned probation or a youth who fails to complete a multiple family intervention program* (Quinn & VanDyke, 2004). Chapter 8 delineates in greater detail the outcomes of the FSP.

It must be acknowledged, however, that it would be naive and risky to assume that first-offender youth have not committed previous offenses or exhibited problem behavior. Often the first-offender youth has simply had "bad luck" and finally been caught for behaviors that are an established pattern or where there were precursors to a pattern of offense, such as school failure, abuse, poor parental monitoring, negative peer group influences, and so on. One common juvenile court procedure is to place a youth on "informal adjustment," indicating that no charge will be filed in exchange for a promise of no further delinquent activity. This serves as a warning and not as an official offense, and therefore in these cases an official first offense is actually not the first incident of trouble identified by the court. It is hoped that the reader does not assume this model can be applied to youth who have an established court record of some length that includes multiple offenses. Such an application would be premature until such time as substantial evaluation of intervention for these youth has been established.

Data summarizing reports from several hundred juvenile first offenders and their parents pertaining to demographic, family, and community involvement are presented, including data related to school status, drug/alcohol status, family structure, family relationships, communication with parents, family functioning, school, community, and church involvement, and peer relationships and influences. In this way, we can establish *a priori* some of the vulnerabilities of the individual and group as a whole. Previous reports of these data have examined some of these variables, including intervention outcomes on recidivism (Quinn, Sutphen, Michaels, & Gale, 1994; Quinn, Bell, & Ward, 1997; Quinn, 1999; Quinn & VanDyke 2001; Quinn, VanDyke, & Kurth, 2002; and Quinn & VanDyke, 2004). The data presented here provide documentation of the effectiveness of a multiple family group intervention for reducing delinquency of first-offender youth.

A second aim of data gathering is to provide information about families to group leaders to help leaders plan group sessions that are most relevant to families. For instance, a juvenile offender group that includes referrals for fighting or assault can incorporate more conflict-resolution activities. A group in which referrals include truancy and school failure can include a sequence of sessions on school attendance, parental involvement, self-motivation, and the like. A group in which referrals are comprised primarily of juveniles between the ages of 9 and 12 can be designed differently from a program in which the referrals are primarily of youth between the ages of 13 and 16. This allows for developmental needs to be shared among the group and addressed in FSP sessions, and allows for interventions to be sculpted in accordance with level of success in their own "life work"— school as well as their family context. A younger-aged FSP group might invite a group leader to emphasize artistic modes of expression instead of relying on the verbal channel of communication. There might be more activities that require physical movement. While an older group of youth might benefit from these same activities, a leader might strengthen communication between parents and youth by relying more on verbal interaction and problem-solving exercises, as these youth desire to claim more independence and need to prepare for experiences with peers and adults (pals, teachers, girlfriends, boyfriends) that require negotiation and interdependence.

First-time youth offenders who are the target population of the FSP typically have not developed a delinquent identity. This makes it possible to incorporate interventions around family support, appropriate peer group development and change, a sense of hopefulness about life, and a dubious but yet still present belief in one's competence or value.

Families

In the multiple family group model described in this volume, no youth can participate in a multiple family group program without family involvement. This appears obvious on the surface when outlining and implementing a multiple family group intervention program. Yet we have experienced how tempting it is to include a youth who may want to participate even when the rest of the family refuses treatment. Often an interventionist will think, "well, surely we can let just one or two youth participate without their families—what would it hurt?" In addition, court staff such as probation officers will refer youth to the program despite the lack of parent interest or commitment. We are obligated to refuse these youth unless a parent or adult can attend who has an ongoing commitment to the identified youth. Actually, without a parent, the consequence to this scenario can potentially hurt a lot.

One negative outcome of including children in the program without their parents is that other youth with family participation may question their own commitment while youth without parents are in attendance. (Parent: "Why do I have to come if Bobby's parent isn't required to?') This presents an unnecessary challenge and hardship to the group leader, who must devote substantial time and attention to building group trust and cohesion. The group leader may also be responsible to the referral agency (e.g., court, school) for insuring attendance.

Furthermore, the richness of group discussion is narrowed when some parents or other adult family members refuse to attend. The possible solutions or alternative perspectives generated by potentially absent parents or family members are not available to the group. For instance, a stepmother of a female youth aged 15 in the program expressed her resentment one night when she told about her husband, who was away all week long each week driving an 18-wheeler tractor trailer while she was expected to monitor the child's whereabouts, making sure she made curfew, got her homework done, and was not in the company of inappropriate peers or adults. She said, "I am not even the biological mother of this girl, and I have to take all this responsibility for her all week while my husband is gone. And when he gets back on Friday night he just wants a cold 6-pack of beer in the refrigerator and expects to spoil his daughter all weekend because he feels guilty that he has been gone all week. I resent it." When the mother finished, another woman in the group spoke: "You know, your story sounds so familiar to me. I had a similar situation with my stepdaughter about a year ago. Could I get your phone number and call you this week, I would like to tell you what I did to improve the situation." This was music to the group leader's ears. This group dynamic is exactly what a multiple family group experience can generate. Families help each other gain a new perspective, a possible solution to a specific problem, and a feeling of support that improves a parent's attitude and can foster a more positive tone in parent–youth communication.

Finally, to include a youth without a family contradicts the theoretical assumptions underlying the approach. Significant and lasting change is more likely to be possible when the family environment is altered to make a more conducive growth-producing group of individuals who care and support each other. The theoretical assumptions underlying this model will be presented that strengthen this rationale for parent inclusion. Also, characteristics of juvenile first offenders and families will be presented in detail in chapter 7, which documents the clear justification for requiring parental involvement in intervention.

Practitioners

Over 1,200 youth have completed the multiple group intervention program in the community through the juvenile court. In over 250 completed cycles of the group, professionals—practitioners/therapists—have been people with specific programmatic functions and relevant academic training.

First and foremost, group leaders are family-trained professionals. Elements of this discipline that leaders are exposed to and that are incorporated into the program are: (1) systemic thinking; (2) a view of human behavior as context-based; (3) an orientation toward solutions; (4) a focus on strengths and resources; and (5) a belief in shared responsibility in human relationships and individual growth.

Important resources for a family-based interventionist include those that emphasize (1) group process (the "shared mind"—discussed in chapter 2); (2) interactional theory in which behavior is seen as embedded in human relationships and social circumstances; (3) a task-centered orientation that offers family members an opportunity to sense change in improved functioning throughout the group program; and (4) a conviction of the value and potential benefits of this intervention model. This conviction is seen in the enthusiasm for this work and enjoyment of human interaction with and between family members and across families. There must be an acceptance of each family's and family member's unique situation and circumstance as well as the potential strengths of each person. Some examples of each group member's strengths are sense of humor, courage, leadership, parenting skill, compassion, and life experience. As important as any college degree or credential, the professional group leader's enthusiasm for the work is crucial to family recruitment and participation.

Community Partners

Adult volunteers from the community can also be important participants in the intervention program. A range of tasks can be enacted by adult volunteers. They can reflect cultural sensitivities not represented in a group with various demographic characteristics. Volunteers can reflect cultural attitudes and ritual behaviors of participating families in the group. Examples of these tasks include the telling of life experiences such as overcoming poverty, feelings of not belonging to the dominant group in a community, and personal hardships that serve to validate the lives of group participants. They can also share experiences about different careers and family obligations of their own that can lift the spirits of parents in the group and give them parenting tips. A bridge, in a way—a therapeutic alliance—can develop between adult volunteers and family members.

College interns who are completing degree requirements can be utilized effectively in the program. This role is particularly beneficial to the group process if professional involvement is limited to one group leader. With as many as five to eight families in a group, interns can reach out to individual family members so that these group members feel connected. Interns can also be a point of contact for information between family members and the professional group leaders. Group leaders may not have access to this information because they have fewer opportunities to visit with these families before and after a session, yet a family may take aside an intern, someone they feel a special attachment to, and freely share an incident, concern, or situation in the family. This can be useful as a way of weaving a group discussion that can bring up this concern at the appropriate time or match the concern with a resource that another family can offer. Information shared by interns can be used to provide additional resources to families, such as tutorial services or family therapy, or to transfer community information such as employment possibilities or community resource phone numbers such as hotlines or referral networks.

Possibly the greatest contribution that college interns can provide is being an instrument that creates for the youth a vision of their future life. Youth begin to ask themselves: "Do I want to go to college?" "If so, what would I want to study?" "If not, what do I want to do when I am that person's age or older?" College interns tell stories of their own family experience as youth and what challenges they faced and how they overcame them, for instance: "What do you do when you are not getting along with your parent, or you disagree on curfew, dating, school behavior, doing chores, and the like?" College interns who describe these experiences usually have the attention of youth because of age similarity and the awareness that the early twenties are a life stage on the horizon for them. The consequence is that youth get assistance in resolving dilemmas with their own parents or life circumstances and their developmental issues such as physiological changes and subsequent psychological effects, peer relationships, and school struggles.

> Shay, a 15-year-old attending the FSP with her mother, complained about her mother's strict curfew rules. Shay's mother, Patti, explained to the group that Shay's curfew sounded strict because she had recently violated the old curfew, which was actually later. But of course Shay didn't mention this. Patti admitted to the group that she could not trust Shay right now because she had told Patti that she was at a girlfriend's house one night when she was actually at the house of her boyfriend who had held a party without any adult in attendance. Anne, a college intern, shared a similar story with the group: when she was 15, she told her mother that she was at a girlfriend's house when she was really in a car with friends driving around. The police pulled them over and found evidence of alcohol, and they were arrested. Anne said that while she was not drinking, she was taken along with the others to the police station, and her mother had to pick her up; she was ordered to juvenile court for a case review. Anne said that while she had learned her lesson at the time, she was not allowed to go out at all on weekends for one month and after that she had three months of restricted curfew. Anne said that was really hard because while she knew she would not lie to her mother again or go to places she knew her mother would not approve of, the trust between them had been violated and it took her a long time to prove herself again. She said that what affected her the most was that she missed some fun events at school, parties with her friends, and overnight trips because her mother could not trust her. Another mother shared with the group that she understood what Patti must have been feeling because she admitted that she had broken a promise with her own mother when she was a teenager and it took a long time for her mother to trust her again. The group leader then asked the group to consider whether they had experienced a similar situation to that experienced by Shay and Patti or Anne and her mother; the question was: How long does it take to trust someone again in the family when they break a promise? While some group members might have used a breakup with a boyfriend or spouse as their referent point pertaining to broken promises as a way to consider the question, others might have been thinking of their own teenage years or the struggle they had had with an older son or daughter.
>   This discussion was richly enhanced by a college intern who could share her own teenage struggle, which Shay and other youth could apply to their own circumstances. Shay had the chance to realize that she had made an error in judgment, that it was an error she suffered from or immediately overcame, and that it was a mistake not unlike one made by others of all generations. Anne's testimonial was an invitation to other group members to share their experiences related to curfew and violations of trust. In the end, the discussion helped Shay

personally absorb the predicament she found herself in and realize that a viola-
tion of trust has consequences but that with time and future promises kept, she
could improve her opportunities to get a later curfew in the future.

Community-Based Programs

Community-based programs to address youth problems have been in existence for some time. Two early studies in the late 1960s in California were
initiated combining incarceration with intense community supervision.
The results were largely the same—equivocal (Stark, 1967; Pond, 1968).
Methods of individual and family counseling, psychiatric consultation,
foster home assignments, and tutoring were included in these projects.
While no superior results were found for youth who participated in community-based programs versus incarceration, there was some evidence
that community-based programs were at least as effective as incarceration
(Harlow, Weber, & Wilkins, 1971). This was supported by Empey and
Lubeck (1971) in their comparison study of incarcerated versus community-based interventions.

There was a mushrooming of programs in the 1970s (Goldstein et al.
1989). Many of the evaluations of these community-based programs
yielded negative or indeterminate results (Rutter & Giller, 1983): "Though
the relevant literature is immense, most reviews have ended with essentially negative conclusions—no delinquent prevention strategies can be
definitely recommended" (Wright & Dixon, 1977, p. 267).

Family therapy approaches, behavior modification techniques, and the
impetus to move delinquency treatment from the institution to community-based programs have been with us for over two decades (Geismar &
Wood, 1986; Greenwood, 1996). Yet at the same time, little has been done
to counter the claims of Illich (1976), Lasch (1977), Platt (1977), and Roth-
man (1978) that the capacity of social agencies to be effective in helping
families has not been demonstrated. The conclusion was drawn by
Famiglie (1981) that: "professionals in their zeal to alleviate the glaring
needs of dependent groups such as juvenile offenders, have assumed, in the
name of the state, the role of parent and have instituted reforms and programs that have often been coercive and intrusive, and that have under-
mined the confidence and capability of families to solve their own
problems" (p. 4).

The primary assumption utilizing the model outlined in this volume is
that families can be and must be more influential in the resolution of
youth delinquency and that youth can benefit from family intervention
whether or not they possess the host of characteristics that lead to further
delinquency. Furthermore, as suggested by Geismar and Wood (1986), the

earlier intervention can be implemented, such as with young, early-delinquent, or status offenders, the more emphasis should be placed on inappropriate family interactions and changing behavior.

The explanation for most of the inconclusive evidence on at-risk, acting-out youth rests on two factors. First, delinquency intervention research suffers from methodological problems. Most studies have had inadequate samples in both size and randomness of selection, inadequate outcome measures, insufficient attention to threats on internal and external validity, a lack of appropriate control groups, and, typical of many studies, inattention to follow-up. Unfortunately, many efforts to address delinquency problems have dissipated because results were inconclusive, despite the fact that many apparently mixed outcomes may have been due to methodological problems.

The second factor that could explain inconclusive results of intervention is the specification and implementation of treatment. Clinicians and investigators fail to define clearly the interventions being used. They do not specify a clear intervention strategy, and no attempt is made to ensure the clear implementation of the intervention strategy. There has been insufficient documentation of strategies employed, as well as additional strategies that were used but which were not noted.

Two suggestions have been made to resolve these problematic facets. First, powerful treatments based on previous successes and sound theory must be considered. For example, "if a strong treatment is used and care is taken during the treatment to ensure that the treatment is actually being implemented as designed, then more positive effects may emerge" (Gottschalk et al. 1987, p. 283). It is vital that any intervention possess *intensity*. Intensity could refer to the number of interventions implemented to effect change or the potency of the interventions implemented. For instance, if a family group meeting is scheduled and implemented in which parents and youth are bored because the presentation is lethargic due to inappropriate content or lack of enthusiasm by the group leader, then the session is unlikely to impact the families to effect change. Or if the method of session delivery is untimely or inappropriate for the age group, the families may respond passively. For instance, if a family group session consists entirely of a two-hour discussion, youth will lose their focus and be unable to manage their restlessness. Sessions must include an active component in which families engage in activities such as role-plays, games, and practice exercises. These activities are not simply intended to make the time go faster for families, but induce a learning modality that allows families to learn something new about each other or to practice new behaviors that lead to problem resolution, family fun, and task accomplishment.

The second suggestion is that certain characteristics of a program's implementation must be carefully chosen. Feldman and colleagues (1983) delineate several necessary facets: (1) the treatment setting should be as similar as possible to the client's natural environment; (2) clients should be able to remain in their homes; (3) clients should receive maximum exposure to prosocial peers; (4) intervention programs should enable clients to take responsibility for their successes and failures; and (5) agencies that offer these programs should have stable financial support.

The family group program presented in this book attempts to incorporate these elements into its structure and content. First, a youth's natural world includes the family and peers and other adults in the community. Second, youth are not incarcerated or, in the vast majority of cases with the exception of identified abuse, not removed from the home. Thus the influence of the family on a juvenile offender remains ongoing despite the potential negative influences it generates. Third, youth are expected to examine their support systems and expand them when possible. In the FSP any adult who has responsibility and ongoing involvement with the juvenile offender or at-risk youth participating the program is encouraged to attend. Youth are guided to change peer relationships when necessary and encouraged to increase involvement with school-, church-, and community-sponsored activities. Fourth, families are expected to accept responsibility for change via assigned homework and parental involvement in and out of sessions, and to seek resources such as school support. Fifth, a family program cannot be managed on a shoestring. Skilled professionals must be compensated fairly, and the choice to hire the least expensive (least trained, least experienced) group leader needs to be avoided. A program session can break down rapidly when an inadequately skilled leader cannot respond effectively to an individual in the group or to the group process overall. The facility must be comfortable; light refreshments can be offered; purchase of materials for group activities is acceptable.

In one FSP session on the topic of effective discipline, a guest speaker, Betsy, came to speak with the families. Betsy was clearly prepared and looked forward to helping parents learn effective discipline strategies. She prefaced her talk to the families by stating: "Of course we know that spanking isn't effective as a discipline strategy." As Betsy proceeded to introduce some new ideas about discipline, the parents began stirring and looking away instead of at her. Some parents looked at each other with expressions of skepticism. One parent rolled her eyes and another frowned. After a couple more minutes, Betsy noticed the parents being agitated and not listening. When she asked if anyone had any questions before she went on, one parent responded: "I don't think spanking is bad at all. I got spanked when I was a kid and, looking back, it was the best thing my parents did." Another parent followed: "Absolutely, there's no getting through to kids unless they know you will spank if you have to." And a third parent said: "These days kids will make you think if you touch them they will call authorities and report you for child abuse. Well, let them, if they think the state will raise them better than me!" It was clear from these comments that the group overwhelmingly opposed the guest speaker's initial premise that spanking was wrong. Betsy knew that she had lost the group right away and had earned no credibility. Flustered, she turned to the FSP leader and said, "could we take a short break?" This was 10 minutes into the session! The group leader sensed the oppositional tone and consented, knowing that Betsy would have to gather herself and plan a different beginning to the discussion on discipline. During the break, while the parents got something to drink and used the restroom, Betsy and the group leader planned a different beginning. This time, Betsy went in and invited the parents to talk about spanking and their attitudes towards corporal punishment. When this occurred, the parents felt validated, even though Betsy understandably struggled due to her views opposing corporal punishment. Once the parents sensed that they were being heard, the discussion opened up. One parent remarked: "Well, spanking my child is certainly not my first option. It's the last. First, I tell them I love them. Second, I tell them I need for them to change their behavior and what they need to do differently. Then, last, I spank if they refuse."

While this last option remains a controversial one and a parental behavior that Betsy and many professionals oppose, the mother's spoken litany of options provided an avenue for discussion and an opportunity to build alternatives. The group leader said: "How many parents say to their children that they love them as often as they think they should?" And: "Tell me more about what you do to help guide their behavior so that it changes and you don't have to spank?" In other words, the group leader must look for opportunities to ask questions that emphasize certain ways of thinking that the group leader believes are congruent with effective parenting behaviors.

The group leader must steer the discussion in the direction of privileging methods that are alternatives to spanking and needs to search for examples from the group and his or her own life that document the effectiveness of these alternatives to spanking.

A skilled group leader is essential to multiple family group success. The influence of a skilled leader on a group begins with enthusiasm. A leader with a commitment to this approach to helping youth with behavior problems and their families contributes to a positive expectancy that with family participation, good things will happen for youth. A group leader carries this attitude throughout the sessions. A leader must also be skilled at managing conversations between family members and among families. It is important to hold the goal of any program activity or discussion firmly in mind so as to navigate the content of the discussion in such a way that increases the possibility of reaching the goal. For instance, the goal of the discussion on discipline and spanking described above was helpful for the leader to keep firmly in mind so that the leader could be guided to prevent parents from feeling alienated and the guest speaker was not embarrassed. A delineation of group leader skills will be further elaborated upon later in the book (see chapters 6 and 7).

CHAPTER 2

The Incomplete Response to Juvenile Crime

Relationships are to child development what location is to real estate.
—Comer, 1998

At-Risk Youth: Crime in Communities

The social science literature beckons for attention to the plight of at-risk youth, who may suffer abuse, neglect, mental health problems, and conduct-disorder behavior. Yet the costs alone to society are staggering and beg the question of how to intervene early enough in a child's development to foster a developmental trajectory that produces positive child outcomes. It has been reported that a high-risk youth who enters the judicial and/or mental health system costs society about $1.3 million (Cohen, 1998). The savings would be enormous if a far greater investment was made in children early in life to help them overcome the risk factors that increase the likelihood of contact with the judicial and mental health systems.

How much of the crime in the United States is caused by juveniles? And what efforts are being made to reduce crime? In the last 15 years the United States has witnessed a nationwide epidemic of juvenile violence (Corbitt, 2000). In 2002 the percentage of the nation's population of children and youth was 26% of the overall population and is expected to increase by 8% by the year 2015 (Godwin & Helms, 2002). While some reports suggest that the overall juvenile arrest rate has been slowing slightly over the last 6 years, a disturbing trend is the increase in violent crimes and young-aged offenders (Godwin & Helms, 2002). Even more striking is the growth of arrests, which is at a more rapid rate than the rate of percentage growth of

27

adolescents in the population overall (Snyder, Sickmund, & Poe-Yamagata, 1996), suggesting that as an age group youth are exhibiting more delinquent behaviors than in the past.

The past decade saw large growth in juvenile arrests for violence, weapons, drugs, and curfew violations. Between 1989 and 1998, courts with juvenile jurisdiction processed 44% more cases. The number of individual offense cases increased by 88% in this decade, property offense cases increased by 11%, drug law violation cases increased by 148%, and public-order offense cases increased by 73% (Puzzanchera, Stanl, Finnegan, Snyder, Poole, & Tierney, 2002). In this same decade, juvenile courts handled 128% more simple assault cases, 100% more disorderly conduct cases, 102% more obstruction of justice cases, 61% more weapons offense cases, 36% more aggravated assault cases, and 29% more robbery cases. Rates of delinquency cases rose in this decade from 48.3 cases per 1,000 juveniles to 60.4 cases per 1,000 youth.

Caseloads for juvenile justice personnel have increased greatly in the last 40 years. Juvenile courts handled more than four times as many delinquency cases in 1999 as in 1960. In 1960 there were about 400,000 cases processed in the court, whereas in 1999 there were 1.7 million cases processed (Puzzanchera, Stanl, Finnegan, Snyder, Poole, & Tierney, 2002). In 1998, on any given day, juvenile courts handled roughly 4,800 delinquency cases; in 1960, approximately 1,100 cases were processed daily. Case rates for drug offenses more than doubled during this time, from 3.1 to 6.6 cases per 1,000 juveniles age 10 and up. Total delinquency case rates rose by 25% from 1989 to 1998. While some categories of delinquency charges have decreased, the trends overall are upward, and case rates of property and drug violations are substantially higher. Between 1989 and 1998, there were increases in all four major offense categories: person, property, drug law violations, and public order. Clearly the efforts made to reduce juvenile crime have not been sufficient. Moreover, many of the youth who are represented in these percentages are repeat offenders, suggesting that those efforts that have been made to steer youth toward a more productive level of functioning that does not include delinquent acts have been insufficient.

Another worrisome trend is the age at which juvenile delinquents are identified and processed. More than half of all delinquency cases involved youth younger than 16 (Puzzanchera, Stanl, Finnegan, Snyder, Poole, & Tierney, 2002). For instance, youth under the age of 15 accounted for 65% of all juvenile arrests for arson in 2000 (Snyder, 2002). The number of delinquency cases by gender also shifted remarkably during the decade 1989 to 1998. The number of cases involving males increased by 35% while the number of cases involving females increased by 83%. The overall female delinquency caseload grew at an average rate of 7% per year, compared to 3% per year for males. The growth in person offense cases was greater for females (157%) than for males (71%) in this decade, with the largest percent growth during this time being drug offense cases (142% and 187%, respectively). During this time, the percent change in case rates was greater for females than for males in each of the four general offense categories.

Juvenile arrests reports in the year 2000 provide further substantiated evidence that the problems of youth are not on the decline. Neither are the threats to public safety in our communities, nor the monetary burdens of processing and disposing of these cases by law enforcement and juvenile courts. And the potential for effective responses by courts to these youth is not likely to improve, given the burden of higher caseloads and restricted resources, unless more effective strategies are designed and implemented. For instance, in 2000, law enforcement agencies made an estimated 2.4 million juvenile arrests of persons under the age of 18, with almost one third (28%) of these arrests being females and one third (32%) being under the age of 15 (Snyder, 2002). As in 1998, the juvenile court delinquency caseload has more than 4 times the caseload of four decades earlier in 1960. According to *Crime in the United States 2000*, juveniles were involved in 16% of all Violent Crime Index arrests and 32% of all Property Crime Index arrests in 2000. The juvenile arrest rate for Driving under the Influence increased 39% between 1993 and 2000, and the arrest rate for drug abuse violations soared in the mid-1990s (Snyder, 2002). Juvenile arrest rates for simple assault grew steadily between 1981 and 1996, from 300 per 100,000 juveniles aged 10–17 to almost 800 per 100,000 juveniles, a rate that has remained to date. On the other hand, after years of stability the juvenile arrest rate for curfew and loitering violations more than doubled between 1993 and 1997 (Snyder, 2002). These behaviors are suggestive of circumstances in which too many youth may experience poor parental monitoring, have few acceptable choices pertaining to time spent during nonschool hours, and have little motivation to participate in activities that enhance their own development and competence.

One major implication of these trends is the burden of case processing and detention in juvenile courts and juvenile justice offices. Detention may be viewed by the court as protecting the community, ensuring a juvenile's appearance at subsequent court hearings, or securing the juvenile's own safety. Detention may also be ordered for the purpose of evaluating the juvenile. The budgetary costs, of course, are high to the local, state, and federal agencies and, in the end, to the public. The number of cases involving detention increased by 25% between 1989 and 1998. This was particularly evidenced with person offense cases (up by 63%), drug cases (up by 55%), and public order cases (up by 44%). And despite the decline in the number of property cases in which persons were detained during this time (down by 6%), these cases still accounted for the largest volume of cases involving detention in 1998.

Petition delinquency cases, or formal processing of cases requiring petitions that request adjudicatory or waiver hearings, burden the courts as well. The number of petitioned delinquency cases increased by 62% between 1989 and 1998. The petitioned caseload increased for all offense categories. For instance, the number of petitioned drug offense cases increased by 152% in this decade. Since 1992, petitioned cases have outnumbered nonpetitioned cases, with 32% more petitioned cases in 1998. Overall, 57% of all delinquency cases were formally processed, and increases over the decade occurred in all race and gender categories.

When the ordinary citizen thinks about juvenile court intervention and disposition, the most likely image projected is one of probation. There is good reason for this commonly held perception, for probation remains the sanction most frequently imposed by juvenile courts. The number of adjudicated cases resulting in a disposition of probation increased by 73% between 1989 and 1998. The likelihood of probation for adjudicated delinquency cases increased for all offense categories over the decade. The increased likelihood of probation occurred for all demographic groups. This percentage increase is even more true of younger juveniles who are 15 or younger (61%) than with juvenile offenders who are 16 or older (54%).

What is to be learned from this trend and from the current practice of placing juveniles on probation? One implication is that probation appears to be a common practice that is accepted by the courts, juvenile justice staff, and, in general, the public. Yet very little evidence suggests that such a practice is effective in curbing further juvenile crime or helping youth live more productive lives. Probation appears to be an increasingly utilized response to juvenile crime, and yet the rates of juvenile crime continue to climb in a vast array of categories. Of course, these increases cannot be tied to the practice of probation alone, as it is known that economic conditions, law enforcement practices and changes therein, and social changes such as increases in family disruption and poor parental monitoring contribute to juvenile delinquency. However, as will be reviewed in this text, interventions that include a focus on behavioral change, counseling, and program involvement such as after-school programs or community-sponsored activities are more likely to be effective than probation, a disposition often symbolized as a stern warning to the youth to curb delinquent behavior. In some cases probation can include direct intervention of the kind just identified; however, in many cases planned interventions that address the problems of youth beyond the delinquent act itself are not integrated into the probationary disposition.

Within the context of crime in the United States, juveniles accounted for 37% of all burglary arrests, 30% of robbery arrests, 24% of weapons arrests, 14% of murder arrests, and 14% of drug arrests (Federal Bureau of Investigation, 1997). Juvenile courts handled 1.8 million delinquency cases in 1998, 1,600 more cases each day than in 1987. Courts in 1996 handled 4,800 delinquency cases per day, an increase of 800 per day compared to

1992, when U.S. courts handled 4,000 delinquency cases a day (almost 1.5 million cases total). Juvenile courts are faced with an increasing and changing workload. Juveniles in all age groups contributed to this increase between 1987 and 1996. As distressing is that juveniles aged 12–17 were as likely to be victims of serious violence as were young adults aged 18–24, despite the general perception that the younger age group would be less likely to be exposed to as much danger. In 1996 residential placement or probation was ordered in 82% of adjudicated delinquency cases. What is sorely lacking are data providing evidence that any substantial benefit is derived from these methods. Juvenile courts are too understaffed to process the number of cases of delinquency. Aside from that, courts do not typically have the resources to provide the intensity or breadth of services needed by youth and their families.

Consequences of Increased Youth Crime Rates

Increasingly, the courts are making a decision to handle cases informally, believing that accountability and rehabilitation can be achieved in some cases without the use of formal court intervention. Of course, this is not generally true for cases of violent crime in which not only are restitution and punishment demanded, but changes in the law have resulted in more juveniles being tried as adults. Yet informal handling can be advantageous to both the community and the offender in many cases of delinquency. Diversion programs reduce administrative burdens and the costs of prosecution, and offenders benefit by avoiding trial and the stigma of formal conviction. Cost estimates of incarceration of a youth range from approximately $16,300 (Henggeler, Melton, & Smith, 1992) to $40,000 according to Davidson and Redner (1988). The costs of incarceration for one youth, including all professional services, in the state of Georgia is approximately $35,000 (Georgia Children & Youth Coordinating Council Report, 1997). Allowing one youth to leave high school before graduating for a life of crime and drug abuse costs society between $1.7 million and $2.3 million, according to the Juvenile Offenders and Victims National Report (Snyder & Sickmund, 1999). This report states that quantitative analysis of this kind suggests the practical wisdom of early investment in high-risk youth. While the juvenile violent crime arrest rate has decreased since 1994 after successive increases from 1988, juvenile property crime arrest rates changed little from 1980 to 1997.

Risks to Successful Peer Group Intervention

The statistics presented on probation suggest that such a disposition is a common court response to juvenile delinquency. Why are there such glaring needs reflected in youth delinquency? One reason is that the responses to juvenile crime have not reflected the knowledge gained in the last two decades that pertains to factors that influence delinquent behavior or to interventions with demonstrated effectiveness. For instance, group intervention *with low supervision* has been found to lead to a higher level of deviance training and further behavioral problems. In the most highly controlled field experiment of 400 youth matched on demographic, behavioral, and physical factors, exposing youth to the best social work interventions of the time resulted in negative results for the youth compared to the control group of youth who were left alone (McCord, 1992). The youth who were assigned to summer camps did poorer than the control group in the three decades that followed (McCord, 1997). More recent studies with adolescents assigned to groups indicate that they have more negative results in terms of tobacco use and teacher-reported delinquent behavior (Dishion & Andrews, 1995; Dishion, Andrews, Kavanagh, & Soberman, 1996). These differences remain three years after termination (Poulin, Dishion, & Burraston, 2001). A feature of these interventions that influences this negative effect may be the manner in which deviant peers can embed deviance-based communication within group interaction contexts. Group discussions that focused on cessation of tobacco use gained more positive peer support, while unstructured times during these sessions fostered support for deviant acts among the youth (Hogansen & Dishion, 2001). This finding suggests that intervention of any kind with a group of deviant peers should not allow any unstructured time, any time when youth are outside the presence of adults, or structured activities that focus on the specific problem behavior such as smoking without attention to positive behavior such as developing family responsibility in school-related tasks and household chores.

Correctional settings cultivate the conditions that foster deviance training. Peer interaction is a staple of institutionalized settings for juvenile delinquents because there are not enough adults nor sufficiently intensive and consistent interventions in these settings to crowd out such interactions. Buehler and Patterson (1996) found that for every one positive behavior exhibited by a youth and reinforced by an adult, there were nine deviant behaviors reinforced by peers in these settings. What is becoming clearer is that the "salience of the peer group in adolescence and the dynamics of the institutional setting appear to be the perfect training conditions for creating a serious career criminal or drug abuser" (Dishion & Kavanagh, 2003; p. 173).

It is clear that intervention that focuses on strengthening family cohesion and communication is necessary, as well as monitoring of youth activities to block this deviance-based communication. This can occur in intervention because it is not driven by the need to emphasize problem behavior such as exists in correctional settings or peer group discussions. In this volume the multiple family group model describes an approach that centers on prosocial activities and plans, privileging family cohesion through family activities, and learning skills to manage adolescent challenges. At no time are youth left on their own, nor are they allowed to have unsupervised time. Every moment is structured with parent and professional leader direction, with an experiential orientation.

One challenge in parent education intervention is the issue of the splitting of parents from their children. Some parents, particularly those who possess hostility and frustration toward their children, may have a difficult time learning principles of parental monitoring and parental supervision because of a lack of readiness. Some parents may feel, in the case of a juvenile offender child, "I didn't do the crime so why do I have to do the time?" In other words, they may have difficulty accepting responsibility for making changes in their lives when their view is that their child is "bad," defective or inadequate. For this reason, including children in intervention can create an intervention atmosphere that fosters better attendance and more openness to the intervention enterprise. Another advantage is that the inclusion of children in the context of treatment with parents allows for opportunities to improve communication, demonstrate affection and nurturing, and detect relationship dynamics that need to be changed.

Another challenge in parent education is convening parents who have high stress due to daily life demands and responsibility for children other than the target child, in this case a juvenile offender. Participation rates for parents in parent education programs are known to be modest at best. The opportunity to participate in a family program whereby the parent views the child as part of the intervention, without the impediments of caring for young children, can increase the chances that parents will attend. Given the literature that builds on family factors in adolescent behavior problems, this is important from the perspective of the public health model of reaching as many parents as possible. While a program may be effective for those who attend, how many other parents who would benefit along with their adolescent children from such an intervention are deprived of the opportunity because of costs and the absence of multiple family group programs? Therefore results of intervention from a public health standpoint are, unfortunately, modest at best due to limitations in program availability.

Family and Community Factors Contributing to Behavior
Problems and Delinquency

It is becoming clearer that family and community factors may be the strongest influences on delinquent behavior (Shumaker, 1997; Dishion & Kavanagh, 2003). Since recidivism is a major problem in delinquent behavior patterns, more effort has been directed at moderating these influences in ways that may reduce recidivism. These influences include poor parental monitoring (Forgatch, 1991, Quinn, Hill, Wiley, & Dotson, 1994; Sampson & Lamb, 1994; Peoples & Loeber, 1994), parental communication including little warmth and great hostility (Johnson & Pandina, 1991; Howing, Wodarski, Kurtz, Gaudin, & Herbst, 1990), parental attachment (Rankin & Kern, 1994), negative peer influences (Romig, Cleland, & Romig, 1989), parental involvement in and appreciation for education (Walker & Silvester, 1991), substance abuse (Dembo, Williams, Wothke, Schmeidler, & Brown, 1992; Trojanowicz & Morash, 1992), marital discord and disruption (Dornfeld & Kruttschnitt, 1992), school failure (Tremblay, Masse, Perron, Leblanc, Schwartzman, & Ledingham, 1992; Quinn et al. 1994; Zingraff, Leiter, Johnsen, & Myers, 1994; Quinn & Van Dyke, 2001), father absence (Brown, Zimmerman, Jenkins, & Rhodes, 1991; Dornfeld & Kruttschnitt, 1992), and poverty (Smith & Krohn, 1995) and its corollary, residing in an underclass neighborhood (Peeples & Loeber, 1994).

In a study of African-American males, social class was not a factor in delinquency; however, parental rejection was a strong predictor in serious delinquency (Gray-Ray & Ray, 1990). Further, social and economic status (SES) was not a factor in delinquency after controlling for parental management (Larzelere & Patterson, 1990). Family poverty inhibits family processes of informal social control, increasing the likelihood of delinquency (Sampson & Lamb, 1994). An empirical test of a social control model examining delinquency prevention and intervention revealed results that were largely reducible to previous educational experiences, poor supervision and unresolvable family conflict, and attachment deficits (Scholte, 1991). Dishion and colleagues have recommended that interventions that promote family management skills may be the most cost-effective strategy for reducing problem behavior in youth (Dishion & Kavanagh, 2003). A parent-focused group on family management resulted in reduced coercive interactions between the parent and youth, and teachers reported less antisocial behavior by youth (Dishion & Andrews, 1995). Results studying the effects of family management intervention were replicated by Irvine, Biglan, Metzler, Smolkowski, & Ary (1999).

Several studies have emphasized the importance of parental investment in explaining variable patterns of coping with social and economic disadvantage (Williams & Kornblum, 1985; Garmezy, 1985), pointing out the strategic importance of methods parents employ to access social resources within the family and their community. The variable that has continued to be ignored is the environment and its characteristics (Geismar & Wood, 1986). The person must be understood within the context of family, community, and the wider cultural context, all of which influence how youth develop. Recent reviews have identified the following risk factors that are associated with adolescent delinquency (Carr, 2001; Tarolla, Wagner, Rabinowitz, & Tubman, 2002):

- poverty
- drug use
- low social conformity
- poor school achievement and dropping out of school
- association with deviant peers
- limited prosocial peer involvement
- low social support
- frequent mobilization (e.g., changes in residence).

At the same time, familial factors contribute significantly to the likelihood of juvenile criminal activity (Tarolla, Wagner, Rabinowitz, & Tubman, 2002):

- lack of parental monitoring
- inept discipline
- high levels of conflict and hostility in the home
- parental difficulties such as drug use/abuse
- psychopathology
- family criminal activity
- low parental affection and warmth
- lack of cohesion
- high stress.

Minimal structure in the home, few rules in the household, and inadequate parental support and guidance are among the greatest contributors to youth offenses (Carr, 2001). Severe and inconsistent discipline practices are also known predictors of delinquency (Hawkins, Herrenkohl, Farrington, Brewer, Catalano, Harachi, & Cothern, 2000). This study and one by Wells and Rankin (1991) found that homes with one parent or where divorce or separation has occurred have consistently shown a higher rate of juvenile delinquency. Child neglect has been shown to increase the risk for delinquency by more than 50% (Widom, 1992), and children neglected or abused are more likely to commit violence crimes (Thornberry, Smith, Rivera, Huizinga, & Stouthamer-Loeber, 1999; Widom, 1992). The empirical literature is clear that overall, delinquency is multidetermined but clearly includes familial characteristics as central to risk for delinquency. Yet attention to these factors in intervention has been slow to form and expand.

At the same time it has also been confirmed that not just any family intervention will do. Nonfocused interventions that rely on encouraging communication and expression of feelings have not been effective. Instead, attention to changing particular family interaction patterns, skill-building, behavioral change goals, and role renegotiation are the kind of strategies that both foster behavior change and decrease the probability of further penetration into the court system. At the same time, it is important to recognize that not every delinquent is circumscribed by family pathology, poor parenting, or family disruption such as divorce or a new boyfriend in the home. This is where a multiple family group intervention program can be particularly helpful. Families are engaged in sharing difficulties that pertain to other aspects of the ecological context. These issues can include school-related problems such as school policies or conflicts, racial tensions, neighborhood and community problems such as physical or drug threats to their children, policing patterns, or peer relationships.

Examining the larger context, there is a strong relationship between disconnected youth, especially male adolescents who are not in school and not working, and delinquency. Nearly one third of those who are disconnected for three or more years have been in a jail or youth correctional facility (Brown, 1996). This compares to 1% for those never disconnected. Risk factors that associate with being disconnected are family structure, parents' education, reading materials in the home, family poverty, educational failure, early age at first sexual intercourse, and suspension from school and associated lack of participation in school activities. For black children, poor performance in school associates with risk for delinquent behavior (Achenbach, Edelbrock, Lynam, Moffitt, & Stouthamer-Loeber, 1993), with the rationale that when formal controls (such as school) are not present for youth to compensate for the lack of informal controls, youth are essentially removing themselves from social control and influence as a result of their frustration and failure in school. Hence "neighborhood delinquents and pressures are free to rush in and fill the void" (p. 195). When a formal control agent loses its power to control behavior as youth do poorly and disidentify with school, this loss has greater consequences for increasing at-risk behavior if school is one of the few agents of control. Despite weakening school influences for some youth, the family plays a crucial role in directly influencing youth well-being.

The family also has a role in determining the manner in which ecological strains are overcome. The strategic position of the families for youth makes them critically important in interrupting the potential cycle of delinquency (Coull, Coie, Dodge, & Coppotelli, 1982). The family can play an instrumental role in intervention with youth.

This text builds on the call by Geismar and Wood (1986), who state that it is unfortunate that some helping professionals tend to see only the resources that they offer as relevant to the problems referred to them. They emphasize that groups such as Alcoholics Anonymous and other nonprofessional helping systems utilize naturally existing helping resources that are indeed useful to many people; the family represents such a resource. The pathological family has great power to hurt; the ordinary family has great power to heal and help, and it has more power to do so than any outside professional. It may need some help from the professional to enable it to recognize and marshal its resources, or it may be able to help its youngster with only support from the professional. With families that do possess this potential (and these are probably the majority of families in at least the less serious forms of adolescent delinquency), the role of the professional becomes that of collaborating with and supporting the family as the primary agency of help for the youngster. "The family, not the professional, is in the central position" (p. 202). It is to this end, the active and consistent inclusion of the family as a resource, that this text is presented.

Rationale for the Multiple Family Group Model

Behavior problems and delinquency in youth remain a serious concern for schools and communities. Juvenile delinquency has become a major problem in the United States (Sexton, 1996). It has become more of an index-offense-level criminal problem than in past years. Sexton (1996) reported that more than a third of all murders in the United States were committed by juveniles under the age of 21. There is an urgency as well as a frustration regarding the resolution of youth violence and the behavior problems of children because community and school safety, family heartache, and the future of society are at issue.

Experts in the fields of child development, psychology, and criminology agree that family system variables play a key role in the development of delinquent and deviant behavior (McGaha & Leoni, 1995). Family-related variables have consistently been shown to be factors in the absence or presence of criminality. McGaha and Leoni (1995) report that individuals who are most tightly bonded to social groups such as family, school, and church are less likely to commit delinquent acts. The attachment and bonding to others through ties of affection and respect for parents, teachers, and others relate to their ability to internalize norms and develop a conscience. The stronger the attachment, the less likely a child will commit a delinquent act.

The multiple intervention program described in the text attempts to take full advantage of these principles. The programs are held in the community in neighborhood settings. For example, programs have been held in black and white churches, a university-based outreach facility, and youth agency facilities. Another option is the utilization of school facilities, which can be a resource for program implementation and a source of advocacy for educational success. Simply conducting a program in a school can promote family–school partnerships.

Another advantage to the multiple family group model is that youth remain in the home to build on ecological aspects of youth well-being. The optimal targeted group of youth is made up of those who have come to the attention of an institution, such as a school or court, for the first time. For instance, juvenile first offenders or youth exhibiting for the first time school difficulties such as truancy, aggression, or insolence are most appropriate because they may not have developed an identity that is often formed when these problems become intractable. For instance, while a wide range of characteristics across youth can occur, first-offender youth are not as likely to have developed a "delinquent identity" nor been psychologically or physically cast off by their families. A youth with newly identified school problems may not be lacking in confidence or academic interest but may be expressing a human dilemma, such as divorcing parents or the death of a close family member, prompting profound sadness or anger. By targeting youth at this age, the likelihood of further penetration into the court system or chronic school failure can be reduced.

Too often the catalyst for professional responses, such as law enforcement or school staff, is an incident that cannot be ignored. This might be a major school violation such as a weapon possession, fighting, or chronic truancy, or a criminal act in the community. Yet there are often indications of a problem expressed by a youth that substantially precede this event in time. Too little, if anything, is done at this earlier time to help a young person. Many reasons exist, including overwhelming demands on professionals, who can give attention only to the most egregious cases, or adults who "look the other way" or minimize responses to behavioral problems because a response requires energy or commitment on the part of the adult, who is highly stressed with other aspects of life or who simply does not welcome intrusions into his or her own life agenda or schedule. However, as Kelley, Loeber, and DeLamatre (1997) state, "the warning signs of early onset of disruptive behaviors must not be dismissed with a 'this too will pass' attitude. Interventions will be more successful if the child has not already persistently performed a negative behavior or penetrated the more serious states of a pathway" (p. 17). Their research suggests that a child who only "tries out" disruptive behavior is at a much lower risk for progressing along the pathway to serious delinquency than a child who persists in practicing negative behaviors.

Gating procedures have been proposed as a method of screening risk and identifying youth in need of intervention at the earliest possible time. For instance, Loeber, Dishion, and Patterson (1984) offered such a design for a three-gate screening procedure in which management practices were developed for teachers, mothers, and families to accommodate sequentially the level of risk and delinquent pattern. Without such screening mechanisms behavior problems remain unchecked, leading to more serious delinquency that heightens the risk and lowers the probability of behavioral resolution. In one of the first longitudinal studies of pathways to behavioral problems, Stouthamer-Loeber et al. (1995) found that the progression of disruptive and delinquent behaviors by 8th-grade boys was essentially ignored. Problems expressed by these boys had been exhibited for six years! Yet only 41% had actually sought help from friends, family, or professionals.

The challenge is to design procedures such that parents, teachers, and professionals who become aware of these problems can convey these concerns and access help. A first step is, as Kelley et al. (1997, p. 18) state, that "parents need to be informed about their children's potential progression into more serious behaviors and about any available community services." This book suggests that an additional step should be mandated or urged. Parents need to be included in community services as an important component of the desired behavior change of their children and a healthier family system to foster healthier development for the future of their children. There is no "magic pill," just hard work, because there are "rarely quick fixes that will redirect a child on the pathway to positive development" (p. 19). Centralizing parents as the "agent of change" comparable to the central position of the children would foster a stronger family system that could be more prepared to help children be redirected toward a more successful life path.

An additional advantage of family programs is that younger siblings are often involved in family programs to provide opportunities for resolving whole-family problems; sibling involvement can prevent or decrease the odds of younger sibling penetration into the juvenile court. Families in the multiple family group are urged to take responsibility for the success or failure of the program from the outset. This expectation of family "ownership" of the intervention experience is conveyed in many ways from the referral stage to the final intervention activity.

One way to build family investment in the intervention is to provide program schedules and topics, both at the referral meeting (discussed in chapter 6) and during the first session, and to invite family members to suggest modifications to the program schedule. They can be offered the chance to voice their interest and concern about certain topics and suggest which need to be incorporated into the program and which should receive less attention or be deleted. Another expectation regarding family responsibility for program success is to require attendance. Attendance is mandatory, and it is explained that the reason is that if someone does not come, "someone present gets cheated because you're not there to help them," since each family's story is expected to have the potential of helping someone else. *Families are more likely to become invested in a multiple family group program if they are counted on to help other families, rather than if they view the program as a punitive mechanism to reconcile a previous delinquent act.* As group experiences unfold, families and family members build social and emotional connections that foster empathy for each other, thereby increasing individual effort.

The leaders review the schedule and topics, and the families are urged to have input, reviewing the schedule and discussing suggested changes for the second session. Another method of securing family investment in the intervention is to encourage group responsibility for individual family transportation problems. A family might say, "Well, I don't know if I can come next week since my car is giving me problems." When transportation difficulties are raised by a family, the group is encouraged to problem-solve about how to help a family get to the program. The group leader can say, "Is there anyone in the group that can help the Johnson family by picking them up?" Often, a family will volunteer to pick up another family on the night of a session. Or an arrangement can be made whereby a family that discovers a transportation problem at the last minute, such as a spouse working late, leaving no vehicle for the parent to get to the intervention program, or a car that simply does not start when they are about to leave for the intervention program, has the phone number of another family that can be called to ask for transportation help to the program.

Family group programs are designed to build ties to the community. Group programs can have several purposes (Pomeroy, Rubin, Van Lianingham, & Walker, 1997). A group comprised of caregivers has the purpose of reducing stress for those who have responsibilities for managing terminally ill or infirm individuals. Other groups have the purpose of forestalling illness or modifying more serious psychological problems (McFarlane, 2002). The multiple family group model described in this volume targets youth who have potential for further delinquent behavior. Curbing delinquency and fostering family bonds provide a greater opportunity to redirect a child's path toward success.

A major part of the program is task-centered. Task-centered approaches tied to developmental demands of youth have demonstrated efficacy (Epstein, 1983; Reid, 1993). Tasks integrate well with psychoeducational approaches because group members can learn from and support each other. This model with youth offenders builds on the concept that group members who are homogeneous—they share a common experience regarding a specific shared problem—are more likely to learn from each other because they "identify" with each other's feelings and experiences. This approach is best used when the focus is in the present; that is, the activities and group discussions encourage forward-thinking and not reflections on why past incidents such as delinquency occurred. Instead the topics, activities, and content relate to strengthening the bonds and communication in the family, gaining parenting skills, increasing parental commitment to monitoring youth behavior, engaging youth to contribute to their community, and beginning short-term (i.e., school) and long-term (i.e., job, career) planning for the future.

Correspondence between Designated Treatment and Its Implementation

In every treatment protocol there is variation between the designated intervention and its actual implementation. There are several sources of variability. If there is no written description of intervention, then each program and each session within a program will vary based on theories held by group leaders and idiosyncratic biases from past intervention experience. If there is a written description of intervention, even a treatment manual or text, it may not be written with the full knowledge of a particular youth or group of youth. Individual characteristics such as personality, temperament, family history, family interaction patterns, school and other experiences, for instance, influence youth in idiosyncratic ways. In addition, unique circumstances of a youth or family also play a part in this variability. Intervention protocols are beneficial in increasing the odds of the probability of success because they are more likely to be built on evaluation procedures and results. Protocols also ensure some level of standardization of the program across sites and leaders. Some variation, however, is expected based on unique family characteristics.

The agent of change (interventionist or group leader) in particular represents characteristics that influence perceptions and actions within the intervention context. The interventionist's theory, academic training, personal characteristics, and life history all influence the decision-making process in regard to what is done within the intervention model. As such, adherence to a text or manual is a function of the change agent's characteristics as well as the characteristics of the family group participants. In other words, who the change agent is does make a difference. One cannot assume that the treatment manual or text is the holy grail. Hence, while a manual or text is extremely important in providing a blueprint for the structure and function of an overall program delivery model, adherence to the model and variation in the model are influenced by the change agent or, in the case of the group model described in this volume, the group leader(s).

The view of causation of youth behavior problems may influence treatment implementation. There are many proposed "causes," for instance, of aggressive behavior. Some causes that have been proposed are: physiological predisposition, culture, immediate interpersonal (conflict with another), immediate physical environment (impoverishment), person qualities (cognitive impairment), disinhibitors such as the absence of social control agents such as adult involvement and monitoring, presence of aggressive cues, and presence of a potential victim (Goldstein et al. 1989). Many of these "causes" or associations can be seen in the data presented in this book for the treatment population in which this model was developed.

A multicausal explanation, or etiology, of acting-out behavior should not necessarily result in the assumption that each youth must receive specialized treatment. Instead, a range of interventions that include individual, family, and community factors can be viewed as a meshing of needs in which group members in the multiple group format can both provide resources (e.g., information, experience, solutions) and receive them from each other.

Many at-risk characteristics exist for these families. Parental conflict, poverty, family structural changes, transitions, and school failure are most common. Chapter 9 provides a youth and family profile of several hundred juvenile first-time offenders that provide a rationale for family intervention. For example, school difficulties, anger problems, or family conflict steer the content and particular topics of the Family Solutions Program. Suffice it to say here that it is important to consider a multiple set of approaches that increase the possibility that a range of interventions might encircle more youth. Recent thinking on this subject led to a proposal that an "interactional or integrated model" of etiology of delinquency may be most helpful (Greenwood, 1996). In this model many pathways to delinquency are possible, and a range of theories, including contextual or ecological circumstances, familial factors, and social learning orientations, can be considered (Emens, Hall, Ross, & Zigler, 1996). In addition, this causality sequence is not unidirectional. For example, weakening of social bonds may increase delinquency, and such delinquent acts reduce the strength of these social ties even further. Parent–youth conflict may sway a youth towards a criminal behavior, and the delinquent act may push the rift between parent and youth even wider, thereby encouraging further delinquency as parents and youth grow more dissatisfied with each other or more pessimistic about their relationships.

Intervention effort must include treatments directed at the youth's parents, siblings, peers, classmates, teachers, and others in his or her immediate community. This endeavor can be further supported by findings that indicate that promoting youth skill development within an environment of incarceration often does not transfer back into the community. This case can also be made for drug-abusing adolescents, for whom inpatient treatment does not generalize to good long-term outcomes due to lack of family involvement or changes in family environment upon return home. Several decades ago Bowen (1965) discovered this with hospitalized schizophrenic patients, who became worse after they were discharged from the hospital. Jules Henry (1971), in his book *Pathways to Madness*, describes his own accounting of this process as a psychiatrist and anthropologist when he lived with psychiatric patients and their families. Family interactions shaped and exacerbated the severity of mental illness in family members. This discovery, along with similar observations during the same era, contributed to a new approach and the growth of family therapy (Hoffman, 1981). Similarly, in more recent decades this has been observed with adolescent drug abusers and adolescent psychiatric hospitalizations, in which patients generally do not thrive after returning home after treatment.

Skill development must be reciprocated and rewarded in the social context of the youth's real world so that such change can be viewed as beneficial to the youth. Family connection produces and maintains a set of interactional dynamics that give meaning or purpose to behavior. When behavior is problematic, dangerous, or developmentally disruptive, this set of communication elements in the family requires alteration.

On Marriage and Multiple Family Group Intervention

One way to consider the vital role of the blending of resources in family group intervention is to compare it to a marriage. Some of the same dynamics of marriage, in a limited and shortened time span, apply to multiple family group intervention. In marriage, two individuals bring unique characteristics that are attractive to each other. These might include beauty, sense of humor, prestige or wealth, work ethic, affection, and career ambitions. At the same time, each spouse might bring certain limitations or vulnerabilities. These might include the inverse of the above characteristics (i.e., lack of humor, uncertainty about a career direction, or impoverishment). Or it might include family background difficulties and past traumatic events such as divorced parents and the lack of a healthy road map for marriage, abuse, childhood illness or disability, or tragic loss of a parent or sibling. Couples in marriage can successfully overcome vulnerabilities by drawing on the strengths of each other to be nurtured when needed, to show empathy when the spouse feels sad or discouraged, and to be led to a happier place by learning more about life from each other in the form of inspirational people, places to visit, or methods of responding to adversity. In addition, like marriage, each family has to make compromises.

As in marriage, a family cannot dominate the discussion, cannot convince other families to do more for them than they will do for others, and cannot demand and receive attention whenever the occasion calls for it. Each family must sometimes put aside their own problem for the problem of another family or must draw back from desiring the central focus, just as married couples with children often forfeit their own needs and interests for the well-being of children who need attention and support.

Multiple family group intervention can create a process similar to marriage in building complementary relationships. If each family is viewed as a spouse, then a family in multiple family group work has empathy for another family, inspires another family, provides a sense of hopefulness, and draws on their own resiliency to boost a family filled with self-doubt or a sense of inadequacy.

CHAPTER 3

Adding Balance: Expanding Relational, Family, and Community Efficacy in Human Service Delivery

If you always do what you've always done, then you'll always get what you've always got.
—Anonymous

It is necessary to reevaluate the utility of human service delivery and to reconsider the utilization of professional costs and services. This book makes a case that the conceptual understanding of resources and the inherent characteristics that they offer youth are too narrowly viewed by helpers in the human service delivery system and by consumers/clients themselves. When the process of service delivery fails, it does so when it lacks a coherent conceptualization of the change process and the associated definitions helpers construct of their roles.

This book addresses the question of what can be done to facilitate human development for youth and families vulnerable to the characteristics known to increase risk factors. New thinking is needed to comprehend the complexity of engaging families and communities in striving for an adequate environment to promote the well-being of youth, and the deprivation/pathology model needs to be rethought in favor of a resource model that advantages youth and families without extreme dependence on public services, agency support, and helping professionals.

One institutional domain, juvenile delinquency and the judicial system, is examined as an example of problematic thinking and program impoverishment. However, much of what is presented here can be extrapolated to other institutional settings, such as mental health service agencies, schools, and adolescent treatment centers. Consumers of human service systems have been viewed largely as recipients of potential resources that, if attained, can improve productivity and well-being and potentially make the consumers independent of such services over time. The conceptual understanding of resources and the inherent characteristics that they possess are often too narrowly viewed by helpers. The process of delivering such services often fails due to a lack of understanding of the change process and the definitions helpers construct of their roles.

Muddled Thinking—The Problem-Solution Dilemma

Family and community have been obscured by the focus on selfhood and the quest for self-actualization. The human temptation to explain social problems using an individual lens helps to simplify the strategies for intervention. Here are 3 examples:

- It is a commonplace that it is "easier" repeatedly to try to correct, punish, or help a student in a school setting than it is to assess, convene, or resolve family processes in which that unmotivated, troubled, or self-doubting student is embedded.
- It is thought to be "easier" to reprimand, adjudicate, or punish a juvenile delinquent than it is to enlist or require a family to appear in court to resolve their abusive tendencies, marital conflict, or personal parental stresses.
- It is thought to be "easier" to control the environment of one drug-abusing adolescent or adult who cannot autonomously get control of the addiction and rid him- or herself of it than it is to vitalize a life wrought with disappointment and failure by reconstructing a social environment that includes affection and tolerance.

Somehow the belief grows that change can more readily appear if the focus of intervention is an individual (youth) rather than a social system (the family).

This tendency to isolate human problems occurs because reconstructing a social environment requires the intentional inclusion of significant other human beings (e.g., a distant father, an unjustifiably demanding stepparent, a destructive and troubled set of peers, professionals with other affiliations and agendas) who are at first seen as part of an overwhelmingly complicated social network. The social environment of a youth includes individual motives, life circumstances, and varied needs that, taken together, cannot be easily or practically joined (i.e., work schedules), or more threatening yet, understood. This myth (of too much complexity to be understood) is somewhat like an inexperienced family therapy trainee who suffers the illusion that seeing one person is actually easier than seeing a family because one life can be understood more clearly than several lives with interconnected linkages. Helpers in human service agencies may routinely adopt a similar approach because of a similar assumption that drawing a boundary around the individual allows for coherence. Such a procedure is also thought to make accountability procedures (i.e., record-keeping) more manageable.

Ten Questionable Reasons a Youth Is Treated Alone

The mainstream of society considers children to be less competent than parents. For example they may be thought of as less mature, less experienced, and lacking in various life coping skills such as managing delayed gratification, possessing sufficient self-discipline, and accumulating life experience. The tendency for adults is to view children as mini-adults, lacking only an equal amount of competence or experience. In comparison to adults, then, children can be seen as deficient or underdeveloped and therefore in more need of attention.

This leads to the temptation on the part of adults to organize themselves to take a superior position. This is evidenced by the responses chosen by adults to when a child deviates from adult expectations. Parents define a child's problems in individualistic terms (i.e., lacking in certain qualities such as compliance, responsibility, or kindness).

1. Since the power to shape current practices of institutions like schools and social organizations is held in the hands of adults, deviations of human behavior and acceptance are defined by adults as well. The result is that characterizations of problems are seen and explained as residing in the child; for example: "that kid is a mess," "what's his problem?" "he is mean," "she is lazy," are more acceptable statements of these deviations than "the family is a mess," "what's the family's problem?" "the family carries hostility," or "the family doesn't accept much responsibility for itself."

2. Further exacerbating the typecasting of children's problems are the mental health insurance policies which require the designation of a diagnosis for an identified patient.

3. School policies and practices, the major domain of a child's "work" life, primarily define aberrant behavior as the child's problem.

4. The predominant societal view holds that success is measured in individual achievement or failure, as with material goods, income, awards and recognition, and professional advancement via promotions and job titles.

5. Families are at the root of the problem; therefore children should be separated from the family toxins.

6. Few personnel exist within educational systems to intervene with families.

7. Few professionals in the helping services are trained to intervene with families.

8. Involving the family in intervention is complicated—it requires juggling work schedules of parents, bringing together conflicted family members such as divorced parents, and persuading family members that they have a part to play in the resolution of their child's difficulty.

9. The view exists that altering the behavior of one person, say a child, is easier or more likely to be possible than altering the behavior of two or more people (absence of a systemic view).

10. Direct time with a youth can be counted, so that a professional's workload can be documented; whereas agency time on the telephone to promote and travel to a site in the community to facilitate collaboration among professionals, and time spent gathering ecological/social/family information are not quantifiable or time-efficient.

These professional or adult beliefs are not nearly as valid as those that espouse them and practice according to them would have the world believe. It is becoming abundantly clear that individuals are embedded in social systems, such as families and communities, that contain reciprocal influences. These reciprocal influences require greater acknowledgment in human service delivery if positive and durable outcomes are to occur. For instance, the value of family intervention such as family therapy for adolescent drug abuse (Quinn, Kuehl, Thomas, & Joanning, 1988; Joanning, Quinn, Thomas, & Mullen, 1992; Todd & Selekman, 1991; Lawson, & Rivers, 2001; Liddle, 1996, 1999) is well known. Results of studies such as these and others identified throughout this book compel interventionists to include the family and must for ethical and clinical reasons supersede the desire for simplicity. Yet the inclusion of the family in treatment is hardly commonplace in most communities.

The relevance of inclusion of family members in other arenas of intervention into human problems is also evident. Bringing multiple families together within the community might be viewed as a helpful approach to resolving both intrafamily conflicts as well as neighborhood problems. A multiple family group intervention plan could be interrupted by a parent who brings a juvenile delinquent daughter to that multiple family group program and says: "You mean I have to stay too? Why?" Or, in a hospital setting, a husband may claim that if his wife's depression can be "cleared up" (chemically treated), he should not be inconveniently or embarrassingly obligated to participate in some kind of marital therapy. In a school situation, when the teacher calls a parent expressing concerns about the child's scholastic failure or classroom behavior, the parent silently questions the need for the call. The parent can be overwhelmed with other life demands; or the parent may have an individual frame of resolving child problems that leads to thinking "you should handle it at school." The thinking of a parent (possibly a professional) might go something like this: "since it is the child who is the student, it is the child, after all, who must learn and graduate to get a decent job, and it is the child who possesses the supposed 'demonic' temperament that requires extinction."

The Darkness through the Individual Lens

An epistemological error is made when the larger circular-causal system is not perceived in the context of human dilemmas (Bateson, 1972). What we typically perceive is a lineal causality in which events are arbitrarily punctuated by time. And due to an inherent desire of advocates to control or influence, certain changes or gains are expected when pressure is applied to particular individual maladies. Advocates expect to give treatment, information, or support, and clients are expected to receive it. Advocates mistakenly desire a constant within this association of giving and receiving because of its apparent simplicity and requirement to adhere to bureaucratic caseworking demands. Another arc in the causal loop must be drawn—the idea that what advocates provide should be dependent on the characteristics of the client and the system in which that client is embedded.

A quick gaze at assessment instruments that are used in case management suggests that family or relational data are often omitted. The following provides an example of how this minimization of family data is suspect:

> In a recent juvenile delinquent case, data were gathered of a young male youth and his current home situation that included information about his custodial parent, the mother, and two siblings. The family endured severe financial hardship and the mother was admittedly unable to provide sufficient supervision of the children. The boy came to weekly multiple family group sessions with a different hair style each week, sometimes with initials or symbols carved into the hair. This suggested that it was being cut routinely. One of the group leaders asked, "So who helps you with your hair style each week?" To which the boy politely responded, "Oh, my Dad's a barber, and I go and see him every Friday." To the team, using an ecological framework, this suggested that this was to the boy a "legitimate" reason for seeing his father in a family in which conflict was severe in the relationship of the two ex-spouses. The boy found his own way of making connections after a marital split. Including the father in decision-making about the boy and his school situation and bringing about a change in the social patterns of his life to promote the father-son relationship became possible. A group leader, after receiving permission from the boy's mother, called the father and told him that his son was participating in a program called Family Solutions. The leader asked the father if he would consider attending, that it would be

helpful to his son, and that his ex-wife would not mind; in fact had she said, "he needs more help than I can give him." The mother confided in the group leaders that she felt all along the boy's father was not doing enough, but the group leaders did not think sharing this with the father would help. However, this inclusion of the boy's father was slow in developing because the data collection method used in the juvenile court did not include an allowance for information regarding family members living outside the home. How much better it could have been if the father's availability had been known at the outset of the program. Strengths in families can be located, but only if a wide social arc of the environment is drawn.

Another short example might serve to mobilize efforts to more fully comprehend the importance of family information:

A mother who was requested to attend a family intervention program for juvenile offenders refused when she discovered that the juvenile court had listed her as the "foster" mother when in fact she was the biological mother and custodial parent. She became incensed and proclaimed that she would rather go to jail herself than to comply with and cooperate with an agency that mislabeled her. The connotation of a foster mother somehow left her with a bad feeling towards those who thought of her as such.

This refusal may be idiosyncratic to this case; however, Yamamoto (1967) reported that with low-income minority group members (the large portion of many caseworkers' loads) unable to afford services, 30% to 40% failed to keep their appointments. What occurs in some of these cases is that struggling children and families, who have voluntarily accessed social service agencies or have been compelled to do so, gather up for themselves a developing distrust of professional systems, which are perceived to be unresponsive to their needs or circumstances.

This point is not meant to level criticism at the already burdened social service systems, educational systems, and the like. Instead, the point is made to document that social problems are inherently fixed at the individual level of comprehension and intervention. Such a conceptual stance disallows a utilization of family and community resources or influences that would in fact bolster strained formal support systems.

It is "easier" to employ a singular lens (within-the-skin focus) because it is perceived that the source of the child's problem is embedded constitutionally in the child's biological system, and certainly if this is the case, then the resolution of the problem is also embedded in that same system. This assumption fits well within a society that prides itself upon and aspires to individual success as measured by income, materialistic gains, and public recognition (i.e., media promotion of sports heroes). A mechanistic rather than recursive lens fixes pathology at a level that lends itself to linear efforts for change, as if a "defective gene" can be spliced or rebuilt to resolve a problematic human behavior. The attitude of parents in some of these instances is: "Let me know when he is fixed and I will come and pick him up."

This line of reasoning, however, has limited the probability of successful outcomes around intervention. The following situation, which occurred to the author, may serve as an illustration. In this case, the description does not involve a youth with behavior problems but rather an elderly man consulting his doctor. Yet the conceptual frame is the same, and serves to illustrate the limitations of it:

An older man of 84 made weekly visits to a physician for ailments that could not be substantiated through tests or examinations. After several visits, the frustrated physician requested me, serving as the behavioral scientist in a medical school, to conduct an evaluation of the man. I conducted a brief interview:

Behavioral Scientist (BE): Where do you live?
Elderly Man (EM): In a nursing home.
BE: Do you have any family members that you see?
EM: I have one son who lives in town.
BE: How often do you see him?
EM: Rarely, I used to see him a lot, he fixed things at my house and cut my grass, but now that I am in a nursing home, I only see him when he brings me to see the doctor.

Here is a context shift that forced a relationship change with problematic consequences. Clearly, while the older man's medical condition may have warranted a consult with a physician, his psychosocial needs were overwhelming. Trips to the physician were a justifiable way for a lonely older man, removed from his familiar environment which heretofore defined his role, to contact his son, who otherwise, as a father, could not give himself permission to ask for companionship. As this notion became clear to the older man—that more frequent contact with his son was something he was yearning for—inclusion of the son in our meetings made sense. Then I followed up with a family session with the older father and adult son. Following a brief interview, I requested that they plan conjoint trips for lunch on alternate weeks to the clinic instead of weekly trips to the medical clinic. It seems that the son assumed that his father's social needs were fully met when he moved to a nursing home.

This example illustrates another limitation of some current approaches to intervention. For a positive outcome to occur in this case, at least two actions were needed. One, the physician, in his frustration, was obliged to seek help from someone else who might possess some insight or answer to the dilemma. This action was remarkable in that such a request was made of someone outside the boundaries of the professional discipline (medicine to behavioral science). This kind of action, while possibly an act of desperation used as an "escape hatch" from the case by the physician, was intuitive and responsible in light of the older man's needs.

The second action needed in the case of the older father and adult son was that the therapist (me) found it necessary to expand the social system of the older man to include someone significant in the man's life. This was accomplished via a series of questions about the man's family. The therapist, then, was pushed by his own conceptual frame to include someone else (the son) in the attempt to resolve the older man's problem. Each of these actions requires a purposive gesture of inclusion. Intervention inclusion is the process of bringing people together to construct a social intervention that often is not routinely considered.

This reluctance toward social expansion of the context is often due to a perception that collaboration is complicated and inconvenient. Also present can be some assessment that there is insufficient overlap in commitment, motivation, expertise, or role enactment; that is, the systems possess cross-purposes or cross-methods (Wynne, Weber, & McDaniel, 1988). The challenge is to bring systems together that may not view themselves collectively or may perceive such efforts as likely to generate poor outcomes.

The consequences of attempts to include more people are often viewed negatively. For instance, disagreements are likely to open up in the presence of others, as with custodial parents who are divorced or a father who is hostile toward his son. Or competition for resources may heighten, as with a question of which of the divorced parents is expected to devote more time or pay more of a child's living expenses. Or a psychological tug-of-war ensues when one parent wants to prove greater loyalty or love than the other parent; the one with a great need to be viewed as sacrificial or more competent battles with the coparent instead of collaborating with the coparent to help support their child. To avoid these pitfalls, families make attempts to locate the blame or responsibility on a person or within a dyad instead of sharing the commitment to strengthen the family and help the child.

Sometimes these fragmented services or partial conceptualizations are simply the function of impracticality or inconvenience. Designing family intervention implies the involvement of more than one individual targeted for change. Instead of the focus on the youth alone, who can come in to see a probation officer during the day, the inclusion of a family requires the negotiation of work schedules, transportation challenges, and other family obligations. *Only a practitioner committed to the necessity of a family intervention has the perseverance, motivation, communication skills, and creativity to convene families successfully in intervention programs.*

New Directions in Social Analysis

The interest in examining new paradigms or approaches grows in part out of the failure of previous and current approaches that emphasize traditional descriptions of pathology and dysfunction. Hoffman (1990) offers the term "art of lenses" as a way of conceptualizing the needed epistemological shift. I will mention briefly just two examples of recent proposals.

An interdisciplinary paradigm is emerging in developmental psychology because the dominant theories of learning have yielded unremarkable results with their conceptual ambiguity (Estes, Koch, MacCorquodale, Meehl, Mueller, Schoenfeld, & Verplanck, 1954). There was skepticism about the generality of findings from controlled laboratory experiments and about the utility of animal models for illuminating complex human behavior. Some years later, Ring (1967) labeled as a crisis the state which he found in his own field of social psychology.

The key developments that contributed to the newer model of inquiry grounded in a contextual framework have been delineated by Jessor (1991). One change in the Zeitgeist was the growing sense that adopting a multidisciplinary perspective was unavoidable. Jessor (1993) points out that psychology heretofore had been "unable to encompass the socially organized environment of human action" (p. 117). What Jessor proposed was a model that includes the individual (i.e., adolescent) nested in the center of overlapping circles that include the family, school, and neighborhood and includes a backdrop that incorporates the larger social-structural, economic, political, and cultural environments. One current and vivid example of the utilization of this design that has grown out of Bronfenbrenner's (1986) "call to context" in studying human behavior is the MacArthur Foundation's support of studies that are multidisciplinary and ecosystemic.

An additional contribution to this contextual paradigm is that proposed by Eccles, Midgley, Wigfield, Buchanan, Reuman, Flanagan, and MacIver (1993), who offered a stage-environment fit. These contributors delineate in insightful detail some examples of school and family experiences that are chronically disturbed because of the traditionalism, rigidity, and marked ignorance of student needs exhibited by educational institutions. One vivid example is the developmental needs of early-adolescent youth, which clash with the immovable and impenetrable structure and size of junior high school and its incongruence with youth's interests, ending in youth maladjustment.

Another trend in this regard is the adoption of the public health model to examine effective interventions to reduce the prevalence of children at risk. School interventions that are universally applied to all children in a school or grade level or those that are applied to a targeted population of children identified as being at risk are based on principles of human behavioral change in context. For example, the GREAT Schools and Families Project (Corporate author, 2004) has developed and implemented a 6th-grade curriculum on prevention of aggression in middle school. The interventions include a student program on how they can resolve differences with their peers peacefully and contribute to a civil classroom environment, a teacher intervention to assist teachers in creating classroom environments that help dissipate bullying and interpersonal conflict, and a 15-week multiple family group intervention for students nominated by their 6th-grade teachers as exhibiting aggressive behavior and their families. The family program attempts to strengthen home–school partnerships, enhance communication and problem-solving, increase effective parental monitoring of children, promote greater self-control and emotional management, and plan for the future. By working with entire schools and implementing a multilevel intervention (students, teachers, families), the hope is that a safer school will result. In this way, while desired behavior change among individual students and families may occur, the intent is to alter an entire institutional environment—the school—to allow students to feel safer and experience fewer aggressive incidents. In this way an intervention is viewed as modifying a social environment—one that exists in every community—a school.

Illuminating Parental Influence

The distillation of influences proposed on child well-being, it seems, may be the relational context of the child embedded in the parental—early adult influence—web. While not exhaustive, there are many studies documenting this phenomenon, including the relation of inept parenting practices and poor parental identification on the absence of child prosocial value commitments (Simons, Whitbeck, Conger, & Conger, 1991); the relation of child maltreatment by parents and juvenile delinquency (Zingraff, Leiter, Myers, & Johnsen, 1993); pathways of disruptive and delinquent behavior (Kelley, Loeber, Keenan, & DeLamatre, 1997); and the relation of parental support and control as predictors of adolescent drinking, delinquency, and related problem behaviors (Barnes & Farrell, 1992). In addition, the early human attachment literature is unswerving in this regard, although its subtleties have not completely been sorted out.

In practical terms, the thrust of programs such as Head Start is the attempt to recognize the value of comprehensive health and social services for a child and family, guided by the theory that a successful school experience requires a conducive family environment. Even within the controversy regarding the effectiveness and appropriate level of support of Head Start, there seems to be a general consensus that "the goal is to improve families' lives and make kids more socially competent, not change their IQs," as reported by Helen Blank of the Children's Defense Fund. More recently, interest has been directed toward helping promote academic preparation in these programs.

The common assumption in either approach is that in these early childhood programs there is a need to help families, many with vulnerabilities including poverty, family conflict, and insufficient parenting skills, to help their children prepare for a successful educational experience. Steinhauer, Santa-Barbara, and Skinner (1984) similarly suggested a process model of family functioning that allows family members to achieve their biological, psychological, and social goals through successful task accomplishment crucial to successful human development. This development would include ensuring health, safety, comfort, and continuing development of all family members, providing reasonable security and autonomy for all, adapting usual patterns of functioning to meet environmental and developmental demands for change, supplying cohesion needed to hold the family together, transmitting to the family the values of the culture, and serving as a mediator between the individual and society. This successful task accomplishment, then, includes basic tasks, developmental tasks, and crisis tasks, and includes six subsystem qualities—paternal, maternal, child, family, social, and marital. From these six subsystems emerges a wave of interactional influences that frame the family as a small group process and structure that determines development, well-being, and level of stress.

This early parental influence that promotes child adjustment can sometimes be mediated by environmental factors such as unemployment and poverty, employment in jobs that inhibit conditions for effective parenting such as night work for single parents, and intergenerational transmission of parental attitudes, behaviors, and norms—mental maps that may have characteristics constraining parental influence that fosters child well-being. Therefore early intervention, such as preschool learning environments, holds great potential for interrupting negative sequences that lead to school failure, destructive social interactions, and juvenile delinquency. This more "outside the skin" approach requires a consideration of the sociocultural conditions that impact the likelihood of success or resolution in problematic family situations.

Context with a Capital C

The pitfall for institutions is that human misery is too often viewed as an isolated expression of personal failure rather than a consequential expression of failed relationships. These failed relationships culminate from a benign neglect, a self-centered compulsion, or a disquieting anger that contagiously infects young children and youth who desperately need, instead, a nurturing experience to solidify their competencies, sense of worth, and social commitment.

Adler contributed an important cornerstone of this idea in his labeling of *Gemeinschaftsgefühl*, or social interest. Other English equivalents of this translation include: social feeling, community feeling, fellow feeling, sense of solidarity, communal intuition, community interest, and social sense (Ansbacher & Ansbacher, 1956). In this account of social interest as a cornerstone of life experience, a central thesis emerges:

> If the conditions of life are determined in the first instance by cosmic influences, they are in the second instance determined socially. They are determined by the fact that men [and women] live together and by the rules and regularities which spontaneously arise in consequence of this. The demands of society have regulated human relationships which had already existed from the beginning as self-understood, as an absolute truth. (p. 128)

This notion of self-other in contemporary society seems almost forgotten. If one viewed the moment-to-moment human interactions and, more specifically, the mental health system and other institutions in analyzing their decision-making processes, what would be found is that the common good is put aside for the perceived well-being of the individual. Of course, at a higher level this is not possible, since individuals are embedded in social environments from which they cannot or do not wish to escape and of which there are social consequences.

A more contemporary tone to the central place that a community has in the life of every person can be found in the following passage: "For before the individual life of man there was the community. In the history of human culture, there is not a single form of life which was not conducted as social. Never has man appeared otherwise than in society" (p. 128). Adler, as a positive idealist rather than a transcendental idealist, proposed that absolute truth is not to be accepted literally but instead offered as a working hypothesis, to acknowledge the human desire of certainty to guide conduct, that the communal life of man is the absolute truth. Adler's justification for this fiction, or working hypothesis, was that all problem cases, from neuroses and psychoses to criminality, have in common their failure to abide by this absolute truth. We may now conceivably add drug abuse, child abuse, and violence of all kinds to this list of consequences.

Not only are human needs understood only in context, so too is human experience understood in context. That is, to understand any individual requires an exploration of that person's past experiences in relation to other significant social relationships, such as family.

Let me offer an example from my own experience of how knowledge, reality, or truth is socially constructed.

> *Quite a few years ago now, 1979, I interviewed men and women (mostly women) in old age to assess needs of the frail elderly to determine the resource obligations of the state of Virginia. Early one evening I drove up to an old farmhouse and came upon an older woman rocking on her front porch in a very rural area of southwest Virginia. I approached her cautiously, introduced myself and explained the*

purpose of my presence, and asked if she would be willing to answer some questions. She happily obliged and invited me to sit next to her. She told me initially that she was 76 years of age. In the standardized interview itself I had to ask her for her birth date in order to verify her mental health status. She told me it was July 5, 1898. Doing a little math, I discovered an incongruence between her report of her age and the actual years between her birth and the current year. I asked her if she was sure of her date of birth, and she said, "Oh yes, my older sister was born in 1896 and my kid sister was born in 1899. I'm sure." Reluctantly, as calmly as I could, I responded by telling her that if she really was born in 1898, then she was now 81 years old and not 76 as she had told me earlier. The woman leaned toward me in her rocker, looked me in the eye and quietly remarked, "You don't say." She seemed confused for a moment. But then she seemed but accepting of this "news of a difference." My curiosity forced me to investigate how this could happen, and the woman told me a story. She said that she had never married and lived alone most of her life, but in her later years her sister's husband had died, and the two sisters decided to move in together. Each year they festively celebrated each other's birthday when it came along. When I asked the woman about her sister, she remarked that her sister had died 5 years previously. So this woman stopped celebrating birthdays 5 years prior to my visit! Thus the woman remained 76 years of age for 5 years because her birthdays were never acknowledged when they came along. I felt bad driving away from her home that evening knowing I had aged the woman 5 years in a 1-hour interview!

I tell this story because the point here is important. Each of our truths is socially constructed. To understand, empathize, analyze, and so on, the condition of another person requires the relational partner (spouse, parent, social service worker, educator) to explore the social experience of that person—his or her history, relational circumstances, and environmental conditions. This is not to say that socially constructed truth is not helpful in life. While fortunately in this case the older woman did not appear to experience any dire consequences of her not knowing her chronological age, too often "statistics" (bits of information) disguise the complexity of a problem. As Mark Twain once said, there are three kinds of lies: "lies, damn lies, and statistics"!

Group life (or culture) allows the individual life to be successful. From this vantage it would seem that if the group life contains pathology, then the individual life cannot be healthy. This in specific and contemporary terms might be applied to school environments, neighborhood environments, and certainly family environments in which human cooperation and civility are sparse. Yet somehow the goal in these environments is often to promote individual growth and development while unfortunately ignoring the social climate that must be conducive to such development and necessary to foster its emergence.

The shortsightedness or limitations of personnel in these contexts results in a lack of attention to the health of a family or school environment. And the public does not adequately understand the unhealthy nature of, for instance, school environments. Often parents are suspicious of their neighborhood and its negative influences on their children but have little power to change such pervasive decay. Policy-makers, administrators, and budget managers tolerate environmental risks to youth because they, too, are overwhelmed with the pervasive quality of these threats. In the end, the public often tolerates neighborhood or school climates that are oppressive or violent because they know so little about such environments. For instance, most schools have a record of violent incidents, and teachers are confronted daily with threats to the safety of the individuals who occupy that space, including themselves; yet efforts to improve safety are insufficient due to the overwhelming number of tasks to which, say, school staff are assigned to improve such environments to rectify these problems.

While family life contributes to the risks some youth carry into school, few schools address family life directly through family group intervention or meetings. Schools are also much bigger than they should be to provide a sense of belonging and safety for the students. And most schools are understaffed, with teachers having an unrealistically high number of students in a given classroom to meet each child's needs, and more is expected with less time to do it. Hence it is not likely that student achievement and success, as well as safety, will be fostered in an environment that minimizes the role of family influences on risk behavior at school.

Two Domains of Problematic Situations

There are several social structures that are deserving of attention as they pertain to human problems. Many of these social arenas contain a problem of "lens-limited" approaches—preoccupation with a youth's individual characteristics—instead of comprehending problems and their solutions. Efforts toward inclusion, that is, expanding the social network of relevant participants engaged in problems defined as individual, are absent in other social contexts as well. Two social structures will be briefly mentioned here: school situations, and youth involved in juvenile delinquency. These two are mentioned for two reasons: familiarity to the author, and the serious implications for the future condition of these structures and our society.

At this juncture it is well established that the condition of a child's well–being is associated with environmental conditions. Two domains of youth problems—criminal behavior and school failure—are illustrative of this phenomenon. Romig, Cleland, and Romig (1989) suggest that social characteristics such as having delinquent friends, lack of attachment to prosocial institutions (schools, church, community organizations), absence of a law-abiding parent, lack of empathy toward others, boredom, impulsive behavior, and drug and alcohol abuse are among the strongest indicators of delinquent potential. These factors have not been established as causal. For instance, association with delinquent peers does not by itself predict criminal behavior, nor does income alone predict delinquency (Institute of Medicine, 1989; Rutter, 1980; Sameroff & McDonough, 1984; Schoror, 1988). There is not necessarily a co-occurrence of delinquency with other problem behaviors, such as drug use, in most cases (Huizinga, Loeber, Thornberry, & Cothern, 2000).

A review of young delinquent children indicates an association between low attachment to caregivers and its important role in later behavior and delinquency problems (Egeland & Farger, 1984; Adams, Hillman, and Gaydos, 1994; Loeber, Farrington, & Petechuk, 2003). In addition, delayed language development may increase a child's stress level, impede normal socialization, and result in criminality (Stattin & Klackenberg-Larsson, 1993; Loeber et al. 2003). The number of risk factors to which a child is exposed and the length of that exposure to these stressors are associated with early-onset offending (Williams, Anderson, McGee, & Silva, 1990). Antisocial parents, substance-abusing parents, parental psychopathology, poor parenting practices such as lack of monitoring (Patterson, Crosby, & Vuchinich, 1992) and lack of positive reinforcement (Bor, Najman, Anderson, O'Callaghan, Williams, & Behrens, 1997), prevalence of physical abuse, a history of family violence, and large family size all associate with early-age offending (Loeber et al. 2003).

Many risk factors are associated with other social systems such as peers and the community environment. However, a recent study found that the strongest predictors of early-onset violence were large family size, poor parenting skills, and antisocial parents (Derzon & Lipsey, 2000). Taking these factors collectively, what is readily apparent is the need for prevention and early intervention to alter developmental trajectories resulting from family influences. Crying out for greater attention is a harnessing of professional resources to build preventive family services, not waiting for intervention to be applied as late as adolescence when intractable peer groups and multiple family risk factors have been in place for a long time. A key theme in preventing child delinquency is "the earlier the better" (Loeber et al. 2003). Since the majority of these risk factors appear to be located in environmental influences (Zigler, Taussig, & Black, 1992), juvenile first offenders are deserving of more attention by the courts and children and youth service agencies. Juvenile first offenders are often past the age at which early intervention would have been optimal for them. Nonetheless, the time when youth come to the attention of school or juvenile justice staff is when family information comes to the attention of authorities (schools, communities, courts) via family data gathering. This first penetration into the school guidance or juvenile justice culture is when parents and families are most likely to be required to make a commitment to addressing the problems of the problem student or offender and the family. Part of this timeliness is due to the court's or school's leverage as the *first opportunity to require intervention.*

Families and Educational Success

The juvenile delinquency data are only one eye-catching trouble spot that contributes to societal ills and undermines the moral fabric of the culture. There have been so many reports of academic (non)achievement nationwide in standardized tests, grade point averages, school violence, and the like that little space in this volume is necessary to elaborate or repeat such horrid statistics. One contributing factor to this educational crisis is the influence of early family instability and dysfunction, family environmental risk, and poor school preparation on the breadth of school failure and truancy. The Edna McConnell Clark Foundation reported that in 1991 some 600,000 children lived apart from their families in foster care, group homes, or juvenile or psychiatric institutions. The United States spent $9 billion to care for children who had been removed from their homes. The Henry J. Kaiser Foundation reported that 43% of all adolescent girls in America will become pregnant at least once before the age of 20. The ramifications of this are not necessary to explain to the reader but, in summary, include fatherless families, poverty, higher risk of child abuse, a next generation of teen pregnancy, and school failure.

> In a Family Solutions Program (FSP) session on education, stacks of play money are laminated and held in a large container. A group leader then proceeds to discuss the relationship between educational success and lifetime financial earnings. Basing figures on U.S. census data, the group leader pulls out of the box stacks of $50,000 corresponding to the data indicating lifetime earnings for high school dropouts, high school graduates, graduates with associates degrees, graduates with 4-year college degrees, and those with graduate education. In this particular session, the reaction by parents and youth is animated as each generation realizes the magnitude of the differential incomes. The youth want to hold the money and discuss what they want to do now to overcome school problems to succeed. Parents may jokingly remark, "Why didn't I get this lesson when I was his [their child's] age?" The interest in this subject is high among parents and children because the stacks of money are a currency that both generations can relate to, and the practical implications of education become clear.

The importance of family partnership in educational endeavors is also well established. An example of the strength of family influence on school success is found in a persuasive article reporting the results of a study of academic achievement of over 200 Indo-Chinese refugee families in several cities in the United States. Evidence was overwhelming that parents were essential to their children's educational success (Caplan, Choy, & Whitmore, 1991). English was not the native language of these students, and yet they performed satisfactorily or above in school. When these researchers examined IQ, personality characteristics, and demographic data among racial and ethnic groups, what appeared significantly to predict success was family environment. Parents set standards and goals for weeknight evenings that facilitated academic progress. This occurred even when the parents' lack of education and English proficiency were evident. The tables in these homes are cleared, chores are completed, and homework begins, older children help younger siblings, and stories are read. Instead of personal efficacy, there is the presence of a *family efficacy*. Parents who attributed greater importance to fun and excitement in their lives had children with lower grades, while parents who emphasized the values of their past family history with children received higher grades.

In a dissertation study, 243 teachers were asked to identify one child from their classrooms about whom they had concerns. Then, throughout the year, teacher contacts with that child's family were tracked. The outcome was empirically established that teachers who had more frequent and varied contacts with their students' families observed the most positive change by the end of the year (Hill-Riley, 1994). The strength of the home–school partnership produced greater success for students. In a comprehensive study of childhood programs on social outcomes and delinquency, Yoshikawa (1995) found that demonstrated long-term effects on antisocial behavior or delinquency are likely if the programs combine intensive family support and early education services and impact a broad range of child and family risk factors for delinquency. These early childhood programs emphasizing prevention and early intervention approaches are establishing cost-effective benefits as well.

Just my reporting of this information or data illustrates the disharmony in the problem-solution congruence needed to eradicate major social problems. Only one reference point is conveniently used—that of the child and the behavior that society categorizes as a statistic. A youth's juvenile delinquency can be unequivocally identified, categorized, and summarized. The same is true for school academic achievement or failure. The life experiences of that youth that might explain delinquency, school failure, and the like are more complex.

Statistics on crime serve a purpose; however, alone they are not sufficient to generate a solution-oriented language to reduce or eradicate youth behavior problems because the numbers do not reflect the interrelatedness of the individual in context. Statistics too often reflect or convey a "pick yourself up by the bootstraps" mentality that allows persons who are not "statistics" a barricade and a drift into the dichotomy of "us-them"; parents may wall themselves off from their own children if they become so difficult as to be intolerable. Instead these statistics should be seen not only as aggregates of individual problems but reflections of social and structural problems. Just as the persons referred to suffer from self-defeating patterns of behavior, so, too, do institutions fall prey to that same pitfall in their efforts to rectify human problems. Very little understanding or inclusion of the family or community of the child is ever achieved when statistics are employed to build policy or program. Research on the school arena over the years has convincingly documented that when parents are involved in their children's education, better attendance records and more positive attitudes about education occur (Henderson, 1989), as well as the most crucial outcome—higher student achievement (Smith, 1968; Epstein, 1983).

Some parents may have valid reasons for parental detachment from a child's education. Some parents may not have benefited from any of the four educational experiences so necessary for learning and academic achievement—a sense of power, a sense of belonging, a sense of fun, or a sense of meaning (Glasser, 1985). These parents may have dropped out themselves, remember school as a place of humiliation or failure, or had no models in their own lives to demonstrate how education could inspire or lead someone to a successful and satisfying life. The family, then, can contribute to the child's experience of failing to consume any of these senses.

The challenge to build home–school partnerships, then, can be formidable. Many continual and varied efforts are needed to help some parents overcome their own sense of uneasiness working with the school in partnership for the sake of their child. Colleagues and I have offered a multisystemic approach using a family–school intervention team to provide direction for educators and parents interested in resolving chronic school problems of children (Quinn, Sutphen, Michaels & Gale, 1994). In this model, the interventionist is meta to the communication problem-solving process and serves as a facilitator of conversation that fosters reconciliation and collaboration among the families and school staff.

Schools themselves are often frustrated because of their lack of success using individual intervention with difficult students. For example, a school counselor who meets individually with a troubled student and provides encouragement or messages directed at self-esteem recognizes that such a student may be going home at the end of the school day to a dysfunctional or deprived family environment. Such an approach becomes a weak and inefficient intervention. We have found that a number of shifts in thinking here can be beneficial, and offer the following principles to guide any family–school meeting (Quinn et al. 1994).

Eight Principles for Successful Family–School Meetings

1. Parent and family behavior changes can affect a child's school behavior and consequently academic and social improvement. *Building a strong home–school partnership for a child is one of the cornerstones of school success.* For example, in a recent multisite project of 37 middle schools working in a family program with students nominated by their teachers for exhibiting aggressive behavior, we noticed that a daily goal sheet mechanism helped some students improve their school behavior (Corporate author, 2004). These daily goal sheets included three ratings by teachers: respect for teachers, respect for their peers, and completing work assignments. Students returned home at the end of each week to share these goal sheets with their parents. Parents checked the goal sheets each week and engaged in discussions with their children about their progress.

2. *Making the problem-solving collaboration more convenient is essential.* Asking parents to choose a time and day for a meeting and considering transportation needs and work schedules are important. Even more important, the nature of collaboration influences results. Asking "Can you meet on Tuesday at 4? That's when the school psychologist will be here," is not nearly as helpful as "What is a time that you (and your husband) could meet with us?" Many educators take the position that if it is likely that a family will attend a meeting at a time that they themselves request, school staff are more than willing to modify their own schedule to meet with the family.

3. The floor is open in the discussion to any participant who expresses concerns. *The goal is to steer conversation toward a consensual pragmatic plan.* Essential ingredients include questions, paraphrasing, and clarification. The goal of a family–school collaborative meeting is to end the meeting with a plan that is agreed upon by everyone in attendance. This plan should be adopted as a shared investment in which each person has a stake and role in the resolution of the problem.

4. School meetings are traditionally loaded with conversation that is unwittingly negative and inhibiting. The motivation to blame is an attempt to deflect personal responsibility and expunge frustration. Talking at levels of explanation is also unhelpful, since analysis

and causation are not concepts that are directly linked with solutions. *In essence, participants are encouraged to move from a "gripe-gripe-gripe" style to one that reflects "What can we do to change it?"*

5. The concept of "dichotomy" is expelled from the model of collaboration. Examples of the kind of dichotomies that are destructive in family–school meetings are being a good child or a bad child (or a good parent or a bad parent); having a good or bad childhood; and being a capable or incapable student. This misguided assumption that a child should be classified in this way in order to be understood (or defend one's behavior) is often expressed in triadic networks in which the school and family, or members within one of these systems, utilize the dichotomy of positions or preferences to differ with each other. This "dance" to shift blame conveniently reduces one's own personal responsibility. This is evident in the adversarial relationship that develops around disagreements about who is at fault: the family, the child, or the school. Of course, *these contests of who is at fault are bankrupt exercises that serve no productive purpose.*

6. A school–family collaboration, like any collaboration between people, requires meaningful conversation that allows good outcomes to emerge. The purpose of collaboration must be identified so that competing cross-agendas do not hamper the constructive interaction needed to achieve a goal. Each participant in the collaboration must be involved. *Everyone needs to feel a sense of belonging to the group, and thoughts and feelings must be invited that express needs and desired goals.* A dominating individual will shut down such shared ownership of the concern.

7. *A description of the problem must be negotiated that excludes the perception of personal inferiority or inadequacy of any individual.* Pieces of information need to be woven together that provide an image of the circumstances and context in which the problem is embedded. Patience is required, as well as some acknowledgment of another person's expertise. Each individual needs to recognize the constraints operating on oneself.

8. *Finally, reviewing, even recording, the plan before terminating any collaboration is helpful.* As any collaboration approaches termination in a given social interaction, questions or final thoughts need to be invited. In this way, motivation and clear direction for action are more likely to occur. Parental involvement in school is strengthened when school personnel enlist parental participation in decision-making and problem resolution. When this occurs,

the impact of the family on a child's school performance can be documented.

Juvenile Delinquency and Family–Community Intervention

Juvenile delinquency is threatening the well-being of families and communities around the country. It is an outcome of a blight that threatens the very nature of the social fabric of our culture and surely threatens the future well-being of the nation. The cost of juvenile delinquency is high. In 1999 there were 1,673,000 cases handled by the juvenile courts in this country, or almost 4,600 cases per day. There was a 37% increase in out-of-home placements between 1989 and just 9 years later in 1998. There were 119,700 out-of-home placements in 1989 and 163,800 in 1998. Between these same years the number of adjudicated cases resulting in a disposition of probation increased by 73%. Probation remains the most likely sanction imposed by juvenile courts. Yet we know very little about the effectiveness of this disposition. Given that 366,100 juveniles were placed on probation, over one third of a million youth receive a disposition that judges, juvenile court staff, and the public know little about pertaining to its effectiveness! It would never be acceptable to families or professionals if there was such little knowledge about adolescent medical or pharmacological treatment.

The financial costs of juvenile crime are high. In 1987 the average cost of care of an incarcerated youth for one year was approximately $40,000 (Davidson & Redner, 1988). One in four schools is vandalized each month, with a cost to the taxpayer of more than $200 million per year (National School Boards Association, 1984). The expense to personal property is many times higher.

Delinquent behavior also has a cost that cannot be put in monetary terms. Nor can it be determined how the quality of life is reduced for those living in high-crime areas, or the reduction in earning potential for the incarcerated youth who becomes impeded academically and vocationally. The effects of delinquency on one's siblings are not well understood but can be assumed to be substantial, as well as the emotional stress on family members (Gordon, Arbuthnot, Gustafson, McGree, & Farrington, 1987).

Social scientists have substantiated the many risk factors associated with juvenile delinquency. Research findings throughout this text are persuasive—that no single indicator has been established as sufficiently robust to predict delinquency. Furthermore, Farrington (1987) suggests that several indicators place youth at risk for delinquency: poor child-rearing practices and parental supervision are influential, as are the criminal behavior of parents and siblings, social deprivation such as low family income, large family size, low educational attainment, and below-standard housing. Forgatch (1991) proposes that parental monitoring is a mediator in the stress and child mental health relationship, while Loeber and Dishion (1983) find that supervision and discipline are predictors of juvenile delinquency.

These findings are presented to document the severity of consequences for persons and communities and to recognize the environmental influences that associate with individual behavior. There are some examples of the importance of a wider lens that can be applied to juvenile offender intervention, including functional family therapy (Alexander, Barton, Schiavo, & Parsons, 1976; Alexander, Pugh, Parsons, & Sexton, 2000), family-based services (Nelson, 1990); the FAST program (McDonald & Frey, 1999), the Strengthening Families program (Kumpfer & Tait, 2000); and multisystemic therapy (Henggeler, Melton, & Smith, 1992; Henggeler, Pickrel, & Brondino, 1999). The value of family-based intervention for at-risk children and juvenile offenders has been effectively documented. It is evident from these studies, and those of our own (Quinn, Sutphen, Michaels, & Gale, 1994; Quinn, Bell, & Ward, 1997; Quinn & VanDyke, 2001; Quinn, VanDyke, & Kurth, 2002; Quinn & VanDyke, 2004), that *family factors associate with juvenile delinquency, and that effective programs require family involvement.*

An example from our own work is the one delineated in this text as a model that moves away from probation and individual approaches for many at-risk youth and juvenile offenders. In this model, a multiple family group intervention indicates a reduction in the rate of repeat offenders, interrupting their continuation in the cycle of criminal behavior. We convene multiple family groups to resolve the offending behavior of their children. Furthermore, these groups are guided to utilize each other's help, counsel, and resources to develop more effective ways of thinking about family life and child development. The family group approach fosters a shared problem-solving activity and offers parents help in monitoring the behavior of children of the neighborhood.

The vast experience with this intervention model has led us to develop an entirely family–community-based approach that is evolving into a mainstream program for youth at risk (see chapter 5, "Development of the Family Solutions Program"). In conceptualizing the program, the goal was not to have a preset program that the participants would have to fit into like a Procrustean bed. Rather, the goal was to create a program that was flexible and adaptable to the immediate needs of the participants. This entailed having a program that was both: (1) structured and consistent with each family program so that the best components found in the program were maintained and evaluation could be undertaken; and (2) sensitive to feedback from the families and facilitators participating in the program (e.g., there are nine optional sessions embedded in the family manual that can be considered relevant depending on the characteristics and needs of the families).

In this approach, families are viewed as doing better when they can voice their ideas together in a collaborative fashion. Each person in each family is invited to share with the other families his or her situation and to tell the story of it. Peers respond from a collaborative level to help normalize the problems, offer other perspectives on the issues, and discover possible solutions.

The program is a flexible one that allows for all parts of the system to provide feedback. Each night of the program, the families are involved in evaluating the program and stating what they want and need that night. While there is a program structure that contains themes (i.e., family communication, value of education, conflict resolution), these are seen as cornerstones much like the foundation of a sturdy building. For instance, one night when the focus was to be on problem-solving communication, the issue of the cost of athletic shoes arose when a parent and youth shared with the group a conflict about purchasing new basketball shoes. This comment led to a group discussion on family finances and family budgets. This led further to the development of a family finance worksheet that families could utilize in their financial planning. Further discussion ensued on the potential violence arising out of a green-with-envy view of athletic wear worn by other youth, as well as the burden to families of financial outlay for unnecessary household purchases.

The program is designed to lead to discussion on topics that are relevant to the particular neighborhood and community. Community leaders (e.g., school counselor, youth services worker) facilitate discussion in such areas as working with the schools, surviving street crime, taking an active approach to safety through parental monitoring, and peer group choices. Eliciting participation and support from the community is a gradual and continual process. Various churches are used as locations for programs that help inform the clergy of the community effort with juvenile delinquents and families. Parents who participated as family members of juvenile delinquents have become facilitators of the group process in subsequent programs. In this way, a down-up motion (family to professional) is as present as much as an up-down motion (professional to family) in which action or change can be initiated or occur within any part of the group structure.

Finally, family advocates, the helping professionals on the project who also serve as group facilitators, are connected to each family in the program to be available for collaboration when further problems may be encountered. These advocates are helpful in resolving a sense of injustice these families feel they sometimes receive from the judicial system. Advocates provide encouragement and a proven allegiance that allows families to resolve their fear or reluctance that they will simply be caught up within another system that will not understand their needs. Using ethnographic methods, in which lengthy interviews with families selected at random were conducted, we have learned what families appreciated about the program as well as their suggestions for improvement. For instance, the youth volunteered that they benefited most from role-plays and experiential exercises; parents expressed appreciation for the manner in which the group became a support in the face of family adversity as well as an opportunity to learn about their own influences on their children.

In this program, intervention occurs at the community level as well. Juvenile court personnel have scheduled court appearances for families to attend that are more sensitive to the families' predicaments, such as evening court hours for employed parents. The implicit consequence is that judicial court staff possess a responsiveness that accommodates to families. The court has responded more quickly to family needs due to the communication with collaborators from the FSP. One example of inclusion of family and community influence in the FSP, is that all subpoenas for hearings in the juvenile court include the parent(s) *and* the youth and can be scheduled at 5 p.m. or later. Not to be in violation requires the participation in such meetings of a parent(s) as well as the youth. Case workers now mirror the language used by the FSP court representative to discuss expectations of parents and youth attending case adjudication hearings. This teamwork requires a belief in the model resulting from feedback to the court by family graduates of the program.

Customer (Family) Requests to a Store Manager (Counselor/Administrator)

There is a much bigger science in the fields of marketing, advertising, and public relations than there is in human service delivery. Yet similar principles often apply. Store managers, corporations, and retail businesses are constantly finding ways to connect with the consumer. They know that without these connections business will dry up. Yet in human service delivery there is very little effort placed on connecting to the consumer, in this case the child and family. We set out to examine what clients said about their therapy experiences, with the aim of detecting important processes that could be generalized to program development and group leader skills.

It is infrequent that the customer (family) has the opportunity to express the experience of engaging with a helper in the human service network. We were struck by powerful family descriptions that shed a light on a darkened area of an interventionist's understanding of what helps individuals and families. Some accounts do exist, and a few brief examples were given above. In this section, a more elaborate set of findings will be reported that could be extrapolated for the benefit of informing service providers. Inquiries were made that allowed clients in family intervention to tell the stories of their experiences. By allowing clients to tell their stories, professionals who intervene can reciprocally receive guidance that helps them become more effective. These stories helped guide the development of our model, including what has to take place first and what has to be continually present that drives the change process toward positive outcomes. We asked 14 families to sit down with someone trained in family intervention—but not their therapist—to describe their experience. We unearthed as many ideas and new insights as could be gleaned from the interviews until such conversations reached saturation; that is, the families were using more examples to make the same point or conveying an idea expressed previously but using different words.

The question can be asked: How do clients describe their therapeutic experiences? Recently we studied this in our own program. There were three domains of meaning that emerged for clients who had completed therapy (Quinn, 1996b). The first domain we labeled *affirmation*. This term was selected because it circumscribes the many comments clients made about the idea that the interventionist had valued and respected the family and each member. This domain was built up with phrases offered by the clients who described the attitudes and behavior of the interventionist. Here are some examples of the phrases offered by family members: "we count," "being able to stay with me" (on my level of thinking or feeling), "extending herself," "drawing me into her life," "being brought into your spouse's feelings without being a dummy," and "not hiding" (showing courage to face adversity).

A second domain was labeled *discovery*, and was comprised of client phrases such as "the light going off," "not clamming up," "throwing questions right back at us," "asking a question I never considered," "putting a new wrinkle on something," "experiencing great organization of the brain," "not knowing its working" (change is occurring), and "giving me permission to take on a new role." Family members appreciate the opportunity to change, to be challenged, and to behave differently and more competently. This is an important revelation in that interventionists are sometimes reluctant to challenge family members to consider changing their attitudes, behavior, or role in the family, especially when they are upset, defensive, or accusatory. These family members were telling us that they appreciated the challenge directed towards them by interventionists.

Despite the occasional discomfort this would create because it placed them in a confusing state, clients came out on the other side with more resources or a better attitude.

The third domain was labeled *congruence*, and included phrases such as "connecting what was happening," "keeping me on balance," "pinpointing the problem," "knowing where I need to go," "putting myself through this little session in my mind" (during the week between sessions), "building up the talk," and "someone who can help in that area." The analogy of a dance is useful here—the idea that for some family members, they felt that good things happened when their interventionist was in step with them. The interventionist understood their circumstances, predicaments, or limitations, and created ways to relate that were relevant and meaningful for that situation.

These client descriptions, categorized as affirmation, discovery, and congruence, are not necessarily original. Nevertheless, they take on a relevance as they reflect the importance of social interaction, relational utility, and the salience of group properties in the production of better outcomes for persons. These better outcomes might be in the form of resolution of personal problems, new and more helpful ways of thinking about self and/or the world, or the experience of productive and respectful human interaction.

An extrapolation of the voices of family members to the human service delivery enterprise might foster some different points of view for service providers as they pertain to collaboration or partnership. First, families are requesting from the service provider some communication that offers a sincere acknowledgment of them. They want to be respected; in a sense they need to know that "How this interventionist is relating to me tells me I count, I matter." This acknowledgment includes a respect for one's needs and situation and a sincere attempt to remain connected ("not hide") and not retreat from the problems in one's life.

Second, families are asking for helpful information or a new idea from the helper that might contribute to the resolution of the problem (discovery). Innovative and cocreated ideas are privileged over standard, predictable, and bureaucratic responses. Examples of the latter might be ideas expressed by another caseworker or a rigidly adamant family member such as "don't worry," "everything will be OK," "I'm sure it must be painful," or "we will see what we can do."

Third, the helper should be engaged in focused interaction that sets in motion actions that make meaningful sense to the family and the helper. These coordinated movements can be more possible when the helper solicits input from family members about whether a plan, its components, and its implementation are sensible and relevant.

This set of ideas leads to two implications that emerge from a relational lens through which to view ecological intervention:

1. The condition and development of human beings are embedded in an ecology that contains certain human interaction, physical conditions, and cultural beliefs. As such, to consider the needs of persons requires the broadest understanding of this ecology, and where needs are unfulfilled in such an ecology, attempts must be made to alter conditions of living in such a way as to ameliorate impediments to development. In more specific terms, it would seem that a greater thrust is needed in society in organizing ecologies at the familial, social, and political levels to promote productive and meaningful life experiences for persons. Hence parental skill development, healthy early-learning environments, and community support resources for parents should be emphasized. Also, intervention programs should begin early in life for at-risk children (Kelley et al. 1997; McDonald & Frey, 1999). An important debate that requires better resolution is at the policy-making level, at which intervention programs that are reviewed and possibly funded are "too little, too late" to help in any meaningful way. These programs preclude the support needed to prevent or ameliorate earlier the human despair and hardship. One example of this call to rethink the point of intervention is the thorough review of the importance of early childhood intervention in preventing juvenile delinquency (Zigler et al. 1992; Kumpfer & Tait, 2000; Wasserman, Miller, & Cothern, 2000).

2. Decision-making in intervention must account for the ecological variables that influence problems of living. Family data are essential in constructing service delivery plans, whether it be within the educational system, human service systems, or family system. A social-context perspective is essential as a way to assess the level of motivation for change in the web of social relations, to determine the locations of resources, and to understand current human behavior. Examples include allowing every decision-making process in educational contexts to include family data as well as family members themselves, juvenile delinquency intervention to include family participation, and mental health delivery to require family (or the significant social network) participation.

When this approach is utilized, it can often include influential persons, such as a noncustodial but actively involved parent or extended-family members who do not live in the household. Of vital importance is the consideration of the inclusion of both parents in a two-parent household in intervention, instead of just one parent, when marital conflict may sabotage intervention efforts. Often, in cases where only one parent participates in intervention in a two-parent household, the parent who attends does so by proxy. The parent who attends "negotiates" or arranges a plan with the spouse to go alone, protecting the other parent (or herself) who has a more conflictual relationship with the children or demonstrates less commitment to the family's well-being. In this way intervention is co-opted, because the division between the "good" parent and the "bad" parent grows wider, which creates more chronic triangulation problems in the family environment (e.g., a more abusive or emotionally distant relationship between the "bad" parent and a child).

The inclusion of both parents in intervention provides the opportunity to soften these rigid complimentary positions of the parents. The presence of both parents makes more accessible to the child the parent who can be helped to be less harsh and more committed to the parenting role. To provide an analogy, in a medical setting, a physician would refuse to initiate surgery without the availability of every necessary surgical tool and piece of equipment in the room. So too, regarding intervention with children, there should be the availability and presence of every resource in the child's ecology, that being all the members of the family.

CHAPTER 4

A Multiple Family Group Perspective

To love another you have to undertake some fragment of their destiny.
—Quentin Crisp (1908–1999)

The Efficacy of Family Intervention

Family intervention programs addressing youth problems have received increasing attention. The multiple family group approach has more utility than the helping professions often acknowledge. There are multiple family group models to ameliorate psychopathology and alcoholism (Steinglass, 1995, 1987; Lawson & Lawson, 1996), family-based social services to stabilize families who are abusive or impoverished (Nelson, 1990), and psychoeducation groups for schizophrenic patients and their families (McFarlane, Link, Dushay, Marchal, & Crilly, 1995; McFarlane, 2002), showing four-year follow-up results using multiple family group intervention in positive parenting programs integrated into primary care services (Sanders, 1999), and structured family intervention groups to address early-onset school-related problems and risks of delinquency (Kumpfer & Tait, 2000; McDonald & Frey, 1999). They all provide support for the utilization of a family–community perspective in delinquency intervention. Snyder and Huntley (1990) propose that early intervention is the most effective with delinquents, and that the family should be a focus of prevention and clinical interventions, with social policy and programs aiming to support the family and its optimal functioning.

Why a Multiple Family Group Model?

There are four major reasons for making the Family Solutions Program (FSP) a multiple family group model. The first is that *many traditional methods of rehabilitation in the form of behavior problem resolution, juvenile crime reduction, and rehabilitation of youth have for too long been ineffective.* Deterrence efforts that attempt to curb criminal behavior using threatened punishments have not provided compelling evidence that increasing the severity of punishment reduces crime (Greenwood, 1996). Probation continues to grow as a case disposition for juvenile offenders, and yet the vagueness generated by such court decisions regarding youth responsibility or resolution has resulted in less-than-persuasive conclusions regarding its effectiveness. In actuality, the certainty with which sanctions are applied is more effective. If a uniform staircase of sanctions is articulated to youth, families, and court personnel, positive outcomes in the form of decreased delinquency do occur. In the case of multiple family group work, this is certainly articulated in the FSP by describing the consequences of participating in and completing the program. In the program described here, families are aware that the status of probation, "informal adjustment," or condition of any other further obligation to the court is removed if they "graduate" from the program. This provides incentive to the families to attend. The family peer pressure operating in the group can solidify the group members and serve to maintain the objective of completion. Once group trust and cohesion are established, group members encourage and facilitate each other's participation.

A more important reason for the family group model is that it is structured as a *community-based model.* Community-based models have been shown to be more effective than institutional placements (Lipsey, 1992). Lipsey found, combining all reported evaluation studies using a meta-analysis, that there was a significant advantage in favor of community programs as compared to large institutional placement. Individual counseling, trained mentor volunteers, vocational programs, and intense deterrent schemes such as Scared Straight have not been shown to be effective (McCord, 1978; Lipsey, 1992). Methods that focus on prosocial skill development are likely to be 10% to 20% more effective in reducing further delinquency than individual counseling or general education (Arenwood, 1996). In addition, bringing youth together in unsupervised or unstructured settings—recreational activities being an example—has not been effective (McCord, 1978; Dishion, McCord, & Poulin, 1999). This potential result is attributed to the element of negative peer pressure that operates in these groups, which encourages delinquency (Elliott, Huizinga, & Menard, 1989). As Greenwood (1996) concluded, "All things being equal, treatment programs operating in community settings are likely to be more effective in reducing recidivism than similar programs provided in institutions" (p. 83).

Another factor supporting the view that community-based programs like the one described in this book generally have greater success is that they are *conducted by private or independent professionals and organizations, as opposed to institutional personnel.* As Greenwood states, "regular probation is effectively no treatment at all" (p. 82). Even intense supervision, probation, and lower caseloads produce negligible results (Petersilia & Turner, 1993). In an interview with a family that graduated from the program, an older sibling of a first-offender youth enrolled in the program remarked, "I wish this program was available to me when I was his (younger brother) age. All I did was show up to check in with the probation officer once a month, but every time I left I thought: but my life isn't changing, and I wanted it to."

Private sponsorship in which well-trained professionals develop and implement a well-defined intervention model appears to be more effective (Greenwood, 1996). This finding is partly due to the likelihood that the researcher or evaluator of a program is more likely to be involved in its implementation. In addition, private sponsorship of programs requires accountability to remain viable. To demonstrate results, a focus on targeted behavior change is relevant. In addition, there are not sufficient incentives in institutional settings for professionals to learn new skills or be rewarded for program development or enhancement.

The third reason for a multiple family group model is that *group processes are particularly valuable for these families, given their apathy or distrust of professional systems.* One of the common fallacies in mental health delivery is the assumption that people who are troubled will seek help from professionals, similar to the manner in which people who are ill seek a physician. However, as stated in the previous section on client expectations, the relationship between the professional and the family is pronounced and serves as the vehicle for discovery and change.

Pharmacological developments and education of society pertaining to mental illness and personal problems have increased acceptability of this aspect of overall health. And inroads have been made with some political leaders who acknowledge the vital part that mental health treatment plays in societal well-being. Health care reform efforts and political dialogue at the national level have encouraged more discussion related to the proper level of mental health coverage acceptable to meet the needs of patients and families. Yet it is widely known that many personally troubled individuals and persons in conflictual relationships do not choose to engage a helping professional in resolving life difficulties. Why is this so? Many reasons exist for this current situation:

Reasons to Avoid a Helping Professional

1. A perception that personal troubles should be kept to oneself or inside the family.

2. A sense that professionals don't share enough common characteristics to understand.
3. Prohibitive costs of seeking help from a professional.
4. A fear that people will find out and think differently of the person(s).
5. A fear that an employer might use such a practice as a reason to fire or not promote or hire that person.
6. The tendency of professionals in mental health delivery, particularly those in private practice, to organize their practices for the self-referral. This professional approach assumes that there are people who acknowledge a personal problem and seek professional help.

Of course, the above-listed reasons for not seeking help must not interfere with the self-referred person. (The self-referred person can be a couple or family as well.) Professionals schedule appointments for these self-referred persons based on the convenience to the practitioner. In addition, the practitioner assumes a high level of motivation brought by the self-referred person. The self-referred person also has financial resources to purchase this mental health service. Needless to say, the conditions in this situation are optimal for beginning treatment and setting ambitious goals. These goals can range from removal of symptoms such as depression or chronic marital conflict to the striving for personal happiness and fulfillment. Some of these goals are unrealistic; nonetheless, such reasons for seeking the help of a therapist are sometimes legitimate.

Yet *as much as we might believe that advancement in the treatment of human problems has occurred, an entire segment of the population is left out of this scenario as it pertains to mental health delivery.* For instance, in the multiple family group model proposed, families will remark, "You know, I knew we had a problem; I just didn't know where to go," or "I didn't want to admit the problems until the court required us to come here." In other cases, the remark takes the form of "I didn't think I could fit something like this into my day; life is so hectic," or "I couldn't afford to seek help for my life problems." These are families that would *never* self-refer due to perceptions that mental health services are for the mentally ill, those who can afford it, those who have more in common with a professional, or those who have the time for it. As a result, many persons and families in our society never reap the benefits of the professional expertise of mental health providers in their communities.

This is analogous to the parent education group leader who invites the public and finds that the vast majority of volunteer participants seem to be doing somewhat satisfactory as parents prior to the start of the program. The reason that parents attend is that they know how important parenting is to child well-being and simply want to assure themselves that they are using ideas and practices that are effective. Those parents who are not aware of their influence simply rule it out. To a degree, the public, the field of psychotherapy, and the social services put into place to accommodate the poor have a higher opinion of the level of benefits they are providing to families in need than really exists.

Those who are required by the public or institutions to attend a human service program due to the consequences of a criminal act are often assigned to professionals who have high caseloads. They may also knowingly have modest academic training or experience due to the financial resources of these agencies but have few opportunities to advance their competencies. The multiple family group program discussed in this book is a vital intervention program because it is offered to the host of persons and families in communities who would likely never self-refer for professional services. In this individualistic society, most professional interventions have been applied to the individual. Even in juvenile court, any counseling services available are primarily offered only to the youth. In fact, there is often a requirement that caseworkers demonstrate and document one-to-one time (hours/minutes) spent with a youth. The belief in such an individualistic society is that the youth must pay the price of a poor choice of behavior, or that the youth who makes poor choices is troubled and in need of special attention.

These beliefs may not be inherently incorrect. However, such a framework for delivering services neglects the environmental context of the youth's existence. There is a plethora of research reports (many of them referred to previously) indicating the association between family and ecological factors and juvenile crime, as well as other child and adolescent problems. Therefore any intervention that ignores such an acknowledgment selects to attempt to repair a youth's life in a vacuum. For instance, building self-esteem as a therapeutic goal for a youth may help a child have a slightly different view of him- or herself upon leaving the counselor's office. The school context may support the youth, which adds to the youth's self-worth within that setting. Yet when that child returns home and hears messages, either verbally or implied through interactional mediums (from a parent), that he is "lazy," "no good," or "trouble," the intervention essentially washes out. If it does not wash out, such communication at least discourages that youth within that context and the community around the home. When a child is told by a school counselor that "whenever you need to talk, come see me" and then returns home to an abusive or alcohol-abusing parent, it is not likely that the brief interchanges in the counselor's office will have much effect.

Self-esteem is not genetically rooted within an individual. Rather, a positive view of oneself is a consequence of interactional experiences in which a child is valued. These results can be derived from family messages conveying the value of a child to the parent or from good outcomes of a child's initiative that in some cases are facilitated by parents. Examples of good outcomes might be a successful experience in an athletic contest, artistic expression, a charitable activity, or an academic accomplishment. The accumulation of such experiences add self-perceived value to the child and a confidence that more advanced initiatives that will produce higher levels of skills or competence are possible. Conversely, a lack of such successful experiences for a child produces a negative perception of self and a growing self-doubt as new challenges are encountered. Experiences that lead to good outcomes can be more realistically arranged for youth within the context of the family and community. This is because their age and standing in the society do not allow them as much opportunity to create these positive experiences independent of adults.

The premise that self-esteem is a child characteristic that derives from interactional experiences provides a foundation for building an intervention model that incorporates parental involvement. Many children and youth at risk who participate in any intervention often begin with the attitude that they are inadequate or irresponsible in some way. It is important that intervention be designed to provide experiences that foster self-esteem and hopefulness. In the multiple family group model, this is done by devising activities that require the involvement of youth. For instance, youth in the FSP must participate in a community activity that helps contribute to their view of themselves as contributors to the community. They may devote half a day to cleaning up or beautifying a school playground, prepare and serve a meal at a homeless shelter, or play bingo and bring prizes at the local senior center. Youth also participate in role-plays that help them understand conflict situations. They also negotiate pledges with their parents to resolve complaints they have with each other. Each of these activities helps build the child's view that he or she has value, can learn skills to be successful in social situations, can contribute to the lives of others, and can overcome adversity.

There are many attributions parents make, like the attribution that a child's confidence or view of his- or herself is built internally, that organize parents to define child problems as located within the child's own skin. Parents may not always say it, but it is common for parents to think about their children: "he is lazy," "she is self-centered," "he is mean," "she is stubborn." This tendency diminishes the likelihood of parents seeking help for their family; rather, help is sought for a child. Professionals frequently respond to these attributions by adopting this mind-set as well, thereby reducing the likelihood of family intervention.

Given the importance of the role of the family in child well-being, as outlined earlier, the multiple family group model requires that the family attend the intervention program. It is a challenge for those who plan and implement the program to convey this expectation to families. This difficulty is due to the very existence of the theme previously mentioned—that an individual's behavior is viewed narrowly as a reflection of personal (in)competence unrelated to the context and isolated within the person (youth).

Throughout this book there will be illustrations of how multiple family group intervention fosters dynamics that promote positive behavior change. The following family members who participated in an FSP are presented to create a lively set of scenarios to examine and demonstrate such group dynamics. While these family members are fictitious, they are composites that comprise actual qualities evidenced in cycles of the FSP over time.

The Cast of Characters

Shay, aged 14, and her mother, *Patti*, were very determined to avoid involvement in the FSP following referral from the juvenile court. Patti was a single mother who worked a day shift in a factory in town. She had two other children, both younger than Shay, and she was adamant that getting to the FSP would be nearly impossible. Shay was truant from school. Patti would leave for work early in the morning, dropping one child at day care and the other at her elementary school on the way. Shay would have no one at home in the morning to monitor her and hence would stay home without accountability to anyone.

Brandon, aged 13, and his mother, *Virginia*, were referred from the court due to a shoplifting charge. Virginia was from the Philippines, and had met her husband, *Mark*, when he was in the military there. They had recently moved to town due to Mark's assignment at the nearby military base. Brandon and his younger brother, *Ernie*, moved frequently as his father was routinely relocated by the military. Brandon and Virginia came to the program without Mark due to his military duties, which often took him away from the base for several days at a time. Since Virginia's family was in the Philippines, she had little extended family support and no close friends in town due to the recent move to the present military base. Her English was broken but sufficient to communicate with others in the group. In fact, she was expressive and enthusiastic, which made her liked by the group because she would always have an answer or response to a question, which saved other group members from having to respond. Virginia would wear a smile as if it was as fixed as the nose on her face and, while she was a petite woman, would wear brightly colored long dresses which matched her personality.

David, aged 15, was referred to the program due to a continual record of truancy from school. His mother, *Jackie,* and father were divorced. His mother worked long hours and rarely knew if David had missed school on any given day. When the school did contact Jackie about David's absence on a given day, she would talk to David and scold him for being irresponsible. Yet her work demands made it difficult to track David's school attendance, and he could miss days without her knowing it. David's father had left the home about a year earlier, and David felt rejected and hurt. David's father was later recruited to the program.

Sam, aged 16, was a large boy, about 6 foot 2, and 230 pounds. Yet he presented as "a big teddy bear." Sam was friendly and polite, and didn't hesitate to talk when he had a chance. Sam played football, but it was not clear whether he was very serious about it or did it because his friends and family thought his physique demanded it of him. Sam had an older brother, *Dan,* who had left recently for boot camp after enlisting in the army. Sam's mother, *Debra,* was married to *Jeff,* who had a well-paying job and came to the group when he was not out of town as a sales representative. Debra was doing part-time work now that the boys were growing up. Sam had gotten in a fight at school resulting in the other boy receiving injuries of a broken nose and wounded pride. Debra and Jeff both believed that Sam was targeted because of his size, and neither was too upset or concerned, believing that Sam did not have a problem because he was not the instigator.

Robert was a 14-year-old African-American boy who had two older brothers, *Steve* and *Jesse.* Steve and Jesse were several years older than Robert and were in and out of the house at various times. Robert's mother, *Joan,* had never lived with either Robert's father or the father of the two older boys. Joan was a school cafeteria worker who was always trying to make ends meet. Since they lived in public housing, Robert often "borrowed" bicycles and used property such as basketballs and footballs from others in the neighborhood. Robert was referred to the program because he did not return the bicycle he most recently "borrowed" and so another family reported it stolen.

Brittany was a perky, tall, sliver of a 15-year-old girl who wore very tight-fitting clothes to reveal her every curve. She was referred for truancy (and during the program was arrested again for shoplifting with another girl). Her mother, *Denise,* was attractive and had a live-in boyfriend, *Max,* whom Brittany despised. He was a truck driver and often not home during the week and hence could not attend the program. Denise dressed similarly to Brittany, in provocative, tight-fitting clothes. Denise worked part-time but depended on her ex-husband's salary for support. Brittany let her physical appearance speak for her and for the first two weeks had a "chip on her shoulder," speaking only when requested and trying to avoid participating in any activity.

The FSP had been tempted in earlier times to allow a youth to participate without the parents' involvement. This is largely due to the strong desire of program leaders to help a youth despite family indifference so as not to deprive the youth of a potentially useful experience. For example, once a juvenile court probation officer knowingly referred a child without the parent's agreement to attend. A difficult, but appropriate, decision was made to refer the child back to the court because of the lack of parent involvement. The probation officer said, "but I know he will benefit from the program." This is a natural desire on the part of persons in the helping profession and is understandable. However, to comply with this request is inconsistent with the multiple family group model. In addition, it could encourage other parents to withdraw, with the idea put in their heads: "If that child's parent is not attending, why should I?"

To settle for such a circumstance of a targeted child involved in intervention without the parent prematurely writes off the involvement of the family. We have found that several approaches are often necessary in an attempt to include the family. This requirement is one reason why mental health delivery is in fact individualistic within institutional settings. The logistics involved in including members of the ecological context of a youth are seen by agencies or professionals as simply too overwhelming. Scheduling conflicts ensue, case management is more complicated, and a vast array of information is too overwhelming when collected from several sources such as family members. Such a view is in part a reflection of the vestiges of psychotherapeutic intervention early in the 20th century, in which the family was seen as the root of an individual's problem; therefore, it was thought, a more appropriate way to work with someone was to separate the youth from the perils of family pathology.

While the family may in fact be comprised of elements that contribute to a youth's difficulties, the family can also be seen as the context for the resolution of these difficulties. Some exceptions to family involvement exist, of course, at various times in a family's progression over time. For instance, domestic violence must be eliminated, and alcohol-related chaos and abuse must be treated for the family to be viewed as a healing agent.

However, these conditions should not serve as reasons to exclude the family or even certain members of the family considered malevolent or personally troubled. After all, in many cases these persons will continue to have an ongoing relationship with the youth and other members of the family. There is an ethical imperative here that interventionists do not sever ties to family members, except for certain abusive and potentially dangerous circumstances. Mental health workers can overstep their bounds by doing so. After all, the caseworker is not the one who will in that child's future schedule and prepare a birthday party, transport the child to important activities, or share family history that promotes values, pride, and self-respect (Pipher, 1996). Professionals need to explore many avenues in designing family inclusion in intervention for children.

One reason for multiple family group intervention is to overcome the shared perception that *mental health providers cannot possibly know what the lives of they and their family members can be like.* Multiple family group intervention removes this obstacle because family members join other families who face similar challenges and share common experiences. Mental health professionals are all too commonly middle-class adults of a different ethnicity from their clients. These characteristics do not represent all facets of the fabric of a society or community. As a result, some of these professionals, such as teachers, officers of bureaucratic institutions, and mental health providers, have not sufficiently accepted or understood many families. While these professionals have competence, they can at times be limited by a pejorative view of family life or a lack of exposure to cultural variation.

Some of these families may have been previously related to in an unjust or harmful way, at least as perceived by the family. Some families recruited to intervention programs have had previous experiences that were dissatisfying. Some of these failed outcomes in recruitment are due to:

- perceived promises that were broken;
- distrust of the referring or recruiting person due to style or stress carried by the professional recruiting the family; or
- the organizational structure that exists for delivering services (e.g., office hours that do not match the family's availability, lack of supervision of recruitment staff, budget constraints that reduce time sufficient to interact with an ambivalent family).

This distrust can be due to previous dissatisfaction with government or community agencies or schools. Class differences between professionals and some of the families can contribute to a mind-set by the families, however valid or invalid, that professionals cannot identify with their predicaments. Family members can possess the following thoughts about professionals:

- "These people can't possibly know my situation, circumstance, or struggle."

- "Their suggestions can't possibly fit in my home or in my life."
- "They travel in different orbits from me."
- "They're going to want to tell me how to live my life like them."

Currently under way in the professional culture is an emphasis on training in diversity. These efforts should be commended. However, what has been underemphasized is the importance of bringing diverse families together in intervention to represent a microcosm of a community in which family members gain experience in real situations calling for understanding, appreciation of others, and tolerance. A multiple family group becomes a "community." As a "community," the group discovers that it shares similar needs and desires, which confirm the value of the person. Members of the multiple family group, or "community," also take an active interest in each other because they are in close proximity to each other and learn about and observe each others' lives. Some neighborhoods in communities provide this support, although unfortunately it is not as prevalent as in the past. For instance, many adults remember their neighborhood when they grew up as a network of adults who took an interest in them as well as sharing the responsibility of keeping them safe or monitoring their behavior. More often in neighborhoods currently, adults "look the other way" if their own children are not involved, or are in such transition that they have little interest in getting to know neighbors.

The second reason for a multiple family intervention model is that *because of a pervasive sense of personal disempowerment or despondency, groups of similar persons provide validation and hope.* Persons who feel disenfranchised or despondent have difficulty accepting information, suggestions, or views from others whom they view as empowered or more positive about their lives. Parents may be tempted to feel that it is "easy for them to say" when dealing with those with whom they feel they share little in common. The group derives ideas, cognitive frames, and prescriptions for behavior changes that arise from members' experiences. The group members, and the group dynamics that organize the flow of language in the group, promote interaction in which the families own the issues they are working out. This is contrary to the intervention frame in which the professional accepts the responsibility for resolving family conflicts. The group discovers what is important to its members while embedded in these interchanges in group discussions.

The topic of parental monitoring and supervision was the focus of one session of the FSP. One mother, Denise, used this opportunity to express her anger and resentment toward her live-in boyfriend. Denise was the mother of Brittany, the 15-year-old daughter of Denise and her ex-husband. Her boyfriend, Max, was an 18-wheeler tractor-trailer driver who was out of town all week. During the week

Denise was expected to supervise Brittany, see that she made curfew and got her schoolwork done, and was not in places "where she should not be, with people she should not be with." Denise stated: "I have to see to it that Brittany follows the rules all week, and deal with her attitude, and all Max wants is to come home on Friday night with his truck and have a cold 6-pack of beer in the refrigerator and to spoil Brittany all weekend because he feels guilty that he has been gone all week. He wants me to feel like he is helping me. Spoiling her doesn't help me! It just makes him feel less guilty! Well I resent it!" At this point, Sam's mother, Debra, who had been listening quietly to Denise's story, responded. She said, "Denise, I've been there, that was the situation I was in with Jeff a while back and we got things worked out. Do you mind if I get your phone number and I'll call you this week and we can talk?" That was "music to the ears" of the group leader because it served as a perfect example of the promise of a multiple family group program for a community to be developed in which families help each other and give each other hope.

Parents enter a multiple family group program as a result of a mandate to participate in an experience that addresses the behavior of their children. They can be held accountable to the juvenile court, for instance, for a criminal offense committed by their children. The context of the engagement of parents and the juvenile court influences the attitudes and feelings parents hold. For example, some parents express embarrassment that their own child has been reported for behavior that violates society sanctions. Interestingly, however, this is not present in many families. If embarrassment is present, the feeling is not nearly as prominent as anger or frustration that they as parents are required to meet with juvenile court officials. In some cases, the parents feel relieved that their children are being noticed for inappropriate conduct and hope that maybe some control will be exerted on their lives by an authority—control that the parents could not attain. In other families, individuals may have disdain for the institution requiring their participation, forcing them to feel more marginalized and apart from the standard of the community.

When juvenile courts were established at the end of the 19th century, a primary purpose was to protect children from harmful sources such as neglectful or abusive parents or living conditions that were inhumane. A more contemporary view of juvenile courts is that they protect society from the harmful or destructive acts of youth. They are agents of the society that punishes children for violating social sanctions. This is not to say that some people do not utilize the court as a source of help. Some parents, for instance, may file "unruly" charges with the court against their own children. This is a result of a parent's sense of futility in his or her own efforts to manage the child in ways that conform to standards set by communities, schools, and the like. Then the court is viewed as a resource. In other cases, the court can provide drug and alcohol education or individual counseling. However, in most cases, particularly as viewed by the public, the court is viewed as an institution that doles out punishment to youth who misbehave in serious and unacceptable ways. Punishment is intended to curb the child's unacceptable conduct. Hence the parent and society can reclaim that child within the social networks related to the child's age-appropriate context, such as schools and extracurricular activities like sports, church, and after-school activities.

The view of the juvenile court as an institution that protects society from youth misconduct and upholds societal standards through punitive actions that curb such violations creates a view of juvenile courts as regulatory institutions rather than as human resources. As such, whether it is a valid perception or not, families, particularly the youth, see juvenile courts as comprised of people who seek not to help them but rather to punish them. In some cases, parents find this role of the court as a punitive agent helpful because it is hoped that such action will "strike fear" into the child, forcing the child to change his or her behavior to avoid further punishment. This change of behavior would then resolve the parents' problem. Either way, the family sees the court as a punitive agent that takes on a surrogate parent role or as simply an adversarial institution that labels them as deficient. Missing from this picture is the view that the court can serve as a *safety net* in which families who would not self-refer can access professional help. This help not only can contribute to the resolution of youth misconduct but can address family environments that inhibit prosocial youth behaviors and emotional well-being. Given the preponderance of the case disposition of probation in this culture (an increase of 73% between 1989 and 1998; Puzzanchera et al. 2002), there appears to be little appreciation by some for the limitations of this punitive or casual approach to juvenile delinquency.

The following is Joan's account of her experience with the juvenile court when required to attend the FSP with Robert:

> You know, when I found out Robert was caught stealing, I had mixed feelings. On the one hand, I was secretly glad that after all my warnings that he didn't heed, he was going to find out what the consequences would be for him. But underneath, I also knew that what this really meant was that my fears that we were not doing well as a family were now confirmed. I just didn't want to face it before, the idea that we needed help. I guess I just kept hoping that the problems would disappear on their own. So I went to the juvenile court for the hearing embarrassed that I would be seen as a failure by people I didn't even know. But on the other hand I was relieved that my son got caught and maybe the court could get his attention that I couldn't get from him. Still, when I went to the court, and they told me we had to attend 10 weeks of the FSP, I thought, "What is that? What good is that gonna do me?" I went the first night angry and resentful. I even said, "Why do I have to be here? I didn't do the crime. Why do I have to do the time?" But by the last week when we had graduation, when at the end of the night the facilitators

invited us as parents to speak about the program, before I realized I was doing it I found myself thanking the facilitators for their sacrifices on our behalf and thanking the other parents for their encouragement and guidance. I had tears in my eye. I wouldn't have asked for this program when I went to the court, but I'm glad it was there for me.

The third, important reason for the group model is that it is cost-effective. This intervention model does not require a separate professional interventionist to be assigned to each family. While cofacilitators are important in group process and logistical management, fewer professionals are needed on average for the families who participate. There are several sources of adult leadership in group work. Volunteers, such as "graduate" families of the FSP, can be helpful in verifying to members of a new group the value of the experience through their personal testimonials. Adults in the community who have a strong desire to advocate for youth can be recruited. Those who wish to learn more about family intervention, such as college interns, can be drawn in, often at no cost. We have been utilizing these resources for many years and have a list of over 250 students in the university who have participated. There is a steady stream of students who want to "be out of the classroom and into the real world." Their independent study or internship experience with us provides them with an opportunity to experience their own usefulness, much like the youth in the program who are required to participate in a volunteer community activity. These college students also discover some of the challenges in working with families that provide a broader educational experience. Some have utilized this experience to shape their own professional plans and have pursued jobs in the helping professions or graduate school.

In essence, the energy and guidance applied to family intervention are derived from the families working together, and these families grow to realize that resource as the program unfolds from session to session. From the outset, group leaders say:

"We are depending on you for the group to be successful";
"You cannot miss a meeting because you would be letting others down; they would think you don't care about them";
"Families would miss out on your ideas if you did not come."

The families help structure dialogue. They help suggest program ideas. They ask about the well-being of each other. While the number of families per program varies, we have worked with as few as four and as many as ten (with ten families, the "name game" lasts a lot longer, but we discover who has a good memory, and it gives more opportunity for group members to help each other). Six families is an optimal number because it balances two important ingredients in a group program: (1) enough people to provide a rich tapestry of human experiences that can be shared and learned from;

and (2) allowing each family to feel a sense of significance in the group and an opportunity to receive attention to their problems.

With two facilitators who are professionals, the service to one family within the FSP multiple family group model can be less than $300 (for ten sessions and between-session contacts). This amount is typically substantially lower than a given therapy regimen. Another way to look at it is within the managed care model. Multiple family group services are gaining momentum. This is for two reasons: (1) groups are viewed as opportunities to utilize broader resources to provide help to families who share common experiences and feelings; and (2) groups are cost-saving measures since one or two professionals for several families are privileged over one-to-one counseling services (one professional and one patient/client). Some managed care companies are paying over $40 per session per family in multiple family group intervention. It is easy to calculate the monetary benefits for the professional who conducts multiple family groups while concurrently providing cost savings for vendors such as juvenile courts and adolescent treatment centers. In this model there are no separations in treatment within the natural support system. While youth and parents may be grouped separately during group sessions, there is no "identified patient" who receives the bulk of resources. The locus of pathology is seamless in that it does not reside within the individual. Specialized treatment for an incarcerated youth can be upward of $400 per day (Carter, 2003). This is not to suggest that the multiple family group model described herein is meant to be a replacement for incarceration. Issues of safety and intensive intervention must be considered; yet the differential in cost should get the attention of the public, schools, juvenile justice, and program administrators who are responsible for the costs of treatment and the justification of later versus early intervention for at-risk youth.

> The costs for this group model are less than costs for individual counseling for a youth or family therapy. Costs are competitive with any funds allocated for use in human services categories. For instance, one-to-one models of intervention, like weekly visits between a probated youth and a probation officer, can be calculated as payment for time with a single youth. In the FSP, five to six families are seen at the same time with one professional group leader and two adult volunteers or college interns. While it is crucial for at least one facilitator to be an experienced family interventionist such as a family therapist and specialist in group work, other facilitators can be adult volunteers who match the racial and ethnic compositions of the group or graduate or postgraduate interns seeking further clinical training, as well as professional youth service workers. Hence, even if four facilitators worked with eight families in the FSP, the ratio of one facilitator for every two families is more cost-effective than individual youth/family intervention. In addition, since not all four facilitators have to be professionals, even fewer payroll costs

are accrued. An additional savings can be achieved if fewer than four facilitators are present. A minimum of two is necessary to provide sufficient structure to the group process, and small group discussion can be included over the course of the program experience.

At no time should at-risk youth in a multiple family group program have opportunities to gather without adult supervision and leadership.

Rationale and Challenge of Parent Involvement

The presence of parents in youth intervention is a major feature that separates this model from many other programs that address at-risk youth. For instance, it is well documented that precursors of juvenile crime relate to family factors. These include: (1) poor parental monitoring (Forgatch, 1991; Quinn, Sutphen, Michaels, & Gale, 1994; Peeples & Loeber, 1994; Sampson & Laub, 1994), even controlling for social and economic status (SES) (Larzelere & Patterson, 1990); (2) absence of effective parental skills such as consistent nurturing (Johnson & Pandina, 1991; Howing, Wodarski, Kurtz, Gaudin, & Herbst, 1990); (3) high frequency of family transitions, including father absence (Brown, Zimmerman, Jenkins, & Rhodes, 1991; Dornfield & Kruttschnitt, 1992), such as geographical moves and loss or gain of family members (separation, divorce, death, new boyfriend) (Quinn, Bell, & Ward, 1997); (4) Substance-abusing and problem and antisocial behavior of parents (Greenwood, 1996; Loeber, Farrington, & Petechuck, 2003); (5) lack of parental involvement in education (Smith, 1991; Walker & Silvester, 1991); (6) school failure (Tremblay, Masse, Perron, Leblanc, Schwartzman, & Ledingham, 1992; Rohrman, 1993; Quinn, Sutphen, Michaels, & Gale, 1994; Zingraff, Leiter, Johnsen, & Myers, 1994; Hill-Riley, 1994); and (7) poverty (Smith & Krohn, 1995) and its corollary, residing in an underclass neighborhood (Peeples & Loeber, 1994). Family poverty inhibits family processes of informal social control, increasing the likelihood of delinquency (Sampson & Laub, 1994). Tracking both younger children and older youth over several years documents the relationships between parental supervision, consistent discipline, communication, and relationship with parents and the onset of persistent serious delinquency (Stouthamer-Loeber, Loeber, Wei, Farrington, & Wikstrom, 2002).

An empirical test of a social control model examining delinquency prevention and intervention revealed results that were largely reducible to previous educational experiences, poor supervision and unresolvable family conflict, and attachment deficits (Scholte, 1991). Several studies have emphasized the importance of parental investment in explaining variable patterns of coping with social and economic disadvantage (Williams & Kornblum, 1985; Garmezy, 1985), pointing out the strategic influence of methods parents employ to access social resources within the family and their community.

Examining the larger context, there is a strong relationship between disconnected youth, especially male adolescents who are not in school and not working, and delinquency. Nearly one third who are disconnected for 3 or more years have been in a jail or youth correctional facility (Brown, 1995). This compares to 1% of those never disconnected. Risk factors that associate with being disconnected are family structure, parent's education, reading materials in the home, family poverty, educational failure, early age at first sexual intercourse, and suspension from school and associated lack of participation in school activities. Our own data with approximately 1,000 juvenile first-offender youth indicate a 48% educational failure rate for any given subject and that a given youth is more likely to be failing every subject than no subject; they have on average 17 unexcused absences in a school year and, on average, 4 suspensions (in-school and out-of-school combined) during the school year. (See chapter 7, reporting data from our own project.)

Poor performance in school for African-American youth is associated with increased risk of delinquent behavior (Achenbach, Edelbrock, Lynam, Moffitt, & Stouthamer-Loeber, 1993). The conclusion drawn in this study proposes that when formal controls such as school are not present for youth to compensate for the lack of informal controls, youth remove themselves from social control and influence as a result of their frustration and failure in school. Hence "neighborhood delinquents and pressures are free to rush in and fill the void" (p. 195). When a formal control agent such as a school loses its power to control behavior as students do poorly and disidentify with school, this loss has greater consequences for these students, whose environments include few agents of control. Yet many of the current programs to ameliorate these circumstances, particularly if these programs do not include early-onset youth at risk, do not engage the family directly in youth intervention nor address directly educational matters.

The FSP as a formal control agent can be a step in the direction of providing clear consequences (e.g., court hearing, probation, school suspension for those who fail to attend with their families) for youth who are embedded in neighborhood peer groups that either result in or tempt youth toward behaviors that are delinquent.

> At a first session of an FSP, each planned activity was completed, beginning with the name game. The name game requires each individual to attach an adjective that describes something about him or her that starts with the same letter as the first name (e.g., Jubilant Jennifer). Each person must repeat the names before introducing their own name and adjective. role-plays and pairs of individuals introducing each other were activities that followed. When the activities were completed for the evening,

families were asked if they had any questions or comments before the session ended. No group member had a question or comment. At that point the group leader raised an issue that she thought would be on the minds of some group members. She said: "Before we end, let me raise a possible concern that none of you have raised, and frankly, I am surprised. My two facilitators and I are both white, and many of the families here are African-American. Aren't there any family members here that seriously wonder whether we can understand you and your lives, your families, well enough to help? I think we should talk about this before we end tonight." There was a short silence. Then an African-American parent said: "Well, you told me you had children. So if you had children, I know we have something in common, and we can all agree that life isn't easy sometimes with children. So I figure your ideas might be helpful to me." Another parent, trying to relieve the tension a little more, stated: "Well, hey, we got a bunch of families in this group that are black, so we have each other, and if we don't think you know what you're talking about, we'll just talk with each other." Laughter ensued. Some of the tension was lifted, and two things occurred. First, by raising the issue of race in the group, the leader was communicating that it is OK to talk about race in this program. And, second, the outcome of the discussion allowed families to feel closer to one another as they expressed their honest opinions. Together, the group raised the stakes for what they wanted to accomplish, indicating that the group was willing to share in the responsibility of creating a successful group experience.

To maintain the objective of child enhancement of well-being without including the family is often shortsighted and impractical. Some would say that it is impractical to include the family. Yes, trying to negotiate with parents the necessity of their attendance in intervention programs can be a challenge. Parents say:

- "Why do I have to come? I'm not the one that got in trouble."
- "I can't, I work."
- "I've got kids at home to take care of."
- "I don't have a way to get there."

When our FSP began in 1992, we even had a few parents who would drop off their child the first night of the FSP and come back at the end. We would actually "plant" program facilitators in the parking lot before the first session to remind parents of their expected commitment so that they could not drive away! We were determined to include parents and were willing to find and close every loophole that would detract from the likelihood of parent attendance.

The likelihood of parental involvement is greater when the commitment to the value of parent inclusion is high and the theoretical stance is unwavering. The empirical evidence for parental contributions to child outcomes of school failure and delinquency are strong, and the existence of current programs demonstrating the effectiveness of parental involvement in intervention with at-risk youth is persuasive. In addition, the recruitment of parents into the program is not as difficult when there is emphasis on the importance and the necessity of their attendance at the source of the referral, such as the juvenile court, when they are referred to a multiple family group program. There must be commitment to the great value that parent/family involvement holds. Without such a focus, the integrity of the group model is lost. For instance, when an invitation for parents to participate in the FSP is made, with the reason being that parents are an integral part of their children's lives and well-being ("you may or may not be part of the problem, but you certainly are part of the solution"), parents view their involvement not as punishment but instead as an opportunity and necessary element in helping the child. Parents are informed in laymen's terms how much is known about the greater probability for a better intervention outcome if they are involved in the program. In this way, the frame is created informing parents that to decline or withdraw from the program is a conscious decision to not offer help to their child.

Intervention for at-risk youth does not appear to match the knowledge base built by child development theorists and researchers. For a century there has been an accumulation of evidence driven by the Russian developmentalist, Lev Vygotsky. He claimed that child development is fundamentally social: it builds through relationships. Children are capable of developing one level of functioning on their own, but a higher level of competence is based on the presence of adults. The difference between what children can do on their own and what they can do socially has been labeled the "zone of proximal development" (ZPD) (Garbarino, 1999). Competence in parenting is based on responding to the child in a manner that provides emotional validation, comforting the child who is discouraged or fearful and encouraging the child who is ambitious and confident. An effective parent expects a child to gather more competence over time and to struggle with disappointment in hopes that overcoming disappointment creates resilience and determination to succeed. With juvenile offenders it is tempting for parents to become upset and angry. However, long-term invalidation by parents leads to rejection, and children lose interest in gaining competence: "that's why widespread availability of ZPD-based parent support and education programs is a critical piece of a comprehensive violence prevention program" (Garbarino, 1999, p. 186). The FSP holds the theoretical tenet that parents must convey their acceptance of their children and act to modify negative behavior.

There are many variations of parental involvement that can be acknowledged to maintain flexibility and meet family situations. A single parent might be encouraged to allow for a coparent to attend as well, unless the relationship is acrimonious. A coparent can be actively recruited, often a father, who does not live with the youth if that coparent is local and available (see the case vignette about the barber described in chapter 3). There are many advantages for a coparent's inclusion in the program. The youth has an opportunity to have available another adult to help in the supervision and guidance of the youth. Of course, if the coparent is a low functioning parent with serious alcohol or violence problems, then such an inclusion is inadvisable. Parents like the barber provide another set of experiences and competencies to share with a youth. In some cases, the possibility of overcoming abandonment problems is possible.

> Jackie, mother of 13-year-old David, came to the court for adjudication and dis-position. A referral was made to the FSP in the risk assessment at the juvenile court. Jackie shared with Laurie, the FSP representative, that David had been doing fine until a recent divorce. Now David did not see his father, Ray, because Ray did not seem interested. A particular problem described by Jackie was that David was currently failing in math, when math had previously been his best sub-ject before this school year (and before the divorce). Jackie said that she was "not good at math," and now that David was doing more advanced math, his father, who was the parent who helped the boy in math, was the only one who could help. Laurie received permission from Jackie to call the father and seek his involvement in the program. It was explained that his son needed his help in math in order to pass and to finish high school, and he would be better prepared if he chose to pur-sue a college degree. Given that the request was framed as one of needing his in-volvement better to prepare his son for life, Ray reluctantly consented to attend. During one of the sessions that focused on family contracts, in which both the par-ent and child negotiate a change that each is willing to make for the other, Ed, as group leader, used this as an opportunity to promote more contact between Ray and David about math help. Ray's pledge was to pick David up from the mother's home on Tuesdays and Thursdays, go to dinner together, and return to Ray's resi-dence to work on math homework or preparation for a math test. With Ed's help, Ray and David went further. On Mondays and Wednesdays, Ray was to call David at 7 p.m. at Jackie's home and see if David needed help that evening, and they would "talk it through" over the phone. Ray had a fax machine and volun-teered to buy one for Jackie, so that David's homework could be sent over to his fa-ther's house for review. Then Ray would call back to tell David how the math homework looked to him.

Grandparents should be considered for inclusion; particularly those that live in the home or neighborhood of the youth in a single parent family structure. A program priority is to include any and all adults who have active participation in the life of the youth. If the youth lives in the home with both parents, both parents should be expected to come unless there are mitigating circumstances, such as a parent who is employed in the evenings when group sessions are scheduled. If other adults live in the home, they are strongly encouraged to come. And if other adults outside the home are actively involved with the youth, we strongly encourage their participation as well. Our belief is that more adults can potentially lead to an expanded social support system. In addition, such involvement provides more opportunities to resolve problems that these adults might be associated with as well, such as family conflicts and allegiances or school failure. In sum, a "parentectomy" intervention that separates a youth from the family and results in parental absence in intervention is an unacceptable option, and a youth must be referred back to the source, such as the juvenile court, if a parent or guardian cannot attend.

It is then important that the referral source, the juvenile court or other source, actively process the case so that the youth and family do not slip through the cracks and end up with no intervention or stipulated responsibility. If the case is not actively reviewed, the perception of the family is that dropping out of the program is inconsequential. As a result, such an experience is shared in the community, and the perception builds that dropping out of the multiple family group intervention program, such as the FSP, is allowable. This misconception leads to other families referred to the program in the future refusing to attend or entering the program with expectations of dropping out or attending inconsistently. Challenges to the integrity of the inclusive nature of the family program must be addressed and overcome.

The impression drawn from this discussion may lead the reader to think that every youth and parent enters the program willingly and with enthusiasm. This is not so, not surprisingly to those who work with youth and parents in mandated treatment. Yes, some parents (and many youth, of course) may come begrudgingly the first night. The anger, embarrassment, or frustration of a parent must be addressed up front. For instance, we acknowledge and overcome parental ambivalence or resentment in the following manner.

We role-play for them how a parent might feel being here. With the group leader or facilitator in the middle of the circle, a role-play ensues in which statements reflecting the range of parent feelings are presented. The leader might say: "I can't believe I have to be here, I had a rough day at work, I have so much to do at home, the house is a mess, I'm missing my favorite TV show, I wasn't even the one who got in trouble." Often parents nod their heads or are heard to exclaim, "Amen!" Then parents are asked to add any feelings that the group leader might have left out. Sometimes parents say that these are exactly the things they feel; but on occasion a parent might sheepishly add that she is glad she is here (e.g., "I have known we needed help for a long time. I am glad I finally found somewhere to go"). A group leader or facilitator then performs a role-play representing a youth. The facilitator offers statements that might reflect attitudes or feelings of the youth (e.g., "I can't believe I have to be here. Well, if I have to come, I'm not gonna talk"; "I could be talking to my girlfriend on the phone"; "I could be at home playing video games"). Again, the youth are invited to call out additional attitudes and feelings not expressed by the role-play.

> *During the initial phase of the first session, one parent, Denise, vociferously proclaimed her irritation with being required to attend the FSP. At every opportunity Denise expressed dismay, frustration, and disagreement with the program requirements. During the role-play of the youth, the facilitator strung together a series of comments that would reflect the feelings of various youths, such as: "Why do I have to be here?"; "I'm not gonna talk"; and "I can't wait for this to be over." When the facilitator asked, "who does this sound like?" expecting to receive a response that "it sounds like the youth here," several members in the circle simultaneously exclaimed, "Denise!" The group laughed heartily at this point, since the question was intended to solicit names of youth. As a result, the group loosened up, and even Denise began to realize the tiresome nature of her complaints.*

There are many strategies that can be useful in developing group cohesion and a commitment to complete the program successfully. Some of these strategies include

1. The name game helps them feel connected as they become acquainted with each other and share something of themselves.
2. The role-plays described above help families appreciate the group leader's sensitivity to the range of feelings and behaviors they carry into the first session of the program: irritation and anger, ambivalence, refusal to participate, and in some cases interest and enthusiasm that maybe this is the program to help them.
3. The dissemination of the schedule of activities with the request for input from the parents offers parents a chance to provide input and helps them feel a part of the meetings.
4. Once a multiple family group program like the FSP has some history in the community and is considered a mainstream part of the human service delivery system in the juvenile court, that history of the FSP can be advantageously discussed. A group leader can describe the kinds of parents that have been helped, what they say about the FSP when they graduate, and the percentages of reoffenses. (These data and family feedback are elaborated upon in chapter 9.)
5. Families who have "graduated" from the FSP are invited to return and share their experiences with later groups of families. This has been a powerful influence, as apprehensive new families hear reports from "graduated" families about the newfound optimism they now have and the closeness that has developed in their family. Families that have a sense that the program has been helpful to

others develop an expectancy set—a collection of beliefs that culminate in an optimistic view of the outcome of the program for them.

A Map for Developing a Family Group Approach

While there has been a widespread effort in advancing family intervention, methodological emphasis that examines issues which provide accountability has lagged (Hughes, 1994). This is particularly the case for family programs that attempt to address seemingly intractable social and family problems such as crime and drug use. In addition, efforts to examine cost-effectiveness have been lacking. Instead, a shortsighted approach has been used to assess changes in attitudes and behaviors, such as parenting measures that assess change in attitudes. This lag partly explains the tenuous nature of some family programs and the effects of budget cuts on human service delivery. Unless a well-substantiated case can be made for the value of an intervention program as it relates to commonly held and shared community concerns about such things as crime and family disruption, support for a program can dwindle. On many occasions professionals who learn about the FSP and become interested in incorporating it into their own service delivery system do so because of the data indicating lower recidivism of youth who complete the program and the consistent reports from parents about the valuable experience it provided them.

Hughes proposes a four-tier model of developing family programs. The first is *content, which includes theory, research, context, and practice,* all of which drive the formation and legitimacy of these programs. The content must be based on sound theoretical and research information (Arcus, 1987; Roosa, 1991), and the context of programs must be clearly articulated. For instance, cultural and family structural variables must be considered so that content is connected to relevance for participants. Furthermore, the current state of practice should be reflected in the program. In the model proposed in this text, multiple family group intervention is a core principle of the program and adheres to recent developments in the field of family intervention.

An example of the importance of clarifying theoretical premises of an intervention model is the commitment to family participation. There are many paths that a family can take to divert from program participation. The following are some of the most common:

- no transportation
- work conflicts
- not my responsibility
- children to supervise at home

- medical problems
- no legal responsibility (noncustodial father, grandparent)

The FSP administrator, program officer, or family group leader must be determined to adhere to the theoretical premise that parent involvement is essential. The group leader must be prepared to remain firm as parents draw on the above explanations to seek permission to be excused from the program. In addition, the group leader must be flexible and ready to negotiate circumstances that help parents feel comfortable with the plan to participate in the program.

The second tier in Hughes's model is *instructional process*. This refers to the articulation of the change process, whether it be in the form of information dissemination or the group dynamics that emerge. The model proposed in this text includes both components—information delivery and group dynamics—out of which emerge new attitudes or behaviors as steered by group interaction. Hughes makes the case that a well-developed program should utilize a variety of teaching activities and formats, such as structured activities and unstructured discussion, to accommodate a wide variety of learning styles. This combination is clearly present in the model developed for families of at-risk youth. Structured topics and activities, are explained, with allotted time for group discussion facilitated by program leaders. A 187-page manual guides the group leader and provides structure to maintain intensity and utilize time efficiently. Probe questions have been formulated to provide program leaders with tools to facilitate meaningful interaction. These probe questions and statements by group facilitators are an essential ingredient in an effective group process that drives desired outcomes (see chapter 7 for more on this topic).

One aspect of instructional process that should not be overlooked is presentation style. A program with very important content may be diminished because the substantive material has been presented in an untimely or uninteresting manner. For example, many of the topics and approaches used in the FSP have been developed and refined based on the enthusiastic response these topics and activities receive when implemented in sessions. When families are unresponsive to program content or activities, a reexamination of presentation style is necessary. In the FSP, a distillation process has occurred over time in which program content and activities have been altered or solidified based on family responsiveness. Families complete written evaluations of each activity in each session. Some groups have a leaning toward group discussion, others prefer group activities that require physical movement and change of surroundings. Finding a balance between the following two components is crucial to the success of a family group session: (1) group activities that generate family cohesion and new experiences for families to engage with each other, and (2) group discussions that bring forth the insights and emotions from group activities that can be shared and hence generate new learning among group members.

It is also important to use relevant examples in program content and activities. These examples should *resonate* with the families, *perturb* their life experiences, and *arouse* their curiosity. For instance, many youth in the program live in single-parent families. In these cases, illustrations of how to prepare a home environment conducive to educational success or positive affect in parent–youth relationships should be grounded in the structure of one-parent families. In addition, many minority families attend the program. Varying attitudes about law enforcement, education, roles of mothers and fathers, and beliefs about discipline must be acknowledged. This is particularly important when youth behavior that is of concern to families ties in to the legal system.

> Sam was reported to the juvenile court as a first offender, and hence was referred to the FSP, because he got into a fight at school. Sam also had a history of irregular attendance. His mother, Debra, was upset at the school because Sam had simply retaliated when another boy pushed him. Sam's father, Jeff, was out of town each week and as in most cases, did not weigh in on the matter. His passivity detracted from the perceived seriousness of the problem. Both boys were disciplined equally, and Debra believed that the boy who initiated the conflict should receive more severe punishment. Both boys were referred to the FSP, but it was determined that placing both boys in the same program would be inadvisable as it would create high tension that would interfere with the importance of creating a friendly, relaxed program atmosphere. Hence they were placed in two different cycles of the program. Ed, the group leader, helped Debra and Sam understand that the program was an opportunity to formulate a plan to improve Sam's behavior at school because, after all, he had been truant and involved in previous conflict situations at school. Ed did not communicate to Debra that she was wrong in thinking that her son Sam was punished too severely. Instead, he tried to help Debra understand that this program was an opportunity she and Sam could utilize. (Because Jeff was out of town, he could not attend to formulate a place to succeed in school.) Ed then asked Debra and Sam to share with the group what the impediments were for Sam in getting to school regularly and in a timely fashion. A discussion ensued among the group members that provided suggestions for removing these impediments and that shared ways in which other parents created structures and procedures at home to ensure regular school attendance. For instance, Denise, who, with Brittney, was in the program due to school truancy, shared what she had done to help Brittney attend school more regularly. Denise said she negotiated with her supervisor at work a slightly different work schedule that allowed her to leave home thirty minutes later so that she could help Brittney get ready for school and prepare breakfast and see her get on the bus. Virginia told the group that Brandon had trouble at school in the past because he moved schools often due to his father's military career. Virginia said

that because Brandon was the "new kid" in the classroom so often he had trouble making friends, but when she learned to talk with the teachers when Brandon first enrolled in a school and alert them to his challenge in making friends, the teachers helped organize classroom activities that fostered friendships between Brandon and a few of the students. Virginia said that it really helped to talk to teachers, even though she had heard before she went that they had too many students to help solve this kind of problem. Virginia suggested that Debra have a conference with the teachers to work together to help defuse situations that led to conflict escalation with peers. Ed permitted Debra to express her frustration with the school, but over time she gradually moved toward thinking and committing to improved school behavior for Sam.

The third of Hughes's tiers in conceptualizing the development of family programs is *implementation*. A program must be structured to fit the life circumstances and expectations of participants. Just as in welfare reform, child care issues must be addressed with program participants if parents are truly to function at a more effective level. Parents may not have the resources to have toddlers and young children supervised at home while they attend a program with the youth who have been juvenile offenders. The time and location of meetings must be considered. The FSP, for example, has been held in churches, counseling centers, recreational centers located at the center of neighborhoods, a university building in the center of an urban area, and education wings of hospitals in locations near family residences. Transportation needs must be addressed, such as locating the program in a building along a public transportation route. In the FSP, families are encouraged to talk with each other about transportation needs. In some cases, families volunteer to pick up other families to attend the FSP. This dynamic contributes to group cohesion and removes unrealistic responsibility for change from the facilitators.

One family, Virginia and Brandon, claimed that they could not attend the program because of transportation problems. They had one car, and Virginia's husband, Mark, was either out of town working at his military job or would regularly have to stay at the base with the car. One of the college interns decided to offer her assistance and pick up Virginia and Brandon for the first night of the program. Once at the family meeting, Ed, the group leader, could raise the issue of transportation needs of the group. He explained Virginia's transportation difficulty and asked if anyone lived near Virginia and Brandon. The leader said that he was not legally able to pick up a family for the program, nor were facilitators (college interns) allowed to pick up families. The leader said that if no family could help Virginia or Brandon with transportation then he was required to refer the family back to the juvenile court for further review and disposition. When families learned of this possibility, they became interested in helping Virginia and Brandon. No family lived very close, but several families lived within 3 miles. The group devised a plan to rotate responsibility for transporting Virginia and Brandon, and each week a different family would pick them up.

FSP facilitators reflect the diversity of the family participants, specifically targeting race, age, and sex characteristics. The FSP utilizes facilitators that are parents themselves, though some facilitators are single or married without children. The FSP even encourages older brothers and sisters of youth offenders to attend, to provide opportunities for problem-solving, mentoring and increased family cohesiveness.

Dan, the 19-year-old older brother of Sam, attended one night while on leave from his military assignment. The topic for that session was conflict resolution. Role–play scenarios were created and enacted in front of the group. One of the role–plays presented demonstrated the limited ability of youth in the program to resolve a confrontational situation relevant to their lives—the threat of one youth physically to remove a "cool" jacket from another youth. David and Robert participated in the role-play. After a period of time in which the two youths had clearly reached a stalemate and the threat of a physical altercation was near, Dan spoke up. The group leader, Ed, encouraged this involvement and asked him to suggest some ideas that could help resolve the dispute before "something really bad happened." Dan stepped forward and suggested a way that the confrontation could be resolved. Ed suggested he role-play this strategy to remove himself from the dispute. Dan described a similar situation that he had experienced and discussed the mistake he had made in that situation and the unfortunate consequence that had occurred. Dan also discussed and demonstrated, with the help of the group leader, several options to resolve the confrontation more effectively, based on recent experiences in the military. The youth in the FSP listened carefully to this brother of one of them, since his youthful age and recent success in the military provided him some legitimacy in the eyes of the group.

Steve, an older brother of Robert, attended one night with Robert and his mother, Joan. Steve was on his own, working and living in an apartment in a town not far away. Steve came because he had been off work that day and was back in the same town as Robert and Joan to get his car repaired. After the program ended that night, he commented to Ed that he wished that when he was in trouble as a youth of about his younger brother's age, he had been required to go to see the probation officer once a week. Steve said, "nothing ever changed. I wish there was a program like this for me when I messed up." This particular statement was shared with Robert, who begin to appreciate the opportunity that the program offered him.

The fourth tier of Hughes model is *evaluation*. Eventually the question will be asked by program or agency administrators, as well as government officials and political leaders and, if relevant, juvenile court judges and court personnel: "Does this program work?" Funds and staff support for programs are almost always quite limited, and questions about whether a program that receives funding and requires staff time is valuable are appropriate. There are many devices that can be utilized to answer this question. They can range from quantifiable data to anecdotal information to clinical impressions. A multimethod approach is ideal because it has the potential to capture program effects in many ways. Without such methods, positive changes may go undetected. The FSP utilizes several methods. First, family ratings of program content of each session are requested. A written rating form is administered to families after session 3, asking them to rate the group leader and the quality of the sessions. Examples of questions families must provide answers to are: "The sessions were lively and energetic"; "My family accepted that part of a group leader's job is to help us change certain things about our family"; "We got much accomplished during the sessions."

Second, families are asked at the final session to share with the group their experience in the program. Consistent positive statements of appreciation for the support received from other families, the chance to engage in family activities that are fun and enjoyable, and learning how to resolve problems that arise in families are three of the most common aspects of these family reports. Finally, recidivism data is routinely gathered to assess whether a youth who is referred to the FSP commits another offense. These data provide responsible answers to the questions raised by judges, juvenile courts, and schools regarding whether youth discover a life path that excludes further delinquency. New communities interested in implementing new programs or funding current ones may have funding only for programs that can demonstrate positive results. In chapter 7 the recidivism data for the FSP are reported.

The primary criterion of effectiveness, however, in a program such as this with acting-out youth and families is whether the program effects a change in aggressive behavior or, in the case of juvenile offenders, whether the program affects recidivism rates? This is the logical question for a referral source such as a judge, therapist, teacher, agency director, budget manager, or local government leader. In the case of juvenile offenders, the rates for repeat offenses nationally vary widely; as Garbarino (1999, p. 212) states: "it is not uncommon to hear an estimated 85% recidivism rate offered, off the record, for the most troubled and aggressive boys by people inside the system, people who know that some of the published research reports over-estimate program success because they only include boys who were positive enough to participate in and complete the program." Reports on recidivism of those sentenced to youth prisons range from 55% in Florida within 18 months of release, to 79% of Utah youth within 12 months of being released, to 96% for California youth within 15 months of release, to 28% of youths from 20 states combined in 1992 (Krisberg & Howell, 1998). The worth of a program for juvenile offenders, then, must be measured by whether such an intervention model can curb such rates, as compared to either the local rate of repeat offenses or the host of national reports regarding repeat offending behavior.

While the intervention model in this text concerns itself with juvenile first offenders, the interest in reoffense rates remains high. Our awareness of this political landscape from the outset made it clear that the primary criterion for program effectiveness would need to be: Does the program reduce repeat offenses? We also believe that adopting such a stance of actively incorporating evaluation at the earliest stage of program development contributed to the growing support and increased legitimacy of the FSP. Later in the text the recidivism rates for several hundred youth who completed the FSP will be reported. By using such a multimethod framework, assessments of parent and youth satisfaction with the program and information pertaining to the quality of program experiences can be accumulated and used to refine program structure and content.

In 1999, the *Atlanta Journal-Constitution* published a story on the growth in numbers of serious and violent offenders. The FSP was featured prominently in the story, and one of those interviewed for the story was Dr. Pete Colbensen, executive director of the Georgia Children and Youth Coordinating Council. This organization funds juvenile justice programs and educational programs for youth and has been instrumental in providing initial support to the FSP as an alternative to existing services. Dr. Colbensen is quoted in this article as stating, "Family Solutions is special, because it has been evaluated" (*Atlanta Journal-Constitution*, 1999). In recent years the priority on evaluation of human service delivery and intervention programs for youth has risen.

> It is routine procedure for a judge, school official, or juvenile justice staff member to be invited to attend the final session of the FSP. At this last session, "graduation," a potluck dinner is served, certificates of completion are presented to the families, What We Like About You cards are presented to the youth, and the leader and guest (e.g., judge) say a few words of congratulations and inspiration to the families. The final activity of the session is a request to the families to share what the program has meant to them, and youth read statements that they have written about their experience in the program. Over time many touching statements have been made by family members. Tears may flow, usually tears of joy for what the program has meant to their sense of value and hopefulness. These statements are heard by the guests in attendance and they contribute to the positive view held about the program and the increasing commitment to support it.

This four-tier framework for family program development is offered as a lens that the reader can use to capture the comprehensive nature of a multiple family group program. Such a lens can also be utilized by program leaders in other communities to provide guideposts in the development of their own program models. In this way, unique features of their own communities, including characteristics of families, competencies of program leaders, geographic features such location and transportation issues, and referral source procedures can be applied to make the program most relevant and workable.

The description of the FSP is offered as a model that addresses needs of courts, families, and communities. Its specific contents and logistics can be revised where necessary to conform to the needs and characteristics of a given community. The stability and durability of the FSP has been a result of an awareness that the needs of professionals committed to youth offenders and the characteristics of the community context in which these families and offenders live must be considered.

CHAPTER 5

Development of the Family Solutions Program

Action is the antidote to despair.
—Joan Baez, folk singer

With the recognition of the body of literature outlined in chapter 4, the Family Solutions Program (FSP) was conceptualized and developed as a multiple family group context in Athens/Clarke County, Georgia, in 1991. The community has a population of 90,000 and a poverty and crime level that is one of the highest in the state. Juvenile crimes include a wide array of categories, among them theft, truancy, unruly/runaway behavior, assault, driving under the influence, and criminal trespass. The FSP was created as an initiative meant to address the concerns and apprehension of community leaders, school administrators, business leaders, the general public, and the juvenile court judges to counter the increase in youth problem behaviors and juvenile crime. Concern in communities was rising, as these youth behavior problems threatened local business, public safety and school achievement.

The juvenile court judge stated in a meeting to a small, interested group of human service professionals (including the author): "I can use all the help you can provide. You're the experts on youth. What can we do and how can I help get it done?" This was clearly an honest and concerned invitation to include expertise from outside the juvenile court system to help interrupt the progression in juvenile cases and the pervasive feelings of a troubled high-crime community. The question then became: "Where do we acquire the resources (staff, operating expenses) to get a program off the ground?" With the support of the U.S. Office of Juvenile Justice and Delinquency Prevention and the Georgia Children & Youth Coordinating Council, the program was launched in January 1992. The central theme shared by those involved was that a family intervention model could be useful in curbing youth crime, given the known associations of family variables and delinquency as well as related problem behaviors such as drug and alcohol use, truancy, and school violence.

The FSP was designed as a multiple family intervention program for juvenile offenders. However, most of the ideas and program activities can be applied to any program that targets youth and families: schools, churches, and youth agencies. You will find in reading this book that many of the components can be utilized with many other problem areas of youth and families, such as drug and alcohol use, truancy, emotional problems such as despair and sadness, first-time juvenile delinquency, and overt family conflict.

Selecting a name for the program was a very deliberate process. The professional group that formed as a result of a common interest in the problem of youth offending behavior met specifically to discuss a name. Many titles were considered. Since the group was interested in a program initiative that focused on positive individual and family change and not on punitive responses to offending behavior, terms were considered that conveyed an optimistic approach in which an expectation of change could be fostered for participating families. The term "Family Solutions" was selected because it conveyed both an emphasis on family participation and an expectation that positive change could occur if a family completed this program. In recent years, the term "solutions" has become a very popular description for new program development and treatment approaches. It is even found in the business world. The term has also been used as a label for entire organizations. In 1991, the term was not common. Despite increasing frequency of the term in mental health delivery, we have retained the name both as a descriptor that conveys possibilities for change and because it is easily identifiable in the local community.

What Does the FSP Try to Accomplish?

The overall goal of the FSP is to foster changes in youth behavior that decrease the possibility of repeat juvenile offenses, school truancy, or problem behavior. The FSP could establish its goal as an approach to curb youth drug use or conduct problems as well, with little modification in program content. The FSP is a 10-session program; however, there are almost 20 session modules available to select from to adapt to the particular vulnerabilities or problem areas reflected in the family group. The formulation of 20 sessions acknowledges the desire not only to address a problematic behavior but to reach beyond this goal to address contextual aspects of family life that contribute to impediments in youth well-being and growth and development. To accomplish this ambitious goal requires intensive intervention that changes: (1) some combination of chronic family conflict patterns; (2) family transitions and resulting maladjustments in family alliances and distrust; (3) perceptions of hopelessness; and (4) a sense of failure and futility in daily life, expressed in, for instance, school failure and peer interaction.

It is our contention that the presence of such beliefs and behaviors cannot, despite the good efforts and intentions of professionals, be combated in large part with one therapist, probation officer, or other family advocate. This is not to say that the trends in mentoring programs and the like are not important. However, many youth at risk may have a long history of traumatic events, developmental failures in tasks such as trust in others based on loss or gain of family members, and school difficulties such as reading. A mentor, whether a caring volunteer or a competent professional, is not intensely present in a consistent manner over the long term to invoke youth and family changes that are substantial enough to create attitudinal and behavior change leading to competent functioning. These youth have frequently encountered family instability in which adults are tenuous beings in their worlds. A mother's series of boyfriends may come and go, or a divorce or death of a parent leaves a hole in a child's physical or emotional world. The sense of abandonment and rejection is strong and often leads either to despair or despondency or to anger or violence over time.

While the outcome goal is reduction in offending behavior, there are process goals that are required to perturb long-standing patterns that lead to offending behavior, in much the same way that intervention for drug abuse (Quinn, 1995), eating disorders, family violence, or depression requires individual and relational changes. Therefore process goals need to be established that are believed to foster different outcomes; in this case, reduction and elimination of offending behavior. We try to make the case that the families themselves are a kind of social capital in which family members serve as resources to each other. Social capital is the presence and utilization of human resources that can be harnessed to help resolve personal struggles or difficult life circumstances. We utilize the families to foster a social network to fill the void remaining from loss of an adult or to strengthen a support network that may rely on one caring adult who confronts a multitude of stresses in daily living.

Process Goals in the Family Solutions Program

As in psychotherapy or a school classroom, there are environmental conditions necessary to create the climate necessary to effect learning and behavior change. In the FSP, the following properties are fostered to attain these outcomes:

1. Try to Create Trust and Willingness to Help Each Other. The first week is a time when we do the name game, role-play what it is like to be here that night, and ask each of the family members to help the role-player express feelings the parents themselves possess. This process goal continues to be a part of the program in subsequent sessions. If a family member forgets one or more of the names and adjectives that come before him or her, ask the group to help. Transportation problems can be resolved with the involvement of other families. Ask who lives near the family with transportation problems or whether the group can take turns each week helping the family get to the group. Or who would be willing to be called by the family if their car does not start or they do not have money for the bus or train.

> *Robert's turn in the name game came, and he was very shy and unsure of himself. He looked down at the floor, hoping to get others to name the group members for him, or maybe hoping Ed, the group leader, would skip him. But Ed did not skip him and gently urged Robert to think of the names that came before. Ed asked Robert to lift his head and look around at the faces of the group members. Instead of identifying each family member in order in the circle as others had, Ed said, "Robert, pick out some one's name you remember and start there." When Robert said, "Super Sam," Ed commended him and asked Robert to continue. Ed then asked the group to keep track of whom Robert had named and whom he had left out. Towards the end of Robert's turn, Ed asked group members to help Robert remember the remaining names. With this technique Ed conveyed early in the program the message that each person would be expected to participate and that helping each other was acceptable and encouraged.*

> *Virginia stated to the group at the first session that she might have to miss some sessions because of transportation problems. Her husband, Mark, being in the military, often had either obligations that would take him off-base and away from home or duties that would keep him at work longer. Ed asked Virginia where in town she lived. Ed then asked the group if anyone lived near Virginia. No family said they lived nearby. So Ed asked the families how many minutes' driving time it would take the families to get to Virginia's neighborhood. Both Patti and Debra said it would take about 10 minutes. Ed asked if Patti and Debra would be willing to be on-call, that is, if Virginia found out that Mark would not be home by the time the group meeting started, could she call them? Patti and Debra said that would be fine, and Ed asked if they would write down their phone numbers on a slip of paper and give this to Virginia. Ed asked Virginia if she would keep track of rotating between Patti and Debra when she had to call for a ride, so as not to burden one or the other. Virginia understood. Her commitment to the program increased now that she was not going to miss meetings, allowing her to be a more active participant in the group.*

2. Draw out Competencies and Strengths of Each Family Member to Provide Help and Support for the Others. For instance, each person is encouraged to move toward problem resolution and away from blame and cause. While discussion of the youth's behavior that resulted in a referral to the program is not avoided, it is minimized so that the group can examine an array of life issues that could enhance their lives.

> One evening Denise came in very angry. It was noticeable to everyone in the group, and it was clear that until her anger was addressed, the plan for the session needed to be temporarily put aside. Ed asked Denise what was wrong, and Denise replied: "Ask her!" (referring to Brittany, her daughter). "She lied to me! I just found out at the grocery store today that Brittany was at a party Saturday night at a house with people I have never met and with no parents there. She knows the rules and she disobeyed." Brittany was noticeably embarrassed and angry at her mother for "outing" her to the group. Denise continued: "I ran into someone I know at the grocery store and she told me her daughter was there and that Brittany was too. When I got home tonight I asked Brittany, and she lied at first, and then when I told her what I knew and that I knew too much already; then Brittany knew that she wasn't going to get out of this one. . . . If this was the first time, I could deal with it, but it has happened before and she breaks the rules. She is just going to have to stay home; no going out at night." Ed responded, "Have you told Brittany this?" Denise said, "Yes, and she doesn't like it, but I don't care." Ed said, "For how long?" And Denise answered, "For a long time, who knows, maybe until she finishes school!"
>
> Ed continued: "Denise, you deserve to be upset about this, after all, our primary obligation as parents is to make sure our children are safe, and at unsupervised parties the chances of children being safe go way down, because alcohol makes people do dumb things, and we know about drinking and driving, and how someone can get killed, and we know about sex, and the possibility of pregnancy, disease, and emotional turmoil. It is our place to be firm about who are children are with and where they are." Denise began to calm herself somewhat as Ed spoke and steered the group towards a focus on what should be done as opposed to the temptation of thinking about how bad Brittany was or how helpless Denise felt. Ed asked the group, "Does anyone have an idea about what to do?"
>
> Joan responded: "Well, I know when Robert stole a bike for the third time and rode in neighborhoods he wasn't supposed to, I had to take desperate measures. I made him stay home, and he did extra chores for me. He not only had to clean his room, take out the trash, and put his dishes in the dishwasher, he had to vacuum the whole house every other day, sweep the garage floor once a week, put everyone's dishes away and mop the kitchen floor on the days he didn't vacuum. And for these extra chores, I paid him money, but after I showed him the money, I took it back and put the money in a safe place until enough was there so he could buy his own bike. I told him I was going to have to find extra money and I didn't know where it was gonna come from. So I told him he was only going to get half of what his brother got for new clothes for the next 6 months. You can bet he didn't wanna do that anymore because he didn't get to see his friends when he had to do all that. I also told him that

if he was caught in neighborhoods he shouldn't be in with his bike, I was taking the bike to my brother's house (his uncle's) so he couldn't ride it. We haven't had a problem since."

Denise listened to the story, although her exasperation with Brittany made it difficult. Denise said she did not think she could trust Brittany anymore and would keep her home until she finished school. Sam, being Brittany's age and feeling compassion for her, responded to that extreme position by saying that he would feel like giving up if that happened to him. When Ed asked Sam what he meant by giving up, Sam said, "I just don't know, but if I had nothing to look forward to . . . I just don't know." Joan said she thought Denise should make Brittany introduce all her friends to her so she could monitor who she was with better, and keep her home on the weekends, but only for a certain length of time, because Brittany would lose hope, give up, and get in more trouble.

Joan said that's why she kept Robert's money, and he could buy a bike, so he knew things would be better in the future and he wouldn't have to do these extra chores. Patti suggested that Denise make Brittany stay home for two weekends by herself, and then spend two more weekends at home but invite a friend over if she wanted. Debra added that after a month Brittany should phone her mother every hour until curfew to tell her where she is and Denise should meet Brittany's friends before she went out at night. As a result, Denise began to put together a plan to monitor Brittany better, to require her to take responsibility for changing her behavior, beginning with restricting her social life for a while, and having a sense of control. The families in the group helped Denise move from feeling helpless to adopting a plan to monitor Brittany and add another perspective to her thinking.

3. Consider the Needs of Parents to Be as Important as the Youth's Behavior that Resulted in a Referral to the Program. While the fact is not ignored that a child behavior problem or juvenile offense was the "ticket punched" to be admitted to the FSP, it is minimized so that the group can examine an array of life issues that could enhance their lives. We think of this as a process of *fast-forward rather than rewind.* The major question is: *How can the future be better than the past as it pertains to the child's well-being and success?* We invest equally in parent change in behavior/attitudes and in youth change. Parents must role-play, speak out, offer suggestions, and participate in activities.

David's mother, Jackie, a school secretary, was quiet and withdrawn in the group, partly due to her temperament or personality and partly due to her sadness about her divorce from David's father. Jackie remained quiet during the first two sessions. At the beginning of the third session, Ed announced to the group that it was time to plan the required community service activity for the youth. Ed mentioned some of the activities that the youth from previous FSPs had participated in, including preparing a meal at the homeless shelter, playing bingo with seniors, and building a bridge over a stream in a county park.

The parents thought for a while without ideas being offered, giving Jackie the opportunity to say that the primary school where she worked had a play area that was overgrown and unattractive. She had been urging the school parent–teacher organization to apply funds towards the beautification of the playground, but they *refused, stating that they had a limited budget and wanted to focus on reading. The schoolteachers thought the playground needed to be improved, but the principal prioritized teacher in-service activities in her budget. Jackie thought the youth with their parents could make it better. Ed noticed that the parents became interested in this idea because the school was in their community and thought they would all benefit, and some parents had younger children who attended the primary school. Ed asked Jackie if she could get permission from the principal to permit the group to take the playground on as their community service. Given Jackie's interest in the idea, he also asked her to contact local department stores like Walmart to see if they would be willing to donate mulch and flowers for the playground. Ed asked if anyone would volunteer to go with her to these department stores. Jackie took leadership for the community service including gathering information on every group member's schedule so that a day and time could be selected for the playground beautification that everyone could attend. Jackie gained the favor of her school colleagues as a result of this stewardship and gained the confidence in the group to participate regularly in all the subsequent sessions.*

4. Create a Forum for All Ideas to Be Heard.   This assumption is based on the belief in "equifinality," the notion that there are many ways to reach the same outcome. No one way of generating new information or behavior prescription can positively affect every youth or family.

There is a metaphor that can be useful in reminding facilitators about unique personal circumstances or readiness to receive information. A 16th-century broadsheet shows a young student sitting in a chair with a funnel on top of his head. Slightly behind the student is a teacher, complete with robe and cap, standing and holding a bucket tipped sideways. Streaming out of the bucket are numbers and formulae which are pouring into the funnel. However, instead of the numbers and equations seeping into the student's head, the funnel fills up with numbers and formulae, and they begin to fall onto the floor. The message here is that a level of readiness and openness to receiving information is necessary regardless of the quality of the information being deposited.

Any comment or partial description by a youth or family member in the group process has the potential to "land" in the funnel and "fall through" the funnel and into the head. This result helps perturb the thinking or behavior pattern of another youth or family member. Examples include parental discipline or monitoring of youth behavior, the meaning of a father's phone calls to a son who needs monitoring of homework, or the value of a mother's new attitude about the capability of a 15-year-old who should be expected to repair a wall he punched through rather than be "grounded" for a month.

One session following the pledge that David and his noncustodial father, Ray, had agreed to: that the two of them would have dinner twice a week and return to

Ray's home for math tutoring, David complained that Ray "got on him" when he called on the telephone to check on David's math homework. David did not like the phone calls always being at the same time on these nights and felt that it "messed up my night." What David meant was that he wanted to have a more flexible arrangement in the evening so he could watch TV and play video games and not be interrupted by these phone calls. Ray responded: "You know David, I'm not doing this to hassle you. Your mother wants me to do it, and I am trying to do my part in helping you grow up. You were failing math before we started this and now you are passing. . . . What more is there to say?" David seemed numb. The entire group was looking at him, waiting for a surly response. Then Virginia, another mother, said: "David, your father is right, you're not going very far without passing your math, but more than that, I am a spiritual person, and I think it is our duty to use our God-given talents, and you were doing fine in math until your father left you, and now that he is helping you, you should be grateful. I know you're mad at him, but you're only hurting yourself by getting mad at him about this." This kind of message from another family can sometimes "open the funnel" that has become clogged.

5. Maintain Consistent Flexibility in the Program Topics and Content. All participants become willing to adjust and alter plans for each program. For instance, when Denise marched into an FSP session on the day that she was informed that her daughter, Brittany, had shoplifted again, she was so angry that it was imperative that the group take this opportunity to help Denise process what happened and construct an appropriate parental response and strategy of intervention. One evening when the Rodney King verdict was announced, the families wanted to talk more about that event than our planned topic, as it was a national story that was in everyone's consciousness. In the case of the horrific 9/11 tragedy, graduation night was postponed as it would not have accomplished its purpose as a celebration.

On the first night of one FSP, when the families examined the schedule of topics, Mark, Brandon's father, who had attended the first night but came only when he was not on military duty, said, "Well, I'm disappointed Brandon doesn't have to face the shopkeeper he violated." Joan added that it bothered her that Robert never had to apologize for "borrowing" other children's bikes without permission. Ed, as leader of the group, took these comments seriously, knowing that his credibility with the families was partially contingent on taking their suggestions seriously, since he invited such input from the families. Ed shared this parental request with the FSP program coordinator, who contacted and recruited merchants from discount and department stores to come and discuss shoplifting and help youth make plans to seek out the one they had victimized and make amends. As it turned out, convenience store clerks and owners refused because they felt it was not going to get children to stop stealing there, and some mom-and-pop stores refused due to the lack of staff to take care of the store. However, large department stores were willing to send staff members, and hence a store manager or chief of security was invited to a session of every program that included shoplifters. The story of how this topic was incorporated into the program as a parent suggestion was retold in each subsequent FSP cycles so that parents believed that their suggestions for program topics were taken seriously and the idea that they were expected to take responsibility for the quality of the program was conveyed.

6. *Use the Vulnerabilities of the Group to Plan the FSP.* It is important to assess the characteristics of families prior to the first group meeting in order to become aware of their greatest needs. If most youth are failing in school, more attention to education is incorporated. This would include discussions with parents regarding plans to increase efforts of advocacy, such as how to participate in a school conference or how to create a home environment that facilitates homework completion or reading. When most youth were charged with assault or battery, more conflict-resolution and anger-management themes and role-plays were used. If several youths have been charged with shoplifting, scheduling speakers who represent department and discount stores can occur, and making amends to the merchant who was affected can be planned. If drinking under the influence of drugs or alcohol (DUI) has resulted in a criminal charge and FSP attendance, discussing drinking and driving laws, and hearing testimonials from those affected by DUI accidents can be arranged, and strategies to avoid such predicaments can be discussed. If a parent has a drinking problem, the issue becomes a legitimate concern. If corporal punishment and its effects emerges as a concern, more focus on discipline strategies is considered than was originally planned.

The data presented in chapter 9 on over 1,000 youth in the FSP document the educational vulnerability of many youth. Our data show that the majority of juvenile first offenders, truant students, and problem-behavior children are failing in school and have an average of three suspensions in a given year and more than ten unexcused absences in a given year. Some have over 20, which can by itself determine whether a student can be promoted. A child can be passing grades but with over 20 days missed can be retained at the same grade level.

David was referred to the program due to truancy; his mother, Jackie, had a difficult time making sure that David got to school on time in the morning. Given that several of the youth had school-related problems, Ed decided to schedule, in addition to sessions on the story of George Dawson (described in chapter 6), the census data, and the stacks of money, a session on parent-student-teacher conferences. After some group discussion on the importance of these meetings but the unsuccessful outcome of many of these conferences, Ed asked David and Jackie if they would role-play a parent-student-teacher conference. Fortunately, this group included an adult volunteer, Tom, who was a teacher who wanted to start FSP groups at his school. Jackie, David, and Tom pulled their chairs to the middle of the circle and role-played a school conference. Ed asked the group to make suggestions to Jackie of what she could say to Tom and what questions to ask. The group had to encourage Jackie to participate because she was feeling defensive in the role-play due to her feelings of inadequacy as a parent for not getting David to school. The group also suggested some things for Jackie to say to the teacher. Both Jackie and David learned from Tom what the school expectations were and also how the school could help Jackie improve David's attendance. In the end, the group helped Jackie realize that there was much more she could do to insure David's attendance at school. Tom, being a teacher, helped Jackie realize that the school was on her side and also had David's best interest in mind.

7. Make Sure to Promote Goals for Changes.   Each family must construct a *pledge, or contract,* that if successful would resolve differences or repeat problematic behaviors. The parents and youth collaboratively decide on a common problem, such as disagreements on curfew time or home responsibilities such as chores. The group of families is divided into pairs, and each pair meets in a separate room or a private space. The facilitator and one family help a second family negotiate their differences and arrive at a resolution. In this way a family can benefit from the perspective of the other family and their own experience managing similar problems and the mechanisms used to resolve such disagreements. Effective communication is promoted, including listening and pacing. We have found that some families successfully follow through on their shared agreements. At other times, the plan did not get completely implemented or implemented successfully. The group leader devotes a few minutes at every subsequent group session to discuss with the families how they are doing with their pledges. Those who are making progress are commended, which encourages them and validates their strengths. *Those families who have not made much progress are asked to do some troubleshooting: What has got in the way or how does the contract need to be altered to increase the probability of success?* While some families make more progress than others, we have noticed that some of these families begin to appreciate the importance of good communication, negotiation, and plans to change. *Their efforts to resolve differences increase as they dislodge themselves from the restricted cycle of rigid communication that ends in the same repetitive, unproductive outcome.*

Shay and Patti had a lot of trouble making a contract. Patti carried a lot of anger toward Shay for her past behaviors, including missing school, and couldn't find a way to cooperate. Patti expected Shay to do the changing and attributed the entire family problem to Shay's choice to stay home. As one of the group facilitators walked around the room to encourage each family to form a pledge, she noticed that both Shay and Patti were crying. The facilitator pulled up a chair and tried to speak calmly to both of them and help them clarify what they wanted from each other. The facilitator started with Patti, since she was so angry and felt that Shay was the one in the family who needed to make changes. Patti said Shay was old enough to get herself up, get her own breakfast, and get the school bus on time. Shay said that it was not easy because there was no one there to get her moving. This made it tempting for Shay to lie back in bed or go slow, and then she would miss the bus. The facilitator asked Patti if, since Shay needed a nudge in the morning, she could make a phone call from work to Shay about 10 minutes after her alarm was set, and say "good morning Shay, I hope you have a good day at school." Patti reluctantly agreed. The facilitator also asked if they could consider a reward if Shay went to school every day in a week. Shay and Patti decided on pizza and a video at home on Friday night, and Shay could have a friend over. The facilitator checked with Shay and Patti at the beginning of each subsequent FSP session to see how their plan was working, giving it greater importance and inviting a stronger commitment from them.

8. Establish a Continuing Quest for Inspirational Experiences. Guest speakers can provide inspiration that will motivate the youth and/or parent to adopt a new attitude or behavior.

Recently, an adult volunteer, a veterinarian at a chicken poultry plant, discussed his crisis as a young man when his plan to be a professional football player was destroyed in college after a career-ending knee injury. He had academic deficiencies that threatened his status. He said, "If the mind can conceive, and you truly believe, you can achieve." This guest speaker went on to discuss how he put everything into preparing for a football career in school and then experienced the painful injury. He had no preparation for doing well in school. He did succeed in the end, but he shared with the group the adversity of being an ill-prepared student and how he regretted not being more prepared to be successful in school. He also spoke of others he knew who did not overcome their athletic disappointments, resulting in alcoholism and unemployment.

More recently, a professional football player was asked to discuss his education history. The youth were extremely attentive, as they identified with him as a "hero" yet someone who had to work hard in school just to be able to have the chance to play college football and become skilled enough to be drafted.

Other inspirational experiences are derived from the many group activities and role-plays that are designed to interrupt the downward spiral of negativity and discouragement. One example is the "traffic jam" exercise (described in chapter 6), in which youth often offer the most inventive ideas for accomplishing the task. The youth draw strength from this exercise because they discover through this activity their abilities and the contribution they can make to others.

A story told about a Texas rancher and Irish dirt farmer is helpful in aiding families to gain perspective and appreciate the blessings in their life. After 30 years on the ranch, the Texan decided he could finally take a vacation. He had always wanted to visit Ireland. During his travels in Ireland he encountered an Irish dirt farmer. Of course, the conversation got around to the land, and the Irish dirt farmer asked the Texas rancher just how big his ranch was. The Texas rancher responded, "Well, let me put it this way, I can get into my pickup truck at sun-up, drive all day, and if I am lucky, I can make it to the other side of my ranch by nightfall." The Irish dirt farmer answered, "Why you know, I used to have a pickup truck like that once!" After the laughter subsides in the group, someone shares the main point of this story. We can all be so busy being envious about another person's life or situation that we lose any appreciation for our own. This is a helpful reminder to families to be more accepting of their circumstances and to be at peace with them, though it does not mean that wanting and working toward making life better for someone or for the family is not a good attitude.

9. Share Information With Families About the Resources That Exist to Help Them.   There is a common temptation for an interventionist to attempt to meet all of the needs of a family. There can be an unspoken and even unconscious belief that intervention success is established only when an individual or family's problems are completely resolved. Often, the most important work of the interventionist is to "unstick" the chronic family cycle of despair, conflict, and poor functioning in areas such as work or relational satisfaction. This shift in itself can produce a "spinning off" of other changes, much like "unjamming" a machine that freezes up or freeing a vehicle that gets stuck in mud.

Life for every human being includes adversity and misfortune. It is important for the interventionist to hold the notion that there are other professionals or laypersons who can provide help, information, resources, and support; professionals need to acknowledge the expertise of others in collaboration on the common goal of promoting the family's well-being. We identify counseling centers, tutorial programs, health specialists, and the value of neighbors and friends. We ask family members, both parents and youth, to share with the group an example of how each has been helped in the past by someone else. Some possible ways they might have been helped is through seeking out information from someone who helped them solve their problem or joining a group such as a religious organization or a support group.

Jeff was able to attend the group one evening with Debra and Sam. When the discussion ensued about how all of us must seek help to make it through a day or overcome a problem, Jeff mentioned a time as a 10-year-old child when he wanted to go to summer sports camp. He had heard that the summer camp his friends were planning to go to was lots of fun, but his single mother could not afford to send him. Jeff heard that there was someone in town, a lawyer, who sometimes gave small amounts of money to needy children. Jeff went to the law firm, saw the receptionist, and marched into the lawyer's office. Jeff told him what he *needed and how much fun this sports camp was going to be. The lawyer opened his desk drawer, pulled out his checkbook, and wrote a check endorsed to the camp for $50. Jeff said it was one of the best childhood experiences he can remember—and now that lawyer is a politician. Jeff said, "And I vote for him every time he is up for reelection!" The group discussed the need to be resourceful and seek out assistance.*

10. Expect Youth to Have an Experience in Which They Give Back to Their Community.   For some it is considered to be a repayment of a debt, something that puts back together something in the community they had fractured. For others, the experience itself provides a feeling of significance that they could mean something to someone else. In this way the youth are provided an opportunity to develop a sense of closure surrounding the criminal offense. They can then leave the bad decision and its consequences behind. In the FSP, youth go to the homeless shelter to prepare meals or to a nursing home to visit seniors and play bingo. Many opportunities exist, and chances for service to others are all around us.

> *One FSP group planned an outing to a local park where they would pick up litter. Once they arrived, there was some litter, but not a lot, and they had finished in 30 minutes. One of the youth in the group, Brandon, told the group that he came to this park often; he pointed to a location where he usually went to hike, and then said, "but there is no way of getting over there right now because the water in the creek is too high." Because this outing was on a Saturday, both Mark, Brandon's father, and Max, Brittany's father, attended the community service outing. Max said: "Well, we have some time. That creek isn't very wide; let's build a bridge over the creek." The youth got excited about this idea of building something. Mark said he and Brandon would go to the Home Depot store to get lumber. Max coordinated the plan at the site, and when Mark and Brandon returned with the lumber, the project was under way. Within two hours, the bridge across the creek was completed and the group spent an hour hiking on the other side.*

Eight Outcomes of Parental Involvement

The inclusion of parents in helping youth at risk is foundational and based on the previous work cited in this volume pertaining to family influences on child behavior problems. One of the foremost family therapy models driven by the principles of systems and family dynamics was the structural family therapy model, which incorporated three essential components: family structure, family subsystems, and interpersonal boundaries (Minuchin, 1974). One of the most valuable contributions of this model was the hurdling of the natural tendency of helping professionals to get mired in the content of a family's problems. When therapists got bogged down in the details of the family's behaviors, they neglected to see how this content simply served to organize the patterns of family dynamics that were so harmful to child development. Seeing the family processes provided a blueprint for changing boundaries, structure, and subsytem rules of interaction.

There is something more in the systemic view offered by Minuchin and his colleagues (Minuchin & Nichols, 1993) that has relevance for the FSP as a multiple family group intervention. In *Institutionalizing Madness* (Elizur & Minuchin, 1989), Minuchin proposes that a systems view of family problems should incorporate the concept of community in a family intervention framework. Without consideration of larger social structures such as neighborhoods, schools, and human service delivery systems in which a family is embedded, interventions are likely to be trivialized and potential family outcomes muffled.

The FSP does not view family involvement simply as a means to increase the probability of attendance of youth. The parent is viewed as an equally vital family member necessary to foster behavior change of the youth and to whom support and resources can be provided. While the group leader refrains from a direct statement to this effect, the parent is expected to consider individual change equivalent to the change expected for the youth. The professionals and group leaders take the stand that the parents and other adults who attend the program because they have continual significant involvement in the life of a youth can benefit from participation in the program. Some of the outcomes of parent involvement in the FSP are:

1. *A recognition of the part parents play in the overall situation of their child.* For example, the games and activities in the early phase of the FSP convey to parents that their involvement is expected to be equal to that of their children. Later activities, including the pledge and educational planning, solidify this expectation.
2. *Renewed enthusiasm and hope for the youth.* It is not common for youth to express their appreciation for their parents' involvement in the program. To most youth this behavior would "blow their cover," it would communicate that they were not "independent" and cannot "run their own life." These characteristics of perceived independence are held highly by adolescents. However, it is clear from the nonverbal communication of the youth that they are very pleased that their parents are present—that they have sacrificed their time to be in the program with them. The parents begin to realize that their children can be enjoyable to be with, do have appealing characteristics like sense of humor and sensitivity, and need guidance. Parents are urged to schedule family time once the program has been completed much as they schedule time to attend the FSP. This shift in attitude helps the children feel more

encouraged and often more motivated to adhere to rules or meet the expectations of their parents.

3. *Improved communication between parent and youth.* As parents learn more about their children in the FSP, they are more able to communicate at an appropriate level, and to be more positive in their interaction.

> *Joan was constantly belittling Robert in the group. She refused to negotiate or sign the family pledge because she claimed that Robert was so defiant that he did not deserve anything from her that would help him. Ed and the group facilitators tried to help Joan understand that encouragement to a child is like water to a plant, it is necessary for health and growth. Other families expressed their dissatisfaction with Joan's negative comments towards Robert; yet Joan was determined to stay the course. For three straight sessions of the FSP, Joan refused to say anything positive about Robert, while Robert was patient and respectful toward Joan. Robert did not argue with his mother or stop trying to comply with his part in the family pledge. Finally, Robert could handle his mother's tirades no longer and stood up and walked out of the room. One of the group facilitators left the group to talk to Robert. At the end of the session Robert returned and even agreed to keep his contract with his mother, which was to express thanks to his mother when she made a meal and washed his clothes. At the end of the third session of Joan's continued criticism of Robert, Ed said to the group that he simply could not continue to be an accomplice to Joan's criticism of Robert by allowing it to continue. He told Joan that he was going to have to hold up a Stop sign (which looked like a road sign) whenever Joan said something negative about Robert in the group discussion. Ed also asked the group members to accept some responsibility for Robert by encouraging him and by being his positive parents while Joan learned how to be supportive of Robert. Beginning at the next session, Ed brought his Stop sign, prepared to hold it up if Joan said something negative about Robert. Twice in the next session Ed had to pick up his sign from underneath his chair and hold it up when Joan began to speak critically of Robert. When Joan saw the Stop sign, she stopped talking, and Ed asked other group members to communicate something positive to Robert. By the ninth session, Joan could speak positively about Robert without Ed holding up the Stop sign.*

4. *Reduced blame directed at the youth by the parent.* With more positive and supportive communication growing, blaming communication is crowded out of the interactions. Like most human behavior, change is not typically made unless something is available that is better or more appealing than the current behavior. Hence blaming communication does not diminish unless another form of communication, a more positive and appealing one, is incorporated into the dialogue. The group leader monitors discussions to promote positive communication, and activities are structured that allow families to experience a more rewarding interaction.

5. *Improved family decision-making skills.* All group activities in the FSP require either intrafamily or interfamily communication and focus on collaboration and enjoyment. Just as the athlete's T-shirt reads "There is no 'I' in T-E-A-M," so too do families begin to have experience with success together. The realization emerges that families can experience win-win situations instead of adversarial, I-win-you-lose outcomes.

6. *Increased resources in which the family as a group resolves some of its problems.* Brandon and Brittany had the opportunity to see their fathers supervise the bridge-building community service activity. The parents were also able to experience the resourcefulness of the youth as they helped design and build the bridge. After this day, they gained a sense of "can-do" about their lives and a greater sense of their ability to overcome obstacles. Parents are uplifted knowing their children view them as competent and resourceful.

7. *Renewed involvement in the overall life of the youth.* As families are urged to set aside time together after the FSP as they have for their participation in the FSP, they leave with more optimism and hopefulness that motivate them to be involved with each other. One exercise that contributes to this motivation is the Parent Recipe that the group constructs and hangs on the wall in their household. The Parent Recipe is constructed by the families during a session and recorded by the leader. It is then presented to the families at graduation (see chapter 6 for details).

8. *Renewed emphasis on school progress and new skills to advocate for school success.* By completing the FSP, parents have learned more about their child's school status and behavior. Families have: (1) role-played a parent-student-teacher conference; (2) been inspired by the life of George Dawson; (3) increased their awareness of education by seeing money stacks using census data for educational level and lifetime earnings: high school drop-out, high school graduate; associates degree, four-year college degree; graduate degree as an avenue to a desired standard of living; (4) set up a home environment for learning; and (5) developed an after-school schedule to increase their advocacy for their child's educational success (see session 5 in chapter 6 for details).

Recruitment and Retention: How Do the Families Get to the FSP?

Recruitment and retention are common challenges in family intervention programs. Some families are disorganized and have difficulty setting priorities and planning and adhering to schedules. Some resent the perceived intrusion of outsiders meddling with their lives. Some families attend because one member of the family is motivated and influences the remaining members. One of the challenges in fostering involvement and generating effectiveness in parent education intervention can be inferred from the following:

> Parents who are very demanding while failing to recognize their child's limitations and needs typify the pattern of physically and emotionally abusive parents, while parents who place few demands and little or no structure typify a neglectful, uninvolved style of parenting. They have been found to demonstrate displeasure in the parenting role, inappropriate expectations of the child, disregard for the child's needs and abilities, role reversal with expectations that the child will meet their needs, beliefs that the child intentionally annoys them, and inconsistent and ineffective childrearing practices. (Cowen, 2001, p. 74)

Given this perspective, some families believe that they have been unfairly blamed by professionals and that is why they have been recruited. Yet we should not overlook the occurrence of some families who possess the attitude that the family intervention program is an opportunity for them. An additional challenge in recruitment is helping put at ease a family that is reluctant to share their lives with other families in a multiple family group intervention program. Some of these challenges and methods of successful recruitment are described in this book, and others have been explicated elsewhere (Quinn, 2003).

Since the FSP was developed initially to address juvenile first offenders, the offending behavior of a youth was considered the entry into intervention. The FSP can be designed for youth with related problems such as truancy or behavior problems. In any case, the initial meeting between the youth and an FSP representative should include the family. In the case of juvenile offenders, a court letter requires the presence of the family in the juvenile court. If the youth pleads guilty, the youth and family are referred to both a staff member of the juvenile court and a representative of the FSP who works in tandem with the court. (See Figure 5.1.) These roles can be subsumed within the same person (a court staff member trained in FSP) if the juvenile court has legitimized the FSP within budget and theoretical domains. That is, juvenile court personnel would need to possess the beliefs related to the importance of family involvement and the potential benefits that can be derived from it. Typically, however, the juvenile is contracted with an agency or organization that serves youth and families and has been certified as a Family Solutions site.

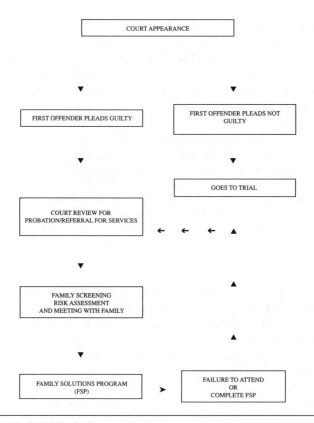

Fig. 5.1 Juvenile First-Offender Program Flow Chart

The importance of meeting the family prior to the first session of the FSP is crucial for several reasons. First, rapport must be built with the family, as parents and youth can have an initial negative reaction about the case disposition or referral. Feelings of anger, fear, confusion, and ambivalence are common. Sitting down face-to-face helps the family begin to see that the FSP is intended to help them and not punish them. In addition, they can begin to see that the person involved is trying to offer assistance. Second, it is important that questions the family has can be answered and that the details of the program are fully explained. This includes location, time and place of the first meeting, that all family members are welcome, and that transportation problems can be remedied. It is also important to send a letter to the family and leave a voice-mail message as the date of the first meeting gets closer. These procedures are intended to boost the show rate on the first night. This is a crucial session in which cohesion and trust are built, and a family that misses this first session is less likely to make a commitment or complete the program.

A risk assessment is then administered with the family in which a comprehensive array of information is collected. This information is examined to assess whether the FSP would not be appropriate for a family. Some exceptions to FSP enrollment might be:

- no adult can feasibly attend the program due to employment;
- the parent has a terminal illness or caretaking responsibilities;
- more supervised care of the youth is required, such as foster placement in cases of abuse and neglect;
- intensive services are needed to address severe emotional or psychiatric problems or drug dependency.

The above circumstances, while they are serious and require further case review to identify more expansive resources, are not as common as some would anticipate but do require attention.

A case has been made in this text that family involvement is crucial to successful intervention and a coordinated effort by the juvenile court, school, or referral agency and the FSP representative. Another advantage to family involvement is the inclusion of siblings. Older siblings can provide credibility with the targeted youth who is required to attend the program. The value of sibling involvement can be illustrated by the following situation:

> *Dan, the 19-year-old brother of Sam, attended one night while on leave from his military assignment. The topic for that session was conflict resolution. role-play scenarios were created and enacted in front of the group. One of the role-plays presented demonstrated the limited ability of youth in the program to resolve a confrontational situation relevant to their lives, the threat of one youth forcibly to remove a "cool" jacket from another youth. After a period of time in which Brandon and Sam had clearly reached a stalemate and the threat of a physical altercation was near, Dan spoke up. Ed encouraged this involvement and asked Dan to suggest some ideas that could help resolve the dispute before "something really bad happened." Dan stepped forward and suggested a way that the confrontation could be resolved. Ed suggested he role-play his strategy to protect himself and remove himself from the dispute. Dan did so and discussed a similar situation that he had experienced when he was younger, explaining the mistake he had made in that situation and the unfortunate consequence that had occurred. Dan also discussed and demonstrated, with the help of the group leader, several options to resolve the confrontation more effectively based on his recent experiences in the military. The youth in the FSP listened carefully to Dan, since his youthful age and recent success in the military provided him some legitimacy in the eyes of the group.*

The following is an example of parent involvement and its contribution to program success:

When Virginia attended the FSP with Brandon, the youth offender aged 13, and her younger son, Ernie, their father, Mark, was in the military and assigned to various bases as an instructor. He lived in the home but had an erratic work schedule. Virginia was new to the community and, having recently arrived from the Philippines, in need of a social network. She tried to become connected by being extremely talkative, always smiling, and very positive about her life despite her longing for her husband's attention, greater acceptance as a minority person in the community, and financial problems. Her life-coping skills were impressive, particularly the cognitive aspects such as her outlook on life which cheered up the entire group as they became more appreciative of her adversity and desire to overcome it. Her children were embarrassed in a way by her enthusiasm and constant talking because it drew attention to them, yet they were quietly proud of her and appreciative of their relationships with her. While Virginia was unusually active in group discussion, other group members entered the program discouraged, quiet, and uncertain. As Virginia put her imprint on this group in the first few weeks of the program, the other families shifted from feelings of futility and despondency to a sense of hopefulness and enthusiasm. One evening, Virginia came to the program with a severe headache. When Ed offered a pain reliever, she said she had taken three before she left home, but her head still throbbed. Yet she continued to participate while rubbing her head and wiping her forehead with a damp cloth. At the end of the contracting activity structured for that session but before the session was over, Ed invited her to consider going home early, since she had completed the task assigned. She was extremely grateful for this offer. Yet before she left, she went to all of the other rooms where families were developing pledges/contracts and individual families were working separately, to say good-bye and apologize for having to leave early. Then, by surprise, the mother offered each of the other children in the group a piece of gum and two dollars. The children did not know how to respond but they accepted before they could understand its meaning. Ed wondered whether some of the parents might take offense, but they did not object in this situation. When Virginia overlooked one child, Brandon pointed it out, and Virginia came back. For the remainder of the session, the group had to function without their "appointed leader" (Virginia). With such empty space, other group members had to become more active. This session changed the tone of future sessions, as other group members felt more comfortable and accepted more responsibility for the group's success, while Virginia's contagious enthusiasm took hold.

There are currently several intervention models that utilize a strengths-based approach to change. They are found under many rubrics, including "brief therapy," "solution-focused therapy," "building family strengths," "family strengths-based model," and even the one described in this book, the FSP.

The basis of this approach is to focus on the utility and presence of a client's or family's characteristics that can promote functional change in the youth. In a multiple family group model, the potential exists to utilize a group or family member who can be drawn into group process to contribute something to another group member's or family's dilemma or difficulty. In the above illustration, one mother's exuberance "rubbed off" on other group members. In addition, her generosity contributed to their feelings of validation and enjoyment about being there.

Other examples of how families are boosted by other family strengths include: (1) one family's story about how they maintain the ritual of eating together each evening strengthened another family's commitment to do the same; (2) one youth's sense of humor became contagious and other youths began to end their silence in the group; (3) one father's belief in tolerating his son's hairstyle was evident when the boy came in weekly with purple-colored hair, which led to a discussion of acceptable dress and appearance, ownership of the human body, and what is tolerable; this led another father to become less rigid in demanding a particular physical appearance of his own son, which led into a discussion by the group of how important it is "to pick the battles one chooses to fight" because differences across the generation are inevitable.

The value of the group process cannot be truly discerned because it is not easy to measure its full effects on group members. Yet the enthusiasm and focus within the context of group interaction is often apparent, and such relevance provides opportunities for learning and change. The common notion of why the families are together (the presence of a youth offense), the unique value of each member's contribution, and the common goal of personal and relational change drive the group process. The group leader who holds these elements as crucial to success can permit the families to share in the responsibility for change.

A core component of the program is the recruitment of families. This is a challenge due to the family's view that "it's the youth who needs help," combined with the ambivalence of their own participation. Planned recruitment strategies to engage families are essential and must be organized and implemented throughout the intervention.

During the review of a family's case in the juvenile court at the time the decision to refer a family to the FSP is made, information about the program is given to them. Some of the important statements made to families include:

- the opportunity to learn how other families manage certain situations;
- the aims of the FSP (e.g., strengthen families, focus on education, decision-making skills);
- requirements of completing the program (e.g., regular attendance, participation, punctuality);

- the date the program will begin;
- the time and place (with map in some cases) of the FSP.

The FSP representative in the court or the assigned court personnel is available to answer the family's questions about the FSP. The FSP representative provides the family with a brochure that outlines the FSP and includes the date, time, and place of the first meeting. About a week prior to the beginning date of the FSP, a letter is sent to the family reminding them of their required commitment (see Figure 5.2). A map to the location and other detailed information is included. We again remind the family that the parent(s) or guardian(s) is required to attend with the youth. The sample letter here can be adapted for a group with a different focus, such as school truancy or other problem behaviors. The important factor is that because some families

_____ (date)
_____ (name)
_____ (address)
_____

Dear _____.
I enjoyed meeting you at the _____ County Juvenile Court. We have been informed by the court that your family has been referred to the FSP to satisfy the conditions of probation. The FSP is a ten-week program that meets one evening per week (and one Saturday). Attendance is required for _____ (the youth) involved with the Juvenile Court *and* _____ (his or her parents).

The first meeting of the Juvenile First Offender FSP is _____ (day of the week), _____ (month and day), 19__ (year) at_____ p.m., at _____ (site) on _____ (street). A map is enclosed. Remember that *parents* and *youth* are required to attend together.

If you have any questions, please call me at (__) ___-____.
We look forward to seeing you there.

Sincerely,

FSP Coordinator

Fig. 5.2 Sample Letter to Families Prior to the First Meeting

possess a reluctance to participate, *regular and clear communication that delineates expectations of attendance is crucial to formation of groups.*

Often siblings will attend, but they are not required to. We find that including siblings gives the family an opportunity to be together and for the siblings to benefit from the program in a way that might lessen the chances of their future criminal involvement or school difficulty. Small children can be assigned to child care or play sessions in an adjacent room. Involving siblings can serve as a primary prevention strategy.

As shown in the previous case example, Dan, an older sibling of Sam who comes to the program while on military leave, can be a valuable resource to the group as the perspective of this person is channeled into the group process.

> *Another older youth, now 19, reviewed his own experience as a juvenile offender and described the probation requirements he was assigned. He expressed his regret that a program like the FSP was not available when he was an offender, and stated: "My life really didn't change going to see the probation officer every week, and that was frustrating. I needed something like this so I could change something about my life."*

Attendance

The importance of multiple strategies for recruitment and retention of families cannot be overemphasized. Methods utilized must be reviewed periodically to determine if changes are needed. For instance, in the program described in this book, we changed the recruitment method as a result of a high number of "no-shows" when the program began over a decade ago. Initially we established an alternative site from the juvenile court to interview families and describe the multiple family group program because we wanted to be seen as a benevolent, not punitive, program. However, we found that many families would not schedule or show up for their appointment following the adjudication hearing or "informal adjustment" at the juvenile court in which they were referred to the program. Or a recommendation or referral would be made by a school administrator or teacher but the family would not follow up. For some families, the process of referral was too confusing, or they felt that the purpose was not clearly stated. In some cases, the family and the referral source were at odds regarding who was to blame and who was responsible for the problem. Others had difficulty scheduling and keeping appointments due to the complexity of their life circumstances and underorganization in family living. Specifically, these families lived day to day or hour to hour, and making a commitment to preserve the time of the scheduled referral appointment several days or a week away was not a skill they had developed.

To remedy the situation, we placed a representative of the multiple family group program (the FSP) in the juvenile court. This liaison to the program tracked the appointments of juvenile offenders and scheduled a time to meet with the families immediately after the court hearing for those families referred to the program. In this way, the program's purpose and methods can be explained. Questions from the family can be answered. Details can be given, such as the time and place of the program sessions. The family can "attach a face to a name." A risk assessment is conducted to assess the family's appropriateness for the program and to plan program topics based on family characteristics.

Subsequent to that meeting, a letter is sent to the family summarizing the family's situation regarding obligation to the court and time and place of the first session. A couple of days before the first session, a telephone call is made to the family as a reminder of the upcoming first session. It is important that phone numbers are double-checked with the family in the interview at the court. It is common for numbers to be inaccurate, outdated, or missing. It is also important to identify the leadership in the family— the representative in the family most invested in the program who can be the family's organizer. This is the person who often must be contacted. If an apathetic family member is contacted, or one who is not accepting responsibility for the court obligation, it is possible that the message serving as the reminder of the upcoming session will never get transferred to others in the family. Every effort must be taken that is reasonable and possible to ensure attendance at the first session.

It is imperative that families attend the first session. The purpose of the first session is to build trust and cohesion in the group and establish a social context for promoting optimal group discussion, collaboration, and empathy. Missing the first session creates a hardship for the family that attends for the first time at the second session. This family can be alienated, and the other families can find themselves at a distance from the family that was absent the first night.

After the first session, the leader/facilitators review the attendance and note any families missing. These families are contacted by phone and reminded that another absence will result in their disqualification from the program and a notice to the court that they will not complete the program.

The rule of attendance in the FSP is that families can miss only one weekly two-hour meeting. Families sign up upon arrival at each session. If they miss more than one, their name is referred back to the juvenile court for further action. (Before long, many family members find the FSP something they look forward to, rather than as a chore or nuisance.) However, a commitment from the program staff to communicate firmly and clearly the family's obligation and the place, time, and date of the meetings is crucial and often requires several methods. On occasion, we find that a family misses more than one session for legitimate reasons—acute illness or family death, or a change in work hours. In this situation, we negotiate another requirement to compensate for their absence so they can still complete the program, or the family is referred to the next cycle of the FSP if a substantial number of sessions are missed for the above reasons. Alternative methods to make up sessions are possible: a volunteer activity in the community might be planned; or a special appointment might be made to have the family watch a video shown during the session they missed and to discuss with a staff member or write a short summary of what was learned. In a few cases, the families have repeated the entire FSP the next time it is offered. If juvenile offenders are the targeted youth group, some of these options must be negotiated with the court, since a probationary status has an established time limit.

A flow chart is included (Fig. 5.1) so that you can see visually how families get to and leave the FSP. They come with a letter from us, they leave with a graduation certificate (discussed in detail in chapter 5). We urge families to place these in a prominent place, such as on a refrigerator or in the youth's bedroom bookcase. The certificate serves as a reminder of the accomplishment. Moreover, we believe valuable experiences can be gained, a changed attitude can emerge, and/or a more effective behavior (i.e., parent–youth communication) has begun.

In the following pages, a summary outline is presented that covers the content of the FSP so you can consider applying the ideas and activities in your community. The FSP manual is over 200 pages and is available to sites that make a decision to implement the FSP in their community (www.families4change.org). In one of our newsletters, we offer a quote: "The dark moment the caterpillar calls the end of the world is the sun-filled moment the butterfly calls the beginning" (anonymous). We hope that this quote will fit your families when you have completed family intervention.

CHAPTER **6**

Program Components of the Family Solutions Program

*Friends are the thermometers by which we may
judge the temperature of our fortunes.*
—Marguerite Power Blessington

This chapter will outline the structure and content of the Family Solutions Program (FSP). The intention is to provide the reader with a view of program content that would permit an assessment of the relevance of the FSP for an agency, organization, school, or court. However, the FSP manual is the complete guide necessary to implement the program. Further information on the manual and training opportunities can be found on the Web site:http://www.families4change.org.

There are topics and related group activities that have remained constant over a decade. These topics are congruent with the developmental needs of youth and the challenges of family life. These topics and activities have also been regularly evaluated by families as being useful and enjoyable. A session evaluation form is administered to both parents and youth at each FSP cycle to assess the family's view of the value of each session. The constancy of activities proven effective is particularly important at the outset of program initiation. One way to think about the goal of a therapist in meeting with a client for the first time is that it should be to do what is required in order to allow the client to believe that the therapeutic endeavor is worthwhile. For the family group leader, the goal is to provide a satisfactory experience for a family in the first session and to provide them with a view of the program as beneficial and worthwhile. In other words, a

129

successful first session for a family can be defined by whether they return for the second session. For most families the first session must include: (1) validation that they are supported and possess strengths; (2) a description of the program that is congruent with their perception of their needs; and (3) a sense that other families have similar concerns or characteristics that allow a family to feel a sense of belonging. If these objectives are not met, the likelihood of a family returning for a second session or possessing a readiness to participate and learn significantly decreases.

While the FSP Teaching Guide provides clear direction to the group leader for conducting each session, the choices of topics and activities embedded in the manual are varied and depend on the characteristics of the families that are identified from both the risk assessment and the family members' participation early in the program. Hence the group leaders are encouraged to have flexibility in designing the program so that it remains relevant and useful for the families throughout the sessions. In fact, in our experience with about 200 cycles of the FSP it is not uncommon for the group leader(s) to modify program components as the FSP unfolds from session to session. The content material in this chapter does not include all curriculum materials for implementing the program. Materials that correspond to activities, such as handouts and worksheets, videos, or evaluation instruments and procedures, are not included here but are in the curriculum. The Session Summaries, which provide an overview of goals, estimated time, objectives, preparation, handouts, and other materials for each session are also not included. The complete Teaching Guide that has been utilized by group leaders is available as part of the training package offered to new communities, agencies, organizations, and practitioners. What is offered here is a condensed version of the Session Background material that comprises the curriculum to provide the reader with a sense of program contents that could be utilized with a group of families with at-risk youth. The content includes material that applies to working with youth offenders and families as well as truant students and youth with behavior problems.

The first session of the FSP focuses on group trust and cohesion. This adheres to the body of literature on group counseling formation in which trust and cohesion are prerequisites for successful group experiences (see chapter 7). Families, like individuals, have a natural desire to associate with other people who share common characteristics. Families also long for validation and hence expect acceptance from others. In the absence of these attributes, families can feel inadequate or defensive, leading to avoidance of the experience. As a result, families may subsequently withdraw from the program. The importance of the first session is elaborated upon for two reasons: (1) because of its strategic importance in group success, including group process and attendance; and (2) to provide the reader with an example of elements that are included in the Teaching Guide, a curriculum that has been used by group leaders working with multiple adolescents and families.

Family Solutions Program: Session 1

Group Trust and Cohesion: The Importance of Session 1

After completing approximately 200 cycles of the FSP, we have substantial evidence that the components of the first session are crucial to the potential effectiveness of the entire program. In particular, these components include: (1) a belief that attending the program will be worthwhile; (2) an opportunity to meet and become comfortable with other families; (3) clarification by the leaders of all questions concerning expectations. In addition, the agreement between the FSP and the referral source, such as the juvenile court or school, is also shared with families so that they are fully aware of the consequences of dropping out. Families also have the opportunity to increase their commitment to attending all sessions, as well as to the content of the program that binds the agreement. Issues that must be covered with the families include: (1) attendance; (2) punctuality; (3) consequence of not completing the program; (4) the reason parent(s) must attend; (5) expectations for participation (e.g., respect for each other, not interrupting); and (6) any problems with transportation.

The leader should acknowledge parent and youth life struggles and state that the central focus of the program is not punitive The FSP is described as a "fast-forward" program and not a "rewind" program. All activities and discussions are intended to be grounded in developing skills and knowledge to meet the challenges of the future and finding enjoyment in their relationships with each other. Our strategies delineated for Session 1 reflect current advancement in our success in linking families from the referral source to the FSP. When the FSP was initiated in 1992, approximately 50% of families would be present for Session 1. Currently the rate of attendance is 92%. A meeting between the FSP representative and the family prior to the first session of the FSP is crucial. Subsequent to the meeting, a letter is sent to the family a week prior to the first session, and a telephone contact is made 2 days prior to the first session.

Welcome (5 minutes)   The room should be set up to convey to participants that the FSP is a collective process in which all family members and facilitators participate as one group. Chairs are typically arranged in a circle. This format promotes eye contact with each other. It also allows facilitators to be part of the group rather than set themselves apart from families. Assuming a lecture position in front of the group or having facilitators sit separately from families works against the collaborative atmosphere that is needed for the FSP to succeed. The group leader and any group facilitators (college students, adult volunteers, group co-leader) should spread themselves out around the circle so that each is sitting next to family members.

Begin the session *no later than* 5 minutes after the scheduled starting time. While it may be reasonable to allow families a few extra minutes to find the location of the room on the first night, it is important that families understand that punctuality is important. The group leaders introduce themselves and extend a welcome to the families. Group facilitators briefly introduce themselves.

Group leaders explain the premises of the FSP at this meeting. One of the key premises shared with each family is that families are crucial to youth behavior change. We believe that (1) families must be included in resolving problems of youth; (2) solutions that promote improved functioning exist within the family; (3) families do better when they can express their ideas and concerns to others in a friendly and cooperative atmosphere; and (4) families can learn from other families.

Session Goals

- The group will begin to develop trust and cohesion.
- Families will begin to feel comfortable and positive about the program.

Session Objectives

- Families will understand the ground rules.
- The feelings of families will be validated.

After completing approximately 200 cycles of the FSP, we have substantial evidence that certain elements must be included in the first session for the program to succeed. These include

- Families will believe that attending the program is worthwhile.
- Families will meet and become more comfortable with each other.
- Instilling the belief that attending the program will be worthwhile.
- Helping families meet and become comfortable with each other.
- Helping families understand that parent and youth struggles are normal and accepted.
- Explaining that the central focus of the program is not punitive.
- Explaining why parents must attend and participate fully.
- Demonstrating that solutions to logical problems, such as lack of transportation, can be found.

- Setting clear expectations and delineation of task of the program leaders and the referring source (e.g., juvenile court, schools) regarding: attendance; punctuality; consequences of not completing the program; participation.

FSP Graduates Share Experiences (15 minutes) One or two FSP graduate families are invited back to the first session of the program to provide testimonials. The group leader invites each member to share his or her experiences of the FSP. This activity contributes to a sense of hopefulness in the current FSP families that the program can be beneficial and worthwhile to them. During the first session, ask returning graduate families to discuss their experiences. This is synonymous with the "word of mouth" phenomenon. The best recommendation about a product, program, or service is from someone who has used the product or service or participated in the program. We strategically build this phenomenon into the FSP by inviting one or two families who have graduated from the FSP to return for the first session of the next FSP. The families who are attending for the first time have the opportunity to learn about the program from families who have completed it. Families who have graduated are positive about the program. They share specific examples of how the program helped them and how their lives are different from what they were prior to this experience. As a result, new families increase their confidence in the value of the FSP and for some, they are helped to realize what an opportunity it is and how it would pass them by if they chose not to come. This positive expectancy is known to be an important contributor to successful intervention (Duncan & Miller, 2000). Clients who believe that their participation in a therapeutic enterprise will provide benefits are more likely to experience success than clients who are pessimistic or ambivalence.

Purpose of the FSP (5 minutes) Distribute copies of the FSP brochure to families. Explain that the purpose of the FSP is to help youth who appear before the Juvenile Court and their families find solutions to personal and family difficulties so that repeat criminal offenses are prevented. State that the FSP adopts the philosophy that the best way to work with youth is by working with their families and the larger community. State to the families: *We believe that . . .*

- Families must be included in helping to solve the problems of youth.
- Families coming together can find solutions to improve family functioning.
- Families do better when they can express their ideas and concerns to others in a friendly and cooperative atmosphere.
- Families can learn from other families.

- Families and individuals do best when they feel part of their local community.

History of the FSP (5 minutes) The following history of the FSP helps families understand how the FSP fits within the overall Juvenile Court System:

- Over 2,000 families have graduated from the program.
- The rate of reoffenses by youth who graduate is much lower than for youth who do not begin the FSP or complete the program.
- The local judge and probation officers show confidence in the program by requiring that all juvenile first offenders be referred to the program.
- We have had families who request permission to participate in the FSP a second time because it was so helpful to them.
- Many families state on Graduation Night that while they were annoyed when they had to come to the FSP in the beginning, they are now pleased that they participated in the FSP.

Court Representative Speaks (if Youth Are Offenders) (5 minutes—optional) Invite a court representative to discuss the court's expectations of the families and what must be accomplished, such as consistent attendance, for families to fulfill their obligations to the court. In this way, the families view the court staff as the authority figure. This allows the FSP staff to maintain a more collaborative role. The message and expectations outlined by the court representative can help strengthen family commitment to the program. The court representative explains that if a parent misses more than one session, the youth cannot complete the program and will be referred back to the juvenile court for further action.

Solicit Input on the Schedule (10 minutes) Distribute the written schedule of topics and discuss why the topics are typically included over the 10 weeks. Topics and group activities are selected based on

- relevance to the life situations of family members;
- whether or not successful outcomes were achieved in previous group interactions;
- needs of the family based on risk-assessment information.

Ask families to share their opinions about activities they like as well as what else they would like to see scheduled during the program. This reinforces the view of the FSP as a collaboration among families and facilitators. With the exception of the first and last sessions, none of the content of the FSP is "cast in stone." Group leaders are encouraged to modify the sessions based on family input so that the program remains relevant and useful for the families throughout the entire 10 weeks.

Invite families to take the schedule home and review it. This will allow shy participants time to think about the schedule and share their views during Session 2. Families who were not prepared to respond to the invitation of providing input can have a week to consider what is important to them and what would help them. The simple request by the group leader conveys that the program is collaborative and that their involvement is expected and the success of program is dependent upon it. Allow time in Session 2 for further discussion of family members' requests for topics and activities.

Establish Ground Rules (10 minutes) Ground rules help a group operate efficiently and achieve group goals. Outline the following ground rules to be used in the FSP:

1. Punctuality is important. Some families have difficulty organizing their time productively; therefore they are prone to arriving at sessions late. Families who come late interrupt group activities and group discussions, hence preventing completion of activities. Lateness may also reflect minimal commitment to the program. In addition, families who arrive at sessions on time may resent others who are late. This can potentially detract from group cohesion. Promise that if families arrive on time, the session will end on time. This will be a challenge for families who have difficulty organizing their lives. Punctuality may become a goal for these families.
2. Attendance is required. Explain to families that their presence not only insures that they will get the most out of the program, it is also needed so that the group can support and learn from one another.
3. Participation is expected. There will be many opportunities to express opinions or describe themselves in the group. Multiple viewpoints increase the probability that the goal of the group activity or discussion can be attained for all participants. In addition, each participant is viewed as a member of a team in which each member's involvement is needed to achieve a planned outcome. Each thought, feeling, or behavior contributes to the building up of new ideas and different perspectives that can lead to change. Tell families to be prepared to express an opinion occasionally, particularly if they have not spoken. This situation applies especially to youth, who are not practiced in speaking in front of adults or who do not possess the confidence to self-disclose. Disclosure is not

built when self-esteem is built. Rather, self-esteem is built when disclosure occurs. Successful experiences promote confidence. Our aim is to provide successful experiences to help youth interrupt their downward spiral of negativity and doubt.

4. Parents must attend with youth for each session (except for the volunteer activity that includes only youth and facilitators). Explain that parental attendance is necessary so that families can learn from and support each other. Stress that youth will not graduate and will be referred back to the court or school for further review if parents miss more than one session. This is a difficult position for facilitators to take, since many parents initially do not see the importance of their attendance in the project.

Important Family members other than parents and youth are encouraged to attend. Sibling attendance is valuable for many reasons. We view sibling participation as beneficial because it

- promotes whole-family shared experience;
- diminishes any anxiety that a parent may have about leaving someone home while attending the program;
- eliminates the problem of child care; and
- provides opportunities for prevention by exposing siblings to the experiences and benefits of the program.

Some parents choose to bring some children but arrange supervision for infants, toddlers, and small children. Other adults, such as a grandparent, are also encouraged to attend, as well as coparents living outside the youth's home. Anyone who has some level of contact and genuine interest in the youth is eligible to attend.

Fathers who live outside the home are especially welcome. A father's presence can provide opportunities for enhancement of communication, resolution of conflict, or overcoming loneliness. Fathers can contribute to group process by recounting characteristics that compliment a mother's influence.

Role-play (15 minutes) Some families may see the program as an interruption of the important things in life that they would rather be doing. Family members might be embarrassed about being there, confused about the juvenile court requirements they have to meet, or nervous that they will have to do something they do not want or know how to do. These feelings must be addressed openly so that the families feel that the FSP leaders understand where they are coming from.

Expressing these feelings allows the group to vent frustrations or express hopes, sets the stage for open and honest communication, and helps families get past their negative feelings. Encouraging families to express their feelings also serves as a form of validation that conveys to families that their feelings are understood and accepted by the group.

The group leaders and facilitators guide the activity by role-playing first the role of a parent, then a youth and finally a facilitator. In this way, participants learn about the perspectives of each subgroup.

At this point in the first session about 45 minutes have passed. Youth in particular can become restless and "leader-deaf." As stated earlier, we fully recognize that parents and youth bring a wide range of feelings and thoughts to the first session of the FSP. They might be angry as parents because they did not commit the offense (e.g., delinquent act, truant behavior). Parents of youth who exhibit behavior problems can be angry or ambivalent about their own required attendance. They may feel embarrassed in front of other parents and naturally try to avoid attending a program. As for youth, the program may be viewed as an interruption of the things in life they want to do. Youth may feel uncomfortable about committing a behavior requiring FSP attendance that impinges on the time of their parents. They also feel frustrated that they are being deprived of activities they would prefer, such as being with friends, watching TV, and playing video games. It is very important to recognize the immediate experience of family members as they enter the room for the very first time and to accept their ambivalence or anxiety. Family members might be: (1) embarrassed about being there; (2) confused about the requirement they have to meet, as spelled out by the juvenile court; and (3) nervous that they will have to do something they do not want or know how to do.

It is very important that these feelings and thoughts be addressed openly so that FSP leaders can convey to families that group leaders have a sense of "what it might be like to be here." To state and live these feelings in the group provides the vehicle for moving beyond these impediments that will prevent genuine and open communication. Identifying the range of attitudes also serves as a vehicle for validating the families by acknowledging their needs.

First, *a facilitator role-plays the experience of the parents in the group*. The facilitator moves his/her chair to the center of the circle and begins to express statements that might be congruent with those felt by parents in the group. Examples are: "I don't know why I have to be here; I didn't do anything wrong"; "I can't afford to be here; I've got so much to do at home"; "I didn't do the crime, so why do I have to do the time?"; and "Coming here makes me look like a bad parent." When these comments were role-played in the group, Mark, Brandon's father, said, "You got that right!" and Joan, Robert's mother, blurted out, "Amen to that!" Then the parents are invited to share with the group additional feelings not expressed by the facilitator. When parents express these in the group, the facilitator repeats them and incorporates them into his/her role-play. Jackie, David's mother, remarked, "I hope something gets through to him here because I can't!" Denise added, "Well, I need help and I'm glad this program is here for us!" Denise's comment helped shape a more positive view of the program for other parents that might foster more engagement and commitment to attendance. The process of soliciting parent input continues until no other parents have comments. The parents begin to feel connected to others, knowing that someone identifies their plight; some laughter can be heard at times because comments expressed ring true or are expressed so dramatically.

When the parent role-play is completed, the facilitator returns to the circle, and another facilitator who will role-play a youth pulls a chair from the circle and sits in the middle. The facilitator begins to remark, "Man, this is a waste (mumbling)"; "I can't believe I gotta come here"; "They don't know what I'm goin' through"; and "I ain't gonna say a thing." Additional comments by the facilitator are strung together, and then the group makes an educated guess that the facilitator is role-playing a youth.

> In the group there was a particularly immature parent, Patti, Shay's mother, noticed by everyone in the group who would whine and complain about being required to come. When the youth role-play commenced, Debra, Sam's mother, remarked, "It's Patti, it's Patti!" Other parents agreed, and everyone laughed. The youth are invited to add their own expressions that reflect their "here and now" feelings. Again, as in the parent role-play, the exercise continues until all comments from youth have been heard and each comment is repeated by the facilitator doing the role-play. David said, "Well if I have to come I ain't gonna talk"; and Brittany said, "My mother needs this more than me!"

Following the youth role-play, the group leader or a group facilitator actually role-plays a facilitator. One of the college interns, Jennifer, dragged a chair to the middle of the circle and began to reveal feelings felt by facilitators. Jennifer began: "It's been a long day, I don't know where I'm gonna find the energy to hang in for two hours tonight"; "these people don't wanna be here. Why should I try; it won't be appreciated"; "I know Ed (group leader) has his own family and feels like he should be eating dinner with them, and here he is with other people's families"; "I don't know if I made the right decision. I have a heavy course load this semester and lots of tests"; "Well, I hope I can help one of these families, but right now I'm not sure how." As in the previous role-plays, those who fit the role, in this case other facilitators sitting in the circle, add their expressions denoting their feelings, such as ambivalence, doubt, and fatigue.

Early on in doing this exercise we realized that not every parent felt negative, and certainly not every facilitator did. Even a youth might not feel negative but was reluctant to express a positive feeling, such as "it's about time someone recognized I wasn't the only one with the problem." One parent asked during a role-play, "Do I have to say something bad or negative? Can't I express my enthusiasm?" After initial surprise, Ed gave her permission by saying, "of course, go ahead," and the parent expanded her feeling by saying that she had been waiting for something like this for a long time—she knew there were problems but didn't know how to change things (with "unruly" youth who are reported by parents, this is known and sometimes admitted). The tone of the group shifts at this stage as family members become more relaxed. Each has heard an expression of their feelings, sometimes with lightheartedness but always with validation.

Icebreaker 1: The Name Game (25 minutes) The term "icebreaker" used to describe an introductory activity among strangers and might have its origin in the statement: "A smile is a powerful weapon; you can even break ice with it" (*Bits and Pieces*, 2003). Icebreakers are used in a variety of group intervention contexts in which people are meeting each other for the first time or under disquieting circumstances. Many icebreaker exercises can be employed that accomplish similar results. Specifically, each person enters a small part of the life space of another so that opportunities for relatedness exist. In time, genuine caring, enjoyment, and/or learning become outcomes of this relatedness. All of these characteristics are prized in the FSP since the group process is the core of the FSP structure and purpose.

Group cohesion begins in Session 1 but gathers steam over the course of the program. We have used the knots game, in which persons must connect and disconnect from each other, the traffic jam, in which persons must reposition themselves to get to the other side based on certain rules, and the toothpick and gumdrop exercise to build towers. Some of these we continue to use to promote cooperation among the group or within families.

The icebreaker game that has been consistently employed during Session 1 for every FSP cycle, however, is the name game. In the name game, persons sequentially introduce themselves by choosing an adjective that describes themselves and that has the same initial as their first name. In addition, the adjective must describe some characteristic of themselves that they own. For instance, I have been known to tell stories that relate to family experiences or invite families to consider an idea about family life that they might apply to their own families. In fun but with some truth, I have always been "Bologna Bill." Family members remember that and even ask other facilitators about me after they graduate, saying, "Hey, how's Bologna Bill doing?" In this group, the following names were offered: Smiling Shay, Peppi Patti, Bright Brandon, Vivacious Virginia, Mobile Mark, Dynamic David, Jumpin' Jackie, Elixir Ed (group leader), Shifty Sam (an athlete), Dependable Debra, Jack-of-all-Trades Jeff, Roamin' Robert, Jolly Joan, Jazzy Jennifer (college intern),

Beautiful Brittany, and Dancing Denise. You get the idea. As each person takes their turn going around the circle, before the person introduces oneself, the person must repeat all the introductions that have preceded him/her. Each person in the circle, then, must listen carefully to remember the names as introduced so they can be repeated. If a person is clearly stuck, a little help from the group is given, without prompting, which enlists group cooperation. However, it is important to restrain anyone who wants to yell out names when it is not his or her turn, so that each turn-taker can be allowed an opportunity to be known and to learn the names of group members. If help is needed, group leaders should refrain unless other families cannot help. The group leader should never help if the leader has a hunch that someone in the group can offer that same input. This is an important element of group leadership: *never offer a comment if you believe someone else in the group can offer a similar or equally valid comment that enhances group discussion.* In this way the group learns to depend on themselves and each other to provide support and guidance to the group.

If there is time before the session closes after each has taken a turn, an open invitation is given to anyone in the group who wishes to do all names consecutively. The group leader can have a prize ready for anyone who can accomplish this task. Sometimes the group members are directed to find new seats, thereby throwing off the order of names learned, and a group member is asked to volunteer to go around the circle identifying the name with the adjective of each person.

Ice Breaker 2: The Toilet Paper Game (20 minutes) Each person takes one to three sheets of toilet paper. They are not told the purpose of the sheets until they have each taken one to three sheets. Participants are then instructed to say something about themselves for every sheet that they have. Another option is to ask group members to pair off with someone who is not a part of their family. They are then instructed to take 3 minutes to learn at least three things about the other person that they can share with the group. In either exercise, the group learns more about each other, which promotes a sense of belonging and comfort. Examples of information people may share include:

> hobbies;
> academic, athletic, or artistic successes;
> occupation;
> exciting adventures in their life;
> exciting adventures planned.

Transportation (5 minutes) Transportation can be a problem for certain families. Our method is to encourage families to take responsibility for this by searching out possibilities, such as the bus system, or a family member or friend who does not attend the program currently. A second option is to ask the families in the FSP to help each other with transportation. Virginia was not sure she would always have a car because her husband, Mark, a military personnel, would sometimes be out of town or late returning from base. Ed asked, "Does any family live near Virginia and Brandon?" Ed asked, "Could any family offer Virginia and Brandon a ride?" When Virginia explained where she lived, Debra volunteered to help out since she did not live far away. This builds cooperation and commitment to each other. It is not uncommon that a family in need of transportation does not actually live too far from another family coming to the FSP. We discuss any transportation needs and invited family members help each other out at this time in the program. In this way the families have already had an experience of cooperation and togetherness that might promote more willingness to help others. At the end of the first session is a good time for raising the transportation issue. To discuss this at the outset of the first night would not likely generate this willingness to help with transportation problems. After two hours together in participating in enjoyable activities, families have a stronger commitment to attend and to help each other.

Ending the Session It is important for the session to end on time to abide by the rule of punctuality and to deliver on the initial promise to release families at the designated ending time. Another important reason to end on time is to end when the enthusiasm and enjoyment are high, so that participants will leave wishing the session had lasted longer. In that way families carry home with them an anticipation for the next session. Facilitators remain to be available to family members who have special needs or requests that they wish to share privately. Examples of concerns that families might express privately include: (1) concerns about other family members; (2) conflicts they have with the scheduled time of the FSP; (3) new problems that have arisen in the family since the risk assessment and interview with the FSP representative present at referral; and (4) specific questions about a youth's situation or problem. Plans are made to accommodate additional requests. These could include a referral to family therapy, if a mental health or counseling center adjoins the site of the program; another educational or social service resource referral; a contact with a teacher; or another review of the case by the court. In most cases, however, these issues are quickly resolved and clarify the appropriateness of the family's inclusion in the FSP.

> *Denise spoke with Ed in private after the first session. Denise showed Ed Brittany's report card and stated that she was puzzled that Brittany would have to come to the program due to truancy. On the left-hand side of the report card, a total of four*

absences were denoted. Denise said, "See, Brittany hasn't missed much school at all. Why are we here?" When Ed looked more closely at the report card, he saw on the right-hand side a place for tardiness to be recorded. In that column was the number 55. When Ed asked Denise why Brittany had been tardy so many times, Denise spoke of her night shift and how hard it was to get up in the morning to get Brittany to school. Ed stated to Denise that it was his best guess that they were referred because Brittany had missed too much class time even though she got to school each day, and that one thing they could work on in the FSP sessions was to find effective ways to get Brittany to school on time. Ed did not blame Denise, or get immediately involved in their morning routine, but saved this issue for examination in future sessions.

Space in this chapter has been devoted to delineating some of the vital components of the first session of the FSP because these components are so crucial to future attendance by families. These components promote a social environment conducive to reaching the program goals. The remainder of the chapter will provide briefer summaries of the subsequent sessions. The FSP Teaching Guide provides a more thorough explanation of each session to guide the group leader.

Family Solutions Program: Session 2
Family Cooperation

Session Goal
- Family cohesion will improve through encouraging good communication and cooperation between family members.

Session Objectives
- Group members will learn to appreciate each other;
- Families will appreciate the benefit of working on tasks together;
- Families will continue helping other families feel comfortable with each other.

Introduction This session helps families learn the importance of communication and teamwork. These skills can help families solve problems that often come up in family life. Many families who are present in the FSP have conflictual family relationships. Family members are often alienated from each other. Often they expect each other to resolve their own problems individually without help. Family members often bring resentment and frustration toward each other into the program. The FSP assumes that the existence of these family processes impedes a willingness to find help and support from each other and to engage in problem-resolution experiences.

There is substantial research indicating the importance of family cohesion in promoting child well-being. Family cohesion is the extent to which family members interact, utilize each other for support, engage in social and recreational activities, and share common experiences in their family environment. This environment is the primary and most natural social arrangement for children in society. Yet it can be the most oppressive or disorganized of any social arrangement for children in society.

The research presented earlier in this volume outlines how youth at risk tend to have low family cohesion. Parents may be uninvolved in the important aspects of a child's or youth's experience. They may not be utilized by their children as confidants. Nurturing is inconsistent or rare. Discipline can be extreme, either chronically punitive and/or abusive or laissez-faire and/or neglectful.

The purpose of Session 2 is to build family cohesion to enhance positive parent–youth interaction within the family. Family interaction can be a mechanism for resolving difficulties, providing nurturing experiences for the youth, and providing guidance. The topic is included early in the program because the exercises that are chosen for the session can be done in a playful and relaxed manner. This helps family members feel positive about being in the FSP as they enjoy and learn more about each other. The ratings by families indicate that this session is the most favored among the sessions of the FSP. The tone of the session is playful and cooperative, which offers families an opportunity to experience each other in a way that is new or underutilized. Family members begin enjoying each other rather than being angry, disconfirming, and disconnected. An often-unnoticed outcome of this session is the gratification that youth receive as a result of their parents' involvement with them in fun and enjoyable activities. This experience often provides youth with confirmation that they are valued rather than scorned.

The families engage in two family cooperation activities. One is an active group activity in which participants work as a team and move around each other on squares to get to the other end. The other is a single-family quiet activity, building a tower as a family with gumdrops and toothpicks. Following each activity, a group discussion ensues. Each activity requires some teamwork and problem-solving to be successful. Group leaders next ask how participants' behavior in this exercise is similar to ways they handle problem-solving in their own lives. Responses from group members after the first activity included the following:

- "Sometimes you feel like quitting when no more moves can be made" (Denise).
- "It didn't come easily" (Virginia).
- "You try to change the rules to get what you want" (Sam).

- "This is a good example of how effort and perseverance can pay off" (Ed).
- "Sometimes you wonder if this much effort is worth it" (Jackie).

As a result of this exercise:

- Youth feel more connection to the adults in the group.
- Youth are validated by adults because they contributed to a successful outcome.
- Parents learn that their children have leadership capability, likability, and creative thinking.
- Group members feel more relaxed about their group experience as they playfully interact in a game that can be frustrating yet challenging.

In one group Ed, the group leader, asks:

- "What did you learn from this experience?"
- "How did you feel about doing this?"
- "How did you figure out a way to work together with the rule that you couldn't talk?"
- "What did you find were the elements of good communication?"
- "How did this exercise and the first one differ from each other?"
- "In which exercise was it easier to communicate?" "Why?"

Group comments related to the second group activity included the following:

- "You had to build a strong base" (David). Ed couldn't help himself: "Oh, what a great insight, David. What can we learn from that?" Virginia responds: "Well, it's kind of like raising children. You have to have a good strong foundation for them to grow up." Ed asks: "Do others agree with Virginia on this?" "Definitely."
- "It wasn't fair—some families had more gumdrops to work with than others" (Joan).
- "Well, that's life, sometimes people start from further back, not everyone has equal resources" (Mark).
- "I didn't realize my son was so good at figuring out things like this" (Debra).
- "You can communicate with each other without using words" (Patti).

"Oh, that's a great insight, Patti, how can we communicate without words?" asks Ed. "Well," Patti responds, "we can hug, wait for someone else to take a turn, and take our turn after they take their turn." Debra adds, "We started the activity by building our own structures separately, then we realized that we were wasting the supplies that way and we could never win unless we worked together and pooled our supplies." Ed responds affirmatively, "So true, Debra. What is the take-home message in this activity?" Sam follows his mother's lead: "It helps to work as a team." Ed quickly responds, "That's a great thought to take home with us tonight, Sam, thanks for offering that to the group."

Family Solutions Program: Session 3
Decision-Making and Consequences

Session Goals

- Youth will modify personal fables and egocentric thoughts that contribute to reoffending behavior.
- Parents will gain communication and parenting skills.
- Youth will understand the consequences of their actions.
- Youth will understand that their actions affect themselves, their families, and their communities.

Session Objectives

- Youth will understand the consequences of youth offending behavior and incarceration.
- Parents will verbalize a greater range of responses for dealing with youth.
- Parents will utilize more effective parenting and communication skills.
- Youth will identify common freedoms can be taken away if they continue down their current path.

Introduction The entire group watches a video entitled *Multiple Choice*, showing real-life situations of incarcerated youth. A group discussion ensues about their feelings and attitudes about juvenile criminal offenses and punishment. Parents are particularly pleased to have this video presented because they have been unable to help their child understand the risks that he or she faces. Sometimes the messenger makes a difference—it helps to have someone else convey the same message to their children.

During adolescence, youth are rapidly developing in all areas. Their bodies are growing at the fastest rate since infancy. They experience new situations that require more advanced social and emotional functioning. And they begin to show more advanced ways of thinking.

Despite these advances, adolescents' cognitive abilities are still immature. In particular, adolescents have difficulty understanding that bad things can happen to them. They often view themselves as invincible. Bad things happen only to other people, not to them. This immature thinking makes it difficult for youth with behavioral problems to accept the consequences or for juvenile offenders to recognize that there will be more severe consequences if they reoffend.

During the first part of this session, youth watch a video depicting the lives of youth who have been arrested and placed in a juvenile detention center. This video will provide a realistic picture of the consequences youth and their families will experience if the youth chooses to reoffend. The video and subsequent discussion help the youth understand that they will indeed suffer similar consequences if they get into trouble again.

Human service professionals who work with youth are well aware of the challenges in altering cognitive processes that underlie youth behaviors. Youth possess personal fables and egocentric thinking that can inhibit responsible behavior. They create self-talk that can lead to thoughts such as "It can't happen to me," or "They won't do that to me." For instance, youth might think that a shopkeeper will not file charges for shoplifting. Or the youth may think that a parent will not request the police or court to intervene if the youth stays out all night. Or, they may believe that the school will not suspend them permanently for possessing a weapon or drugs. Some youth might think that being arrested a second time will simply result in the same consequence as the first time, despite the warning of a judge or parent. Simply put, a youth may tell a story to him- or herself that is quite different from the reality of laws or court procedures. As a result, a youth may not believe that the consequences of certain behaviors will be invoked. The youth does not believe that sanctions such as an arrest, probation, and/or other requirements such as counseling or mediation will be imposed.

View Videotape (30 minutes) A video of youth in incarcerated settings, called *Multiple Choice*, produced by the Georgia Children and Youth Coordinating Council, helps some youth visualize the consequences of continued offending behavior. *Multiple Choice* vividly portrays the anguish that Georgia youth experience in detention and incarceration as a result of criminal behavior. The stories are true and presented dramatically. The presentation is moving and generates a curious and heartfelt reaction from families who view the video. It can evoke anger and annoyance with the courts, the legal system, the youth, or some other part of society. The video may also evoke relief on the part of some parents who have repeatedly warned their children about the consequences of their antisocial behavior and to make better decisions to stay out of trouble. Hence parents are pleased that the message is being sent by someone else. We have found that the youth talk excitedly about the raw footage showing a hole in the floor as the "bathroom"; interviews with youth living in these settings who express deep hurt and regret; the hot, dusty, heavy-lifting work assignments on the property; and the restrictions in living conditions. The youth are overwhelmed by the exposure to this kind of life. The youth watching the video quickly become somber and quiet. This change in demeanor is an outward sign of the impact of the video.

We also find that the parents approve of the viewing of *Multiple Choice* because it supports the efforts parents have made to warn their child about the consequences of unacceptable behavior and, possibly, continued offending behavior. We have found that exposure to this element does not unduly upset youth. There is no attempt to shock youth or create a frightened or traumatic reaction. Rather, the experience helps youth visualize the oppressive, restrictive, and lonely environment. The goal is to help youth realize that these settings are places to avoid. Instilling this belief will help youth grasp the possibility of living in an environment such as those presented on the video without the determination to change their attitudes and behaviors that will allow them to avoid such places.

Discussion (45 minutes) Following the videotape, the group leader initiates a discussion based on group members' reactions to the video. Emotional reactions typically vary, and there may be divergent views expressed in reaction to viewing *Multiple Choice*. Some group members, particularly parents, are pleased that their children have been exposed to a vivid portrayal of the consequences of criminal behavior. Others may be disturbed that youth are incarcerated in this manner. Some believe it to be unfair. Leaders can promote discussion by asking questions such as:

- What is your reaction to what you saw?
- Did you know you could go to jail or a youth detention center for [whatever crime or behavior was exhibited]?
- What needs to happen in your life so that this doesn't happen to you?
- How would you go about making it happen?

Examples of comments made by youth include:

- "It wasn't fair for that young girl to be put in jail just because she was sitting in the truck not knowing that her boyfriend was committing a crime at the same time."
- "It's no fun being in there."
- "I didn't realize how much they missed out on."
- "That's not going to happen to me!"

Examples of comments made by parents include:

- "It's good that these kids see what could happen to them if they keep this up."
- "Punishment doesn't seem to fit the crime sometimes, but that's the chance you take."

The group leader can elicit more discussion with questions such as:

- How could a bunch of kids have gotten themselves into this situation?
- What happens to a youth's future?
- What happens to a youth's reputation?
- Can a youth be deprived of an education if suspended from school?
- What can parents do to help prevent this outcome?

After leading a general discussion of *Multiple Choice*, the group leader ends by asking:

- What did you learn from this video?
- Do you think it will change you in anyway?

Finally, the group leader concludes by pointing out that youth should not feel threatened or manipulated by the discussion. However, it is important to emphasize that the stories are real because youth do not want to be deceived or simply warned of potentially harmful outcomes. They need to know that their peers have experienced a consequence they never would have predicted for themselves. The youth observing the video begin to comprehend that their opportunity to choose will be taken away if they are placed in a secure facility away from home.

Parent Activity: Discipline and Punishment Many parents of youth offenders have limited parenting skills. They may rely on corporal punishment to force compliance and to promote acceptable behavior. They may have few verbal skills that nurture and support their children. Some have insufficient understanding of child development and therefore do not understand their child's attitudes and behaviors. Parents often do not listen to their child and may have little desire or skill to negotiate with their adolescents. This session on positive parenting is intended to enhance communication skills of parents and to explore options for managing behavior. The session helps parents broaden their awareness of the part they play in the well-being of their child. Parents also gain a sense of what they can do to foster change in their child.

Effective parenting requires understanding, good communication, and knowledge of appropriate ways to discipline youth. Many parents need to learn how to listen to, encourage, and negotiate with their child. It is important for parents to require youth to follow certain rules that insure their safety. In most cases, however, parents should be willing to negotiate or reason with a youth who wishes to change or modify a rule. Rules need to be changed as youth mature and gain new skills. This session helps parents gain communication skills and effective methods for disciplining older children.

Group leaders and facilitators should be familiar with the information in the parent handouts before leading the session. For example the leader may want to stress the importance of having realistic expectations for youth, limiting youth's choices, and being consistent in disciplining their child. The leader should encourage parents to feel comfortable expressing their beliefs about discipline. This is a good time for parents to learn from other parents alternative ways to influence their children effectively in positive ways.

Discussions about appropriate discipline can often be sensitive or emotionally charged. There may be parents who say "I give him a good whoopin' when he needs it." "After all, I got it when I was a child and it didn't hurt me any." The goal for the group leader should be carefully to promote a discussion on appropriate alternatives to corporal punishment or threats. One important and effective alternative is to establish in the youth and parent a mutual understanding of the consequences of a particular behavior. This helps the youth and parent become aware of the action to be taken if a rule has been violated. What happens if chores are not completed? What happens if curfew is violated? What happens if the youth is in an unacceptable location? The parent and youth should have a clear understanding of the consequences that will be imposed in each situation. By imposing agreed-upon consequences, the negative emotion and power struggle is removed from the situation. This allows the relationship to be preserved.

Handouts on praise and encouragement are distributed. Tips for effective discipline are provided. The group leader can ask each parent to answer questions about communication and then total their scores to determine how well they communicate with their children and family. The leader(s) then ask questions, such as:

- Is this a fair representation of your communication skills?
- If not, why?
- From this assessment, is there anything you've learned that you would like to work on?

If the group discussion turns into negative comments about the youth, ask the following questions:

- When was the last time you said something encouraging or positive to your youth?
- What did you say?

Have each parent respond so that the group can benefit from each other's strategies, and incorporate them into their own repertoire of strategies of encouragement.

Go around the circle and have parents share the last encouraging or positive statement they made to their child.

Discuss the importance of encouraging/praising their children as well as encouraging/praising themselves. Take turns practicing praise with each other. For example, ask:

- Can one parent praise another for communication skills that they have seen another parent use with their children during the program?
- Could someone begin the discussion about enhancing family communication?
- Who has an example of how they use each of the communication skills listed?
- Is there is anything they use that is not included on the handout?
- Are there any techniques on this handout that you might want to try or use more?
- Who can give an example of how they would use one of these techniques?

The goal is to provide parents with a wider range of communication skills. The probability of accomplishing this goal is greater when parents are asked *open-ended questions* that allow them to respond with what they do well, so that responses can be mulled over by all the parents and potentially incorporated into the parenting practices of other parents. These open-ended questions are more likely to allow them to detect their own blind spots that are destructive or discouraging. Blind spots are those messages that parents let fly without a filter. A filter is a metacognition, a standard that a parent employs that conforms to a desired attitude or behavior expected in the child. Sometimes filters shut down for parents during times of heightened anxiety or stress. This results in messages sent by parents to children that are hurtful or confusing to them. When open-ended questions are asked by the group leader, parents have a better opportunity to identify these blind spots—times when they send destructive messages.

Identifying Discipline Techniques (30 minutes) Distribute helpful hints on discipline and invite parents to identify any tips on the handout that they use successfully. As the group leader, ask for someone to describe how he or she successfully uses these techniques.

Next, ask parents if they would consider trying any tips listed that they either do not use or do not use well.

In a future session, the leader can request that families return and share their list of helpful hints; ask:

- How have you been able to incorporate these tips into parenting practices?
- If you have trouble using these helpful hints, what gets in your way? Why can't you add more positive and encouraging comments in your repertoire of communication skills?

The group leader should encourage a group discussion that allows families to help each other.

Establishing Consequences (30 minutes) Finally, lead a discussion that helps parents identify appropriate consequences for misbehavior. The group leader begins this discussion and elicits parent comments by asking open-ended questions such as:

- What are the situations with your child in which you find yourself frustrated?
- When does your child break a certain rule regularly?
- What do you usually do about it?
- How come your response doesn't work?
- What could be done differently to inspire better cooperation or behavior management?
- Has any parent here found a solution to that problem? What is it?
- If you are reluctant to invoke the consequences, what keeps you from doing it?
- Are there any rules that need to be renegotiated because they are no longer relevant or age-appropriate?

Group leader questions such as "What could be done differently about . . . ?" "What keeps you from . . . ?" and "How do you effectively . . . ?" are open-ended and allow for the expansion of viewpoints and ideas that can be shared to benefit the entire group. Encourage the group to explore these questions and each other's responses. This will permit the parents to educate each other about effective parenting. Also encourage the group to make suggestions to each other as they describe what works for them.

- "Which of the suggestions that have been shared in the group do you all think Patti could benefit from the most?"

- "Since Debra has trouble with her schedule to monitor Sam some-times, which of the ideas or strategies that the group has men-tioned would be the best ones for Debra to consider?"

Ending the Session Routinely, the group leader should ask the parents if they learned anything from the discussion and how they plan to use this information on encouragement and effective discipline in the future. Try to complete the discussion in a timely manner so that all parents have some new ideas or strategies to try to incorporate into their repertoire.

Family Solutions Program: Session 4
Want Ad of the Ideal Other/Contracting

Session Goals
- Parents and youth will learn to communicate their feelings, needs, and expectations to each other and will pledge to make efforts to resolve interpersonal problems.
- Youth will receive confirmation that their parents are supportive of them.

Session Objectives
- Parents will reevaluate their participation in the life of the youth.
- Parents will understand the effect of their behavior on the youth.
- Youth will realize the importance of appropriate behaviors.
- Parents and youth will sign a pledge.
- Parents and youth will reflect on their own part in the parent–youth relationship.

Introduction This session strengthens families by promoting the bonds that parents and youth need to bolster child well-being. The importance of expressing feelings and working together is emphasized as it can lead to a better life together. The session also identifies specific family concerns and helps families solve their individual problems. In addition, the session re-quests that parents and youth engage in self-reflection regarding their competency within the relationship.

One often-necessary step is to help family members learn how to com-municate with each other when working out contracts. This skill is often lacking in families with chronic relationship problems and often results in a continuing series of disappointments. Parents need to have a plan for im-buing specific communication skills in the relationships with their chil-dren. Some of these skills include: (1) sharing concerns honestly; (2) expressing hopes for themselves and each other; (3) eliminating blaming statements, which inhibit problem-solving ("You never get your chores done"; "you never let me do anything"); and (4) successful negotiation when disagreements occur or competing interests are expressed. Families are encouraged to use statements that directly state their requests ("I need you to . . .") as well as self-disclose what they would do to make the relationship better ("I would be willing to . . .").

Another important step for families is to develop specific plans of action (i.e., homework time, curfew). It is not uncommon for families to descend into a downward spiral of negative interaction as blaming and frustration creep into the negotiation. Sometimes the group leader or facilitator may need to "float" around the room to stop this spiral and infuse the interaction with encouragement, honesty, and direct statements about what they will do and what they want from each other. Youth often are reticent in these interactions because they feel they will be criticized by their parents or have little confidence in their verbal abilities. One required feature in the formation of contracts is the ability to verbalize their feelings and ideas appropriately. Youth involved in the FSP often have little skill in expressing needs and wants in socially acceptable ways.

It is important for parents and youth to understand their roles in the family. Parents sometimes have blind spots about how certain characteristics, such as frequent criticism, affect youth in a negative or discouraging manner. Youth typically react to such criticism with defensiveness and arguing in order to rebuff attempts at parental control.

Want Ad The group leader begins the discussion by saying:

> Sometimes as parents we wish that our children were different. Maybe you wish your son or daughter would study more or be more cooperative. Youths sometimes wish that your parents would let you do more things that you want to do. Maybe you wish your parent would give you more money or not hassle you so much. Or maybe you wish your parent would be friendlier. We're going to ask the parents to get together as one group and the youth will meet in a separate group. We want each group to pretend that you are writing an advertisement for the newspaper because you wish you could have a different son or daughter (if you are a parent), or a different parent (if you are a youth). You want to search for the best one. Each group is to list on the flip chart all of the characteristics that you want in an ideal parent or ideal child, so that you can find the best one. This list can be qualities you would like in a youth or parent, or they can be positive qualities your youth or parent already has.

Parents report first on their list of qualities that will appear in the Want Ad for the Ideal Child. When parents make a report of their group results from the flip chart, the following items often appear:

- hardworking;
- smart;

- loving;
- respectful;
- cooperative;
- kind;
- religious;
- responsible;
- sense of humor;
- not easily led.

The group leader asks the youth: "Which one of these would you guess your parent added to the list?" Surprisingly, the youth often guess correctly! This adds some fun to the exercise, and prizes are given.

Then the youth present their list of characteristics in their Want Ad for the ideal parent:

- be fair;
- give me money;
- be friendly;
- don't yell;
- give me the car;
- let me stay out late;
- keep promises.

There is a moment of self-reflection that serves to invite both parents and youth to review their own behavior in relation to each other. This process inhibits criticism of each other and helps both parents and youth focus on their own role in the relationship. Since youth have an opportunity to give parents feedback about their parenting, parents are suspended in the unusual place of being quiet and pensive. They are obliged to assess their own role and potentially make modifications in their behavior. A message is sent about the characteristics that are valued.

In one session, Ed instructs: "I would like to ask each person to identify one characteristic listed that they think their child (or parent) already has." The identification of a particular characteristic is a form of validation and encourages the person to continue exhibiting this characteristic. Go around the circle, asking each person to choose one characteristic on the list that they wish their parent (child) would do more of. For example, Virginia said, "Be respectful; don't be rude and talk back." Brandon said, "Keep your promises."

Encourage family members to clarify what is meant by their statements. For example, Virginia's son, Brandon, said, "Be friendlier and not hassle me so much, and keep your promise." When Virginia asked what Brandon meant, he said "sometimes you promise on Tuesday that I can go out Friday night if I do all my chores. But you change your mind at the end of the week and make me watch my little brother." Ed, the group leader, responded, "It is courageous for Brandon to express this to his mother. I hope, Virginia, you can think about this and make sure Brandon can trust you when you make an agreement with him."

The following case example illustrates an outcome of the Want Ad exercise that promoted more cooperation and appreciation of one another:

> *One boy put on the list of characteristics of a parent, "won't bug me" because he complained that his father, who lived elsewhere in the community, called him every night to see if he got his homework done and whether he needed help. Three other youth immediately challenged him. One said, "I can't believe you're complaining that your father calls you every day to check on your schoolwork. My father left when I was three years old and I haven't heard from him yet." Another youth said, "My father left last month and he hasn't called yet." And a third said, "You really should be glad that someone cares about you." Not only did that boy think differently about his father's telephone calls; the father who attended the group felt validated. The father was assured that he was doing the right thing by calling and should not give up because his son was rejecting him. This illustrates the persuasive quality of group interaction that affects group members' attitudes and results in stronger relationships.*

One outcome of this exercise of reflection that parents and youth engage in is to assess to what extent they approximate the idealized parent or child that is expressed in list form generated by the group. Where characteristics identified match those that parents or children exhibit, the discussion contributes to validation and serves as a reminder to continue exhibiting that particular characteristic. Overall, the activity puts a positive spin on role competencies. For a parent, the exercise serves as reminder of the importance of examining one's own role effectiveness. Parents sometimes have blind spots, a lack of awareness of how certain messages conveyed affect their children in a negative or discouraging manner. One of them is incessant criticism. This activity serves as an opportunity for the parent to reevaluate his or her participation in the life of the youth, by (1) detecting the negative effect of that behavior on the youth; and (2) incorporating a positive or appropriate behavior listed among those on the flip chart. For example, if a statement on the flip chart for the Ideal Parent is: "keeps her promise," then a parent can assess her own behavior pertaining to following through on her commitments or promises and increasing her commitment to do so.

Similar effects can occur for youth. They can be open to thoughts about how their own behavior influences their parents without being given direct instructions for change that can be felt as criticism, leading to yet another experience of failure or insignificance. The older the youth is, the more likely such criticism is met with defensiveness and argument in order to rebuff attempts to be controlled.

Family Contracts Distribute the contract handout, *Just Between Us, A Pledge* (see Figure 6.1). This handout helps families establish contracts.

 What is one thing your son or daughter does that bothers you or you wish he or she would change? What is one thing your mother or father does that bothers you or you wish she or he would change? Sit down together now and share with each other what that one thing is that bothers you or you wish he or she would change. Then agree to change that one thing so that it doesn't bother the other person anymore or would please the other person. Complete the pledge below and place it on your refrigerator when you get home so that you can both be reminded of the pledge you are making throughout the week. You will be asked to report each week to the other families in the FSP how your pledge is working out. Try to set a goal for keeping this pledge until the end of the FSP. Finally, plan a reward that is something you both enjoy for reaching your goal.

Parent Pledge
I, _____, pledge to (name of youth)_____
_____
_____
_____.

Signed:
_____
_____.

Youth Pledge
I, _____, pledge to (name of parent)
_____
_____
_____
_____

Signed: (Name of youth): _____

Our reward for keeping our pledge will be:
_____
_____
_____
_____.

Fig. 6.1 Family Pledge

In one meeting, Ed begins by saying:

> *In order for families to be successful and work well together, there has to be mutual understanding about how family members will live together. For instance, it is hard to prepare a meal for the family if you don't know when people will be home or ready for dinner. Family roles also have to be agreed upon. Who does the wash? Who prepares meals? Who cleans up? These roles are like rules that family members follow so that everyone can live in reasonable harmony and get necessary tasks done. Sometimes families have conflict because these rules are not followed or they are no longer appropriate. For example, rules for an adolescent need to be different from those for a young child. As a result, rules will need to be renegotiated as children grow and mature. If rules cannot be agreed to or renegotiated, then family life suffers and important tasks don't get done. Your family may have, or had in the past, situations that led to disagreements about rules. Tonight we are going to offer you the opportunity to identify a rule or situation that is problematic for your family. Do you disagree about a rule? Are you frustrated that a family member doesn't follow a rule? If so, what is the rule that is a problem? Each family will discuss an issue that especially concerns them. For parents, this could be curfew issues, completing homework, or youth being around undesirable friends. For youth, you might want to talk about curfew, privileges or parents not keeping promises. Each family will work on an exercise that could help resolve the situation.*

The pledge card is distributed and families separate and move into smaller rooms or private spaces. If there are facilitators, each works with a specific family. Facilitators actively help family members communicate more effectively. They help them refrain from interruption, requesting that they express their needs or requests more clearly, encouraging them to communicate honestly and directly. Most of all, they encourage a collaborative setting in which each person is open to compromise or modification of a request from one another.

When the contract has been negotiated, each family member signs it. The families gather together and each family outlines their contract for the other families. *In this way, each family has proclaimed their plan publicly. This adds a sense of commitment and accountability.* The group leaders and facilitators check in on how the contracts are going in subsequent sessions.

> *Debra said she would give Sam the car on Saturdays to go to the weight room and have lunch with his friends, and Sam pledged to stay out of further trouble with people at school. Their reward was to go to a pro football game if they succeeded for one month. Brandon said he would do his chores, and Virginia pledged to keep her promise and permit Brandon to go to football games on Friday nights. Their reward was to have Virginia's husband and Brandon's father, Mark, stay with little Ernie while the two of them went to the mall to have lunch together. David pledged to bring his assignment book home each night for Jackie to see and initial, and Jackie agreed to cook David's favorite meal once a week. Their reward was to rent a video one weekend night after David's special meal. Shay and Patti pledged the same thing, to be home at the same time to eat dinner together, and their reward*

was to go bowling together. Robert agreed to be home on time for dinner and to stay home to do his homework during the week, and Joan agreed to give Robert an allowance for jobs he did at home so he could earn some money to buy a bike or whatever he wanted. Brittany was adamant that she was not going to agree to anything unless her mother, Denise, broke up with her live-in boyfriend, Max. Denise refused, and they reached a stalemate. Both were angry during the negotiation and both were crying. Denise agreed to ask Max to permit her and Brittany to do something fun each Saturday, even though Max was home only on the weekend and expected time with Denise. Brittany agreed to stop seeing the friend who had shoplifted with her.

These families have difficulty communicating about chronic problems because the interactional pattern is entrenched in negativity and frustration. There is an absence of positive statements expressing shared responsibility for the difficulties. Instead, there is an abundance of comments indicating a lack of personal responsibility and attributions of negative characteristics of another family member. Some of these communication skills include listening, using "I" statements ("I would be willing to . . .") rather than "you" (blaming) statements ("you never get your chores done"), and breaking behaviors down into specific plans of action (i.e., homework time, curfew). Another important component of contracting is helping youth verbalize their feelings and ideas. Often youth have little skill in expressing needs and wants in socially acceptable ways. The group facilitator is active in helping family members communicate more effectively. This includes helping them refrain from interruption and express their need or request more clearly, and having a collaborative setting in which each person is open to compromise or modification of a request from another.

Family Solutions Program: Session 5
Education

Session Goal

- Youth and families will emphasize education in their daily lives and identify and attain educational resources.

Session Objectives

- Youth and families will devote more time to educational activities.
- Youth and families will recognize that they can benefit from interacting with others who can meet their needs.
- Youth and families will understand that accessing resources can make a person's life better and will become more willing to access those resources.

- Families will develop networks that can provide new information needed to resolve difficulties or fulfill needs.
- Youth and families will emphasize education in their daily lives and identify and attain educational resources.

Introduction There are strong correlations between delinquency and educational difficulty or failure. School is the "work life" of youth. Not to be successful in school, where they spend the majority of their waking hours, fosters discouragement, self-doubt, and a sense of inadequacy. School failure also results in poor preparation for the world of work. This is not to suggest that everyone should go to college, only that a child needs to develop fundamental reading and math skills and a basic knowledge of how to participate as a citizen in society. Regardless of how much is accomplished in behavioral or family intervention such as the FSP, youth will continue to be at risk for behavior problems. Furthermore, they will face adult obstacles to success, such as unemployment, divorce, and drug or alcohol problems, if they drop of school.

Data from several hundred youth in the FSP shows that half were failing reading, English, math, and science and almost half were failing social studies. Some youth have long histories of academic failure and behavioral problems; for other youth, problems in school developed only recently. Approximately 38% were failing math, approximately 47% were failing English, with only 20% making a B or better average, approximately 42% were failing science, and approximately 41% were failing social studies (see Table 6.1).

Due to educational failures of their own, some parents cannot or do not stress the importance of school success for their youth. Parents may not appreciate the benefits of education and hence their home environments may not be conducive to reading or doing homework. Problems with parent–teacher conferences in the past or failure in communication with the school may discourage parents from playing an active role in promoting school success.

This session is designed to encourage families to foster school success. In addition, the opening discussion permits families to evaluate their progress in fulfilling the contracts developed in Session 4. Since some of the family contracts pertain to pledges to increase the emphasis on education, this type of ongoing encouragement and support is often needed by family members as they develop new ways of working together.

To begin the session, the group leader discusses contracts as a strategy for embedding the family pledge into the weekly commitment for every family in the program. Each family is asked to report on how the contracts are working out. Those families who report progress are congratulated and

Table 6.1 Numerical Grade Average of 580
Juvenile First Offenders

Math Grade	Percent
0–49	8
50–59	10
60–69	20
70–79	24
80–89	20
90–96	18

English Grade	Percent
0–49	19
50–59	11
60–69	17
70–79	33
80–89	16
91	4

Science Grade	Percent
0–49	6
50–59	20
60–69	16
70–79	27
80–89	24
90–97	6

Social Studies Grade	Percent
0–49	5
50–59	16
60–69	20
70–79	32
80–89	19
90–94	8

utilized as models for other families to aspire to fulfilling their family pledges. With families who report that their pledge did not work in the past week or that progress was minimal, the group leader encourages them to modify their plan. The group leader seeks help and encouragement from the group for these families. A modified family pledge, shaped by the group on behalf of those families who were not satisfied with their progress, is established before moving into the heart of the session topic. The families are encouraged to continue working to fulfill the contract during the coming week.

The Importance of Education The topic of school and academic achievement is introduced by stating that education is essential for adult success and fulfillment. Regardless of how much is accomplished in the FSP, failure to address school problems will result in youth graduating from the FSP program with a major portion of their lives—school—ignored. School is the work of youth. Parents are informed that not being successful in school is likely to cause their children to feel inadequate and discouraged and leaves children unprepared for the world of work. To be successful at work and in life, the point is made by the group leader that all young people need to develop basic reading and math skills, and a knowledge of how to participate as a citizen in society.

> Ed, as group leader, explained that data from youth who have attended FSP in the past show that many youth are struggling in school. Ed distributed a handout to the parents and youth with data summarizing the grades of all youth who have ever begun the FSP. Ed elaborated on this handout by explaining that there are strong correlations between recidivism and educational failure or difficulty. Ed tried to make his point very clear: "School is the work of youth, and if they experience failure in school, they may view themselves as failures." Ed said, "It is our job to see to it that every young person here feels positive about themselves and believes that they can be successful in school."

School Status of Juvenile First Offenders Data collected on passing and failing school subjects were collected only from juveniles who participated in the FSP. This was for the purpose of using these data to determine who is in need of academic help and the nature of the interventions needed. In sum, approximately half of the first offenders who completed a risk assessment ($n = 580$) were currently failing any given subject. And they were more likely to be failing every subject than none at all.

In addition, unexcused absences, absences not permitted by the schools that include a parent note, were very frequent. Many youth had over 20 days of unexcused school absences per year. A figure this high can place a student at risk for failing a grade automatically, regardless of grades.

The majority had been suspended from school at least once, and many of them than once. The following data support our decision to include the topic of education, including parental skills to prepare parents for effective participation in school conferences and parental advocacy through home-based support. Collecting the data has the benefit of providing parents with realistic views of the children's educational experience. The group leader presents the data to the group during the session(s) on education to provide a rationale for the group theme for the session. The data provide an objective perspective to the parents that can sway their thinking if they have not been affected by school contacts or information that the child has shared. Parents who have underemphasized their role in advocating for their child in the educational arena require factual information that provides a sobering look at the precariousness of their children's educational experience.

While we make it clear that the group data in no way indicate to parents what *their* child's school status is, the data hit the mark for enough of the youth and parents in the group that a serious discussion can unfold with leader facilitation. The data are presented to each FSP group based on current overall data on youth who have ever participated in the FSP. Only 12% were considered to have no problems with school grades or behavior. One of the ways a mind-set on educational concerns within the group can be built is by presenting data to the families on the academic difficulties of youth. We do so by sharing data of those in the current group of youth as well as a data summary, such as Table 6.1, representing at-risk youth overall who have attended the FSP. We do this by placing on large sheets of paper on an easel or wall the listing of grades for youth, average number of suspensions from school due to behavioral difficulties or school rule violations, and average number of unexcused absences from school. Of course, we are certain to state to families that these data do not necessarily implicate an individual youth in the group, that any given youth might be doing well. However, the odds that some youth in the group are having school difficulties are high based on overall data and data collected from the school on the youth currently in the group. The following is an example of data presented to the group based on the number of youth who have appeared in the local juvenile court. In the following, these data represent 580 youth who have been referred to the FSP:

Absences The average number of unexcused absences during the current school at the time these data were collected was 17 days, with the range from 0 to 97 days. Prior to the first FSP session, a request is made to all schools representing the youth referred to the group to send current school status information. Specifically, information on grades, absences, and suspensions are requested. As a result of this procedure, one could conclude that the mean number of unexcused absences for an entire school year would be much higher than 17 since FSP groups meet throughout the school year and therefore data are collected at various times during school year.

Suspensions Over 48% of the youth had been suspended at least once during the previous year, and 31% had received two or more suspensions for the year. In addition, 68% of the youth reported that they did not regularly participate in any school activities such as sports, clubs, or school-sponsored organizations or activities.

Overall School Functioning Parents are asked at the time of the risk assessment prior to the first FSP session for their views of their children's

Table 6.2

My Child Has:	Percent
No school problems	12
Recent problems with grades	20
Recent problems with grades and behavior	38
Long-term problems with grades and behavior	29
Dropped out/been expelled	2*

* This is a low number because the mean age of youth in this sample is 13; therefore, most are not near the legal age for being allowed to drop out.

school experience. Specifically, the school data shown in Table 6.2 are collected from parents and this serves as a summary of results from the youth/family risk assessment interview. Parents are asked: "Which of the following statements best describes the school situation of your child."

One of the group facilitators summarizes these data that are posted on the wall for all family members to see.

In one group, Ed then asked:

- "Which parents here tonight have been having concerns about your child's progress? Why?"
- "Do any of the youth have conflicts with their teachers? What kind?"
- "How many parents attend parent/teacher conferences or visit the school? Why or why not?"

In response to these questions, parents are likely to express frustration and discontent with the schools or their children. Some will report that they do not know if their child has homework or not, or that they do not know how their child is doing because they never get grade slips. Others will mention that they are frustrated that the school never calls them unless there is a problem. Some will express frustration that their child skips school or does not want to do homework.

The group leader explains that "it is important that families create a home environment that fosters school success. The next activity will help families consider how they spend their time together." Each parent and youth is given a handout called "My After-School/After-Work Schedule," and asked to consider a typical day. Everyone completes the handout, and parents and youth are asked to volunteer how they typically spend their time between 4 p.m. and 11 p.m. Then a group facilitator asks, "How many of those hours were spent on educational activities?" Most parents and youth will realize that their activities during this time are not focused on education. Many youth have little or nothing listed that pertains to education, and parents often have lists that include making dinner, washing clothes, watching TV, and so on. Any parent or youth who identifies a school or educational related activity is commended. For example, the youth might report on the time spent doing homework assignments, reading, or going to the library. The parents might report on how much time they spend helping with homework or reading. They might also report if they have designated an hour for quiet time without television.

The group leader or facilitator asks, "What does the schedule they have listed tell you about their emphasis on education? Is the time you spend on school in line with how important you think education is?" Most families will say that the schedules do not include enough emphasis on education. When asked if they feel this is good or bad, or if it really does not matter how they spend their time, most group members will probably feel that they should spend more time on educational activities.

Activities like this should not end with an awareness of a problem or circumstance *without* specific planning regarding how they will solve the problem. Parents and youth should be urged to consider how they can modify the situation to improve their family life to promote child well–being. In this case, families are given a second schedule of a typical weekday, "After-School/Work," and asked to develop a schedule that includes more education-related activities. After the group is allowed time to complete this activity, group members are asked to share some things they learned from analyzing their schedule. The group leader asks them to share at least one activity they plan to change so that their schedule includes more educational activities.

> Ed asks the parents to give examples of how they will help their children fulfill their plans. Debra says: "Monitor TV watching and turn off TV during homework times"; Denise adds, "Encourage a reading time"; Joan offers, "Be available to help with homework"; Jeff says, "Sam should read on his own," and Mark, a military man, states, "Discuss current events." Ed ends the discussion by complimenting the families on their progress and reminds the families that "when they return for the next session they will share their progress with each other."

Parent–Teacher Conferences It is important for parents to have a constructive relationship with their children's teacher. A poor relationship puts a strain on the youth and can adversely affect the youth's success in school. Sometimes a parent feels frustrated that a school conference did not result in a specific plan for the youth's improvement because the conversation did not get past blame and defensiveness. The following questions help jump-start the family group conversation about parent-school conferences:

• How many wish you knew more about your child's school life and progress?

- Has anyone had a disappointing conversation with a teacher?
- What made the conversation difficult?
- What can be gained from parent–teacher (and youth, in some cases) conferences?
- How can parent–teacher conferences be made more successful?

After parents respond to these questions and sharpen their focus on parent-school conferences, the group leader organizes a role-play situation so that parents can implement some of the ideas they have suggested. The leader suggests that the group role-play a typical parent–teacher conference, and says, "think of a time that you have participated in or a conference called by a teacher because of concerns the teacher has about your child." The leader pulls two chairs into the center of the circle and asks one of the group facilitators who had been a teacher to play the role of a teacher. (If a group leader is a teacher or there is an adult volunteer or group facilitator in the FSP who is a teacher, the role-play can be enacted in a very realistic manner due to his or her experience as a teacher in parent–teacher conferences). Ask a parent to play the role of a parent. After the role-play, the leader asks:

- Were you satisfied with the way you conducted yourself?
- How close were you to getting the information you wanted?
- Did you feel you were listened to by the teacher and that this understanding might help the child? Why? or why not?

If someone other than the group leader role plays the teacher, the group leader can ask these questions:

- How did you feel about being the teacher?
- Did you find yourself to be effective?
- What was it like to be a teacher?
- What were the demands of being a teacher?
- How do you respond to an upset parent?

Finally, the leader encourages the group to provide comments by asking:

- What reminded you of your own personal experiences in parent–teacher conferences?
- What suggestions do you have for how parents might encourage positive parent–teacher relationships?

Note that all questions are phrased as open-ended invitations for discussion and not options for "yes" or "no" responses. A central element of any exercise is the group discussion that ensues following the activity. The After School/Work Schedule and the Parent–Teacher Conference can be opportunities to ratchet up the commitment of parents to their children's educational success. The goal is to strengthen their role as advocates for their children in education pursuits. The questions listed above can offer the possibility that parents will begin to examine their own role as advocates and to convey to their children that they expect success and that as parents they are available to help them in this quest.

Family Solutions Program: Session 6
Conflict-Resolution

Session Goal

- Youth will learn nonviolent ways to resolve conflict.

Session Objectives

- Youth will understand alternative methods to resolve conflicts with peers, school officials, and parents.
- Parents will become more vigilant in supervising the conflict situations of their children.
- Parents will contact those who can help reduce their child's risk of conflict, such as school personnel or other parents.

Introduction The primary emphasis of this session's focus is on the daily conflicts that youth encounter. Parents may be unaware of the potential harm that can come to their child in the immediate surroundings of their school or neighborhood. Youth may brazenly choose to go to places that increase their risk of danger. They may also find themselves in situations in which they are challenged in some way to resolve a relationship predicament. For instance, youth might face a bully or dealing with a confrontation in which they are challenged because of something they had done previously that offended someone else. Due to this danger, it is important for youth to be trained in how to resolve their conflicts nonviolently.

Some youth will need help overcoming inappropriate responses to conflict. These inappropriate responses may occur for many reasons, including poor knowledge of basic social skills, low self-worth, and feeling deprived, which may cause youth to seek validation in any way possible. Youth who offend often have difficulty managing conflict in their lives. In fact, the lack of conflict resolution skills may be the very reason that the offense occurred. Many youth are arrested for crimes such as assault or theft.

There can be many reasons why youth are lacking in conflict resolution skills:

- Effective conflict-resolution skills may not be modeled by parents and other family members.
- Family members may use intimidation or inappropriately use their authority. As a result, youth also use intimidation and fear to get what they want.
- Youth who live in single-parent homes may have few opportunities to observe persons of the same generation, such as parents, working out differences. As a result, a youth who tries to work out a problem with another youth (someone of the same generation) has no template or map to follow.
- The youth may have no experience in observing people compromise or seek resolution to their differences.
- Youth may have a series of unsuccessful experiences that result in high levels of frustration and discouragement.

Some youth may have fewer material resources, such as money or clothes, than others. In these cases, a youth may feel deprived and possibly cheated. Out of frustration and resentment, the youth may seek these resources in devious or illegal ways, such as stealing from someone or intimidating someone to get something they want.

It is important for youth who are intimidating others to learn more effective ways to meet their needs. When youth lack material resources, it can be helpful to explore ways to help the youth "feel like others"—to provide a sense of connection or belonging. Youth also can be encouraged to accept their circumstances as "not of their making." Youth need to become aware that all people can find themselves in problematic situations that they feel are due to no fault of their own. At the same time, youth can be encouraged to overcome these feelings of inadequacy through pursuing their education, locating work, or finding personal satisfaction in things other than material possessions such as more clothes, jewelry, music players, and more cash.

In this session, youth will identify conflict situations that arise and will develop effective methods for dealing with these situations.

In one meeting, Ed begins the session by setting the backdrop for this session:

> Conflict-resolution skills are needed both to handle the normal difficulties youth experience in their social environments and to overcome inappropriate behavior that some children demonstrate. Youth may find themselves in the wrong place at the wrong time or may be asked to come to the aid of a friend who is being victimized or challenged. Conflicts also occur in social situations in which there is a great

need for acceptance. For instance, two boys may fight over a girl (or vice versa). Or two girls who are best friends may have a falling out, and one tries to seek revenge by telling lies about the other or by making a new friend in order to make the former friend jealous. A boy may find himself in a situation where a group decides to commit a crime. Effective conflict-resolution skills will be helpful in these situations. What are some examples of youth conflict?

The group calls out some examples. The group leader/facilitators ask youth to identify conflicts that they encounter with peers, parents, or at school. Their answers may include:

- skipping school and getting in trouble with the principal;
- conflict with a teacher;
- fighting over a boyfriend or girlfriend;
- confrontation with someone who threatens to take my jacket;
- use of the telephone;
- pressure to take drugs and use alcohol.

Ed asks the youth to develop skits that illustrate several of these situations. Ed and the group go to a different room while the group facilitator works with the parents. In this session, all the youth worked together because Shay was still carrying resentment that she was fired from her fast food job because she mistreated a customer. Shay told the story of being assigned the drive-through window. Two men pulled up to the speaker and gave their order. In giving their order they also used vulgarity and tried to confuse her by changing their order several times. Then when they received their order through the window, one of the men said he had ordered a milk shake and didn't get it. Shay said that she told the man he didn't order a milk shake, and the man yelled at her. Then the other man in the vehicle said he was supposed to get an apple pie, and Shay lost her patience and her temper and said, "Just get out of here!" The men then asked to speak to the manager. Shay was fired over this incident because the manager said she did not treat the customers courteously. Shay told the manager what they had said at the speaker and at the window and the manager said, "Shay, you still have to handle jerks like that without causing a scene; it's not good for other customers to see an incident like this." Shay thought the manager should have taken her side and not fired her over this incident. The youth liked this story for a skit and Ed assigned roles and rehearsed the skit several times, each time encouraging the youth to slow down and make sure every part of the story was depicted so the parents could understand it.

The youth group with group facilitator assistance creates two endings for each skit:

1. a destructive or conflict-escalating way to resolve the conflict; and
2. a conflict-reducing way to resolve the conflict if Shay had a chance to do it over again.

The group facilitators in the other room asked parents to describe conflicts that they encounter with their children, at work, or with a significant other. Parents often report conflicts related to children:

- conflicts with a coworker who was competing for the same promotion;
- listening to their child's loud music;
- having a disagreement with the automobile mechanic;
- their child not completing chores;
- their child not doing homework.

While Ed worked with the youth, two of the group facilitators worked with the parents, and began by asking the parents to discuss and share possible strategies for resolving conflict situations. Parents were encouraged to give suggestions and share experiences that might help other parents. Parents prepared one skit that illustrated a conflict situation with their children, providing first a negative outcome and then a more positive outcome.

The parents and youth reconvened and the youth, then the parents, presented their skits.

Usually the skits begin by portraying a negative or destructive outcome. As each skit is performed, the group analyzes the situation and discusses what contributed to the danger or trouble. The youth repeat the skit, this time demonstrating a more positive outcome. It is important to redo these conflict scenarios so that youth practice a productive resolution to the conflict, one that is just and safe. In this way, youth gain a vision of how to resolve conflict appropriately as well as confidence in their ability to manage such a situation. As each skit is performed the second time, ask the group to identify what contributed to the better outcome.

After all the skits were presented, Ed asked, "What are the advantages of resolving conflicts?" The group provided the following responses:

- keeping your job!
- preserving safety, because you don't want to upset volatile people if you can avoid it;
- reconciling disagreements;
- decreasing anger;
- increasing skill in handling peer influences without it ending in trouble.

After this last comment in the group, Sam mentioned that he knew someone at school who got a "busted lip" because he wouldn't give up his jacket to a bully. Ed asked, "What should a person do in this situation?" Sam said, "You gotta fight 'em for it or everyone will think you're a wimp and they can take advantage of you!" David remarked, "That's easy for you to say because you are so big, Sam, but I'm small and there are bullies at school who would hurt me bad." Ed asked the group,

"What should David do if he got into this predicament?" Sam extended the discussion: "Let's talk about peer pressure." The group discussed options. Jackie said, "One is to walk away from the situation." Virginia added, "Know where to go for help, which teacher or office person in the school is likely to help." Patti said, "I would rather they take your jacket than to beat you up, we can work to avoid this again by getting help from the school, but you might not ever recover from an assault."

Nineteen-year-old Dan, the older brother of Sam, attended the FSP on the night of the conflict-resolution session while on leave from his military assignment. After a period of time in the skit in which the two youth clearly reached a stalemate and the threat of physical altercation was near, Dan spoke up. The group leader encouraged this involvement and asked him to suggest some ideas that could help resolve the dispute before "something really bad happened." Dan stepped forward and suggested a way that the confrontation could be resolved. Ed suggested Sam role-play this strategy to remove himself from the dispute. Dan discussed a similar situation that he had experienced, outlining the mistake that he had made in that situation and the unfortunate consequence that had occurred. Dan also discussed, and demonstrated with the help of the group leader, several options to resolve the confrontation more effectively based on more recent experiences in the military. The youth in the FSP listened carefully to the brother, since his youthful age and recent success in the military provided him some legitimacy in the eyes of the group. Ed encouraged the parents to reassure youth that it is acceptable that they walk away from conflict situations with peers or strangers in some situations.

Discussing these peer pressure situations also provides parents with an appreciation of the stress their children may experience when interacting with peers. Some parents believe that their children's lives are without complication or challenge when they are not around. While many parents have a knowledge or even preoccupation with their children's well-being while at school, in the neighborhood, and with their peers in other places, there are some parents who have more of an out-of-sight-out-of-mind perspective. This is problematic because parental monitoring is crucial to helping youth make good decisions and to keeping them safe. It is important for parents to be sensitive to their children's circumstances in the world of peer pressure and identity formation. For example, many youth are under the impression that parents would be upset if someone took their special jacket or new tennis shoes. After all, they know their parents worked hard for the money used to purchase these items. Parents need to point out that their child's life is much more valuable than a pair of shoes or a jacket. If, in discussing this situation, this message does not come through early, the group leader may have to encourage parents to convey their priorities—the well-being of their child versus keeping a material possession.

The group facilitators invited the parents to conduct their role-play. Debra went first and portrayed a situation she experienced at home while participating in the FSP. Brandon's father, Mark, who attend this session, played the part of Sam. Mark and other parents enacted a scene in which Sam and his friends trashed the house while Debra was gone. This included putting a hole in the living room wall. Then Debra came home, saw the disaster, and yelled at Sam, "You're grounded for a month!" Mark, as Sam, acted mad and blasted back, "No way am I gonna play in a football game Friday and come right home! And I'm not gonna miss out on the day at the lake Saturday." (Sam enjoyed watching someone role-play himself.) Debra interrupted, "Yes you are, you're gonna miss it all!" Mark said, "Oh yeah? Just wait and see!"

The first role play ended, and then Debra started the reenactment. The reenactment was constructed at the same time the original role-play was created to portray this conflict. Debra was coached by Ed, the group facilitator, to consider options that would help Sam experience the consequences of his blunder while his mother was gone. Ed asked during the rehearsal, while the youth were in another room preparing their role-play, "Just to be sure, how old is your Sam?" (Ed knew Sam's age but wanted to make a point by helping the group focus on Sam's potential to fix what he had damaged.) Debra responded, "He's fifteen." The group facilitator asked if it was possible for a boy of his age to repair the damage. Could he get a piece of Sheetrock or patch the hole? Could he rent carpet shampoo equipment (with his own money), and clean the carpet. Debra said he could take the money from his allowance and rent the equipment, but that the hole was too big to patch. But he probably knew someone capable of getting Sheetrock (which he would pay for) and could recruit someone who knew how to work with Sheetrock to help him repair the wall. After the skit was enacted in this second form, and a group discussion ensued, Debra said, "You know, I realized that I had been treating my fifteen-year-old son like he was ten. It was eye-opening to think about how I had been interacting with him as a child, rather than as a young man. This solution made a big impact on me and it changed my way of relating to my son."

Family Solutions Program: Session 7

Volunteer Community Activity and Parenting Practices

There is widespread belief and considerable evidence that youth who participate in helping other human beings benefit themselves. They benefit by increasing their sense of significance that they can affect other people in a positive way and by receiving gratification that the lives of other people are better as a result of their efforts. At-risk youth sometimes sense that their lives are insignificant because they are neglected. A lack of success in school and minimal involvement in community activities such as athletics, church, or artistic endeavors add to a sense of insignificance. Society is often not designed in a way that fosters youth participation in their communities.

Many parents, as well, express concern that their sons or daughters seem interested only in themselves. Parents view their children as self-centered and only gratified when they receive material things that make their lives more convenient or comfortable. One parent recently remarked in a session: "When I was child, Christmas came once a year; now it seems children expect Christmas to be all year. I'm only liked if I make it possible for my daughter to get something she wants." Furthermore, some parents expect that the FSP will require their children to make amends for their criminal offense—to repair what they "broke" in the community—such as stealing from a merchant or home owner, physically hurting an adversary such as another youth, or giving or selling harmful substances to another person. Therefore we require that each youth participate in a volunteer activity that contributes to the well-being of another person or group of persons.

Volunteer Community Activity

Session Goal

- Youth will realize that they can affect other people in a positive way and will discover their own value.

Session Objectives

- Youth will feel gratified that other people's lives are better due to their efforts.
- Youth will experience increased self-esteem.
- Youth will realize that they can affect other people in a positive way.

The FSP routinely requires that all youth participants develop and implement a community service activity. One such activity is the preparation and serving of a meal at the local homeless shelter. The youth have the chance to see others who have a life full of struggle. These youth sometimes feel more fortunate than they did prior to this service. Also, such an experience instills a feeling of goodness about themselves for helping others. Finally, working together as a group bonds the youth and promotes a spirit of cooperation.

A wide array of volunteer activities can be made available to youth to fulfill this requirement in the FSP. Every program in every community can choose to fulfill this commitment in its own way as an FSP group. Other examples can include playing bingo at a senior center (youth bring prizes for the residents when they win) or beautification projects at a school playground or local park.

Parenting Practices

Session Goal

- Parents will assess their parenting behaviors and explore new behaviors.

Session Objectives

- Parents will identify successful parenting behaviors.
- Parents will extend their range of parenting skills.

While youth participate in a community service activity, parents have an opportunity to discuss their parenting experience freely without the presence of youth. This can allow them to be candid, which provides opportunities to examine and possible modify problematic parenting behaviors.

The group leader suggests that the group further consider the material on communication and discipline that was provided in Session 3. The leader promotes discussion by asking questions such as:

- How do you feel about your parenting effectiveness at this time?
- How have you been successful in interacting with your son or daughter?
- What do you still want to improve on or resolve with your son or daughter?

The leader invites parents to discuss the progress they have made in parenting since Session 3, when they assessed their situations and identified ways to increase their skills.

Family Solutions Program: Session 9

What We Like About You and Peer Pressure

Young people, like all of us, value the comments others make about them when their strengths are acknowledged. Such statements contribute to self-worth and promote positive relationships when the source of these comments is their parents.

What We Like About You During the FSP, all parents get to know all of the youth in addition to learning more about their own children. In some cases, parents can identify characteristics in other children that the child's own parents have not seen or have stopped noticing. Since

Sam, What We Like About You Is . . . .

(Parent): _____

_____

(Parent): _____

_____

(Parent): _____

_____

(Parent): _____

_____

(Parent): _____

_____

(Parent): _____

_____

(Parent): _____

_____

(Parent): _____

Fig. 6.2 Greeting Card

parents have had many opportunities over the nine sessions to relate to other youth, they can provide support to these youth. At graduation, each youth will receive a card (see Figure 6.2) on which each parent has identified one of the youth's strengths. These cards are colorful and have artistic designs that symbolize each youth's interests (sports, music, etc.) and a title that reads: "[Jason, for example] What We Like About You!"

Each parent writes something positive to each child, including his or her own child. While youth are preparing conflict-resolution role-plays, parents pass these cards around the table for each to sign. In this way, the presentation of cards at graduation night is a surprise to the youth. Some examples include: "Sam, you are a natural-born leader"; "Brandon, you are lots of fun and have a great sense of humor"; "Brittany, you have a great

smile and will be a good friend to those you meet." On the night of graduation, each child will read these comments in front of the adults and verbally proclaim these positive characteristics. This proclamation can
enhance a youth's feelings of worth and competence. Siblings can also be
given cards to acknowledge their attendance and participation and to
boost their feelings of worth and confidence.

Peer Pressure Adolescents also need to develop skills that permit them to
deal with peer pressure. At this age, fitting in with the crowd is of utmost
importance to young people. Not all peer pressure is bad. Having friends
who do well in school, who have good relationships with their parents, and
who volunteer in the community is likely to encourage positive behaviors
in youth. Unfortunately, youth at risk, such as juvenile offenders, are more
likely to be friends with youth who are not doing well in school. They may
be in trouble with the juvenile justice system themselves. It is important
that juvenile offenders be given the skills needed to develop new friendships and to avoid situations in which negative peer pressure may cause
them to get into trouble again.

To initiate a discussion on peer pressure, the group leader asks parents
and youth to describe situations in which peer pressure resulted in negative or destructive outcomes. Parents might describe experiences from
childhood in which they were influenced by peer pressure as well as adult
situations involving peer pressure. Youth might share current or past situations with a friend or peer group that resulted in a poor outcome. The
leader asks each group member to share one idea from the discussion that
he or she feels will be useful in dealing with peers.

Mystery Bag Prior to the session, three bags are prepared that vary in their
visual appeal. The best prize is placed ($2, candy, and/or a small book) in
the least appealing bag. The second-best prize is placed in the second most
appealing bag (pack of gum, candy bar, coins). A minimal prize such as
two coins, a stick of gum, or a piece of candy is placed in the most visually
appealing bag.

To begin the exercise, three youths are recruited and consecutively select one of the bags of their choice. After all three youths have each selected one of the bags, they are asked to open their bags and show the
items to the rest of the group. Often the most appealing or decorated bag
is chosen first.

> Ed begins the discussion by asking Robert about what he thinks about having
> picked the most attractive bag with so little in it. Robert's frown reveals his disap-
> pointment. Then David is asked what he thinks about getting a piece of candy and
> a quarter and a dime; he responds, "Oh, well, at least I got something." And Shay,
> who ended up with the plain brown bag but with two $1 bills, a candy bar, and a

pack of gum, cannot hide her smile. Shay is asked what she learned from this exercise; she answers: "Well, I can't say I would have chosen this if I didn't have to, but I guess it means you never know what is on the inside." Ed asks the group to comment on what it might mean that the very attractive bag had no prize. Joan, Robert's mother, is delighted that Robert didn't have much in his attractive bag and says, "It just goes to show how you can get attracted to things that don't turn out so great." Ed emphasizes the importance of Joan's comment: "Yes, appearances can be deceiving, can't they?" Ed then asks, "Who can give an example of a time when they were deceived by how things appeared?" The group generates the following thoughts:

- someone you thought was a friend in the beginning but turned out to just want something from you;
- buying something on sale that fell apart;
- an attractive girl or boy I liked who turned out to be mean when I didn't do what they wanted.

Family Solutions Program: Session 10

Graduation Night

The final FSP session is always Graduation Night. The experience is a ritualistic one in which families have the opportunity to acknowledge their accomplishments. The activity provides a sense of closure that the juvenile's problem behaviors have been addressed. More important, the youth and families have increased their resolve to meet the challenges ahead of them and have newly developed skills to enhance their daily functioning. Families feel an anticipation that their future together can be better.

Session Goal

- Families graduate from FSP with a sense of accomplishment.

Session Objectives

- Families will experience closure concerning the youth's offending or other problematic behavior.
- Families will experience feelings of optimism and hope for the future.
- Families will complete a program evaluation.

Graduation night is a celebratory occasion in which families have the opportunity to acknowledge their accomplishments. The activity provides closure. The youth behavior that resulted in referral has been addressed and the obligation to the referral source or court has been fulfilled. Families typically expect that their future together can be better.

Inspirational Speaker After a potluck dinner, the invited guest for graduation night has frequently been an effective speaker who has a message for youth and families. Sometimes the speaker is a representative from the referring source, such as a juvenile court judge, school principal, or caseworker, who congratulates the families on their accomplishments and urges them to plan and live a future that is successful and satisfying.

Then families are asked to share with the group what they see as their accomplishments and what the program has meant to them. This provides evidence of the program's effectiveness. These testimonials build a positive view of the program in the minds of the referring sources or judges that fosters their continued collaboration and support. An adult volunteer in one of the FSP cycles was asked to provide some words of inspiration to the families because of his rapport with the families and his previously persuasive comments in group discussion. After telling a life story of his own in which he had to overcome extreme adversity, he ended his message by saying, "To all of you, I say: if the mind can conceive, and you truly believe, then you can achieve!" The group applauded vigorously.

Presenting Diplomas Following the speaker, FSP program certificates/ diplomas (Fig. 6.3) are presented by the group leaders or facilitators. The certificate contains the names of all family members who participated. In addition to the youths' accomplishment, this highlights the families' accomplishment. Each group facilitator presents certificates to the families whom they have gotten to know the best over the course of the program. Each family is called to the front one by one, and a facilitator shares some words about the family's accomplishments and what they did over the course of the program to improve themselves and their family. Applause follows the presentation of each certificate.

As a group leader or facilitator presents the certificate and calls the family to the front, compliments about the behavior of the youth or family are articulated. For example, the following compliments were offered in this group:

- "When Robert came in the beginning, he was not eager to be part of the group. He ended up being an important contributor."
- "I saw Brittany and her mom as a ball of anger in the beginning; it's good to see how they have started to respect each other and work things out."
- "I remember in the beginning how Brandon's father said he couldn't make it to the program, but we all appreciate how he sacrificed to be here and added to our work as a group; and it seems that Brandon is glad that his dad cared enough about him to come."

Certificate of Completion

Awarded to

Joan Johnson
Robert Johnson

Presented by

the Family Solutions Program

Tuesday, June 22, 2004

Dr. Bill Quinn
Group Leader

Kadie Coker
Facilitator

Fig. 6.3 Certificate of completion.

- "You remember how we were all worried about the way Shay solved her conflicts in the conflict-resolution scenarios. It sure was impressive the way she learned to deal with conflict without the destructiveness."
- "Sam—what can you say about Sam that we already don't know? He always had something useful to say, and everyone expected him to talk first because he was so thoughtful about things. All the youth knew that he was going to be their mouthpiece. I can't imagine how we would have accomplished so much if he wasn't here. He is going to be leader in whatever he does."

Presenting Greeting Cards Following the presentation of certificates, each youth is presented with a personalized greeting card, "What I Like About You." This card contains the comments written by each FSP parent during the previous session, denoting a positive attribute of that child. Each youth comes up one by one and is asked to read out a few of these comments in front of the group. This activity provides an opportunity for youth to acknowledge their own good qualities in a public manner, thereby strengthening their belief in these qualities.

> *Brittany reads her card to the group: "Brittany you came in to the group acting like you had no use for us, but you realized that we were your friends and wanted to see you be successful." "And you cooperated with your mom more and more as the sessions went along." "You are a determined girl and you will be successful when you figure out what you want your life to be." Sam follows: "Sam you are kind and smart." "Sam, thanks for your courage to always share your opinions." Robert comes up to receive his card, and reads aloud: "Robert, you tried to get lost in the group, but you were cooperative when the group asked you for your ideas. Robert, you have more confidence in yourself than you think, you can accomplish a lot." Shay came to the front of the room and read her card: "Shay, you were so negative when you came, but you had the strength to change without feeling manipulated by the group. You had a habit of blaming others, but we know now that you only did it because you were so unsure of yourself, but we saw a lot of good qualities in you, you are funny, creative, and generous." Brandon followed Shay: "Brandon, I know your mother embarrassed you sometimes because she was so intense about the program, but it is obvious that you stick up for her and help her when she gets overloaded with things. You are considerate and loving."*

Parent and Youth Comments At the end of the night, we offer parents and youth the opportunity to make any comments about their experience before the program ends. Often parents will speak about what they have learned or how they changed their attitudes or feelings about the program, their children, or themselves. This acclamation allows parents to express their forgiveness of their child, personal regrets and blame, or vision of the future. The end result is an atmosphere that is uplifting and hopeful.

> *Brandon dressed in a shirt and tie for graduation. When parents and youth were invited to share what their experiences were like in the program, Brandon came up to the front of the room and said, "Thank you all for being my friend, I hope I never see any of you ever again!" The group laughed, as they understood what Brandon meant—that he hoped he would not make a bad decision that would require him to attend the program again. Denise said, "I really appreciate what you did for me the night I came in here so mad because I had just found out that Brittany got caught shoplifting that day." Mark apologized for not coming to more sessions due to work and for having such a low opinion of it. He said, "I surprised myself—this group taught me that I need to spend more time with my children." Sam said he liked every session, and didn't mind coming; and Debra said she was looking forward to hearing how everyone was doing in the future.*

Booster Sessions

Human service providers are becoming more aware that many intervention models must require provisions in their protocols for follow-up or maintenance resources to achieve positive results. For instance, aftercare programs are in favor because of the perceived intractability of problems such as alcoholism or drug addiction. Studies of psychotherapy effectiveness have demonstrated that in many cases changes due to treatment effects "wash out" over time. Significant changes that can occur in a group context can be snuffed out or diminished when the group members return to the natural environment, which has not changed significantly to accommodate the personal change gained in the group. In addition, groups can become important social resources for individuals if trust and cohesion are developed during the group process.

Many parents have asked for continued meetings following graduation. They may request this for different reasons, some of which include:

- a concern that the changes made in the group are not going to last without help from other group members,
- a desire for social relationships that have been established to continue, and
- as opportunities to make more changes after the designated time length of the program ends.

There are several ways booster sessions can be organized. One is to schedule group meetings on a monthly or regular basis. During these meetings families can be asked to describe how their lives have been since graduation. Families have developed a concern for each other during the program, and such family reports help satisfy their curiosity. Group members are asked to share ideas or suggestions about how they have helped each other in the family and what problems have been resolved. Families can also share which problems continue to challenge them. Finally, a discussion can be encouraged by a group leader that allows families to prepare for future challenges or problems and to seek advice or support from other families in the group.

Another approach to booster sessions is to schedule reunions in which families from several cycles come together. Families find a larger support group in which to provide validation for each other. In this way some families will know each other, and others will be new, allowing them to expand their support group and learn from new families.

The FSP group leader has the benefit of a curriculum guide to provide structure to the group for each session. In addition, this guide helps ensure consistency across cycles of the FSP. The FSP curriculum guide includes the following:

- a delineation of goals and objectives;
- background and information related to the each session topic;
- the activity overview;
- materials needed;
- preparation necessary;
- handouts;
- videotapes;
- description of activities;
- case vignettes; and
- evaluation tools.

However, it must be acknowledged that families vary widely and the needs, interests, and chemistry of each group varies widely. Therefore there are twice the number of topics and session plans as there are sessions in a program. This allows group leaders and families to select the most relevant and appropriate topics for their situations for some of the sessions.

CHAPTER **7**

The Multiple Family Group Process

There is no house like the house of belonging.
—David Whyte

We must remember that everything is ordinary or extraordinary. It is our minds that either open or close.
—Natalie Goldberg

Families and Groups

The multiple family group model described in this text integrates family processes with small-group dynamics. However, interventions with families and those with small groups were developed separately beginning in the early part of the 1900s. Actually, the precursor to both movements may have been influenced by the lively debate between Rousseau and Diderot and their followers throughout the previous century about what had priority—the individual or the society.

This debate was picked up by social scientists who tried to establish whether groups and families were products of either the individual or the larger system. The case has been made in this book (see discussion of this issue in chapter 1) that recent decades (such as the "me" generation) have privileged the individual over the group in many domains of society, including treatment approaches in which the frame of "patient," or "client," is universally employed. This frame comes complete with demands from the health insurance sector requiring a patient to be designated, diagnosis be attached, and a set of rules delineated pertaining to the patient/client's benefits, such as maximum number of treatment visits.

During the early part of the last century, social scientists began studying natural groups in society, hoping to resolve political problems using some of the contentions made by those arguing on behalf of Rousseau and Diderot. In 1920, William McDougall, a social psychologist, published *The Group Mind*. In this text he outlined how a group's continuity depends in part on the group being an important idea in the minds of its members. To be a group there is the presence of boundaries and structures in which specialization of function could be defined. The group emphasizes the importance of customary behaviors that could provide a sense of stability for persons through the prediction of certain actions.

Later Kurt Lewin gave us field theory in which he proposed that the group is different from and more than the sum of its parts. In the social realm, this meant that persons comprising the group became more than the sum of their individual personalities. An important idea generated from this theory was that group interaction became superior to didactic presentations for changing ideas and behavior.

This idea of the group being more than the sum of its parts has prominence today in the field of family therapy. For example, if a therapist wants to help a husband to be more affectionate and nurturing of his wife, it would be best to help him do so in the presence of his wife rather than alone with the therapist. In this way, the husband can experience himself in a different and more competent way within the context of his wife, with the hope that a changed definition of himself would have benefits for himself as well as his wife. Lewin offered the notion of "quasi-stationery social equilibrium," demonstrating that change in group behavior requires an "unfreezing" and "refreezing" of members' beliefs and behaviors. An idea emerging from a group member's life experience and shared with others must rattle the customary beliefs and behavior of the group or individual group members. Only then will group members be prepared to accept change.

Another aspect of small group dynamics that contributes to good outcome is group atmosphere. Some important dynamics embedded in this social climate that a group must incorporate and sometimes reconcile are: (1) cohesiveness; (2) level of structure in groups; (3) authoritarian and democratic processes, as operationalized by teaching and rule-setting versus collaboration and thematic building up of topics or roles; (4) scapegoating in groups; (5) the contribution of friendship choice to communication channels; and (6) the level of emotion and emotional content encouraged by the leader (Nichols & Schwartz, 2004). The success of the group experience is dependent on establishing the level of each of these variables in concordance with the aims and preferences of the group.

In families, it is often true that not everyone is present in treatment to be changed in some way. Many come, sometimes begrudgingly, to solidify the notion that one person must change. For family members with a self-perception of innocence or blamelessness, the mind-set and communication strategy is one that implicates another family member, such as an acting-out adolescent or neglectful marital partner. These family members may be anxious or worried about the person who has been defined as the problem. However, these responsible but "blameless" family members often do not make the connection that the behavior of the person whom they are concerned about has anything to do with them. This is quite a remarkable notion to some—that one person's behavior or emotional system is connected to anyone else. Nonetheless, it is somewhat common in these families to possess the notion that "If you would just change—everything would be fine."

In family therapy, multiple groups were initiated by Peter Laqueur in 1950 in which four to six families would meet weekly for 90 minutes (Nichols & Schwartz, 2004). Laqueur and his cotherapists would conduct treatment using group therapy principles, such as structured exercises, to increase the level of interaction and intensity of feeling (Laqueur, 1966, 1976). Families were used as "cotherapists" to help confront members of other families. This strategy to draw on families as cotherapists was believed to counter the threat of harmful conflict or emotional upset in the family that would result if more personal positions were taken by family members within the same family.

It was thought that families could not do as much "reality-testing" when family members challenge each other, compared to group members who would challenge family members, because the stakes were higher in intrafamily interaction. Family members have to return to the same place together and carry on their existence with each other. Therefore groups comprised of different families can invoke some level of confrontation or debate that may not be possible in family treatment.

Robert MacGregor and colleagues developed multiple impact therapy as a way to have maximum impact on families with disturbed adolescents in crisis (MacGregor, 1967, 1972). The families would come and spend several days in intense therapy with a large team of professionals. Although multiple impact family therapy is not practiced currently, it contributed to the developments of family intervention models such as the network, experiential, and Milan therapies. These therapies have further established the utility of family involvement in treatment including extended and surrogate (e.g., long-standing friendships that take on family roles) family members.

There are many kinds of social groups that originate in different ways and serve varying purposes. The family group has a "species-survival purpose" (Becvar, Canfield, & Becvar, 1997). Groups are formed consciously for specific purposes: (1) some as an evolving experience in which participants share life space; (2) some that perform tasks that are more easily managed by a collective; (3) others formed to attempt to manage stress or survival issues more effectively. Each member brings a story to the group (Becvar et al., 1997)—a particular account of how and why one joins and participates in the group.

These stories may have similarities and differences across members. For instance, a similarity in a group of families with youth offenders or drug users is that they share a common characteristic—a group of youth who are all offenders or drug users. At the same time, members may differ in their view of that identity. Some parents may believe that a child should not really be labeled as an offender because the child may have been influenced by another youth who offended, or the other youth "got off" and the youth in the program may have simply "got caught" but does not deserve to be there. Or a drug user may claim that others, like parents or school officials, are overreacting. It is not uncommon that in two-parent families one parent will minimize the drug problem and the other is consumed by it, resulting in parental conflict pertaining to the management of the problem (Quinn, Kuehl, Thomas, & Joanning, 1988). Drug users may minimize their use and therefore their need to attend meetings. One parent may be upset or angry about being in the group, another might be secretly pleased knowing that the opportunity to resolve a chronic family problem is available.

These examples of varying perspectives that family members hold about group participants serve to remind us that few assumptions can be made initially about the mind-set or emotional state of group members. And group members can travel different routes to get there. In a remedial group, one that forms because of a perceived shared deficit or problem, we cannot even assume necessarily that the group agrees it shares the problem. This is particularly true of a mandated group, a collection of people who are required, say by a court, to participate in a group program. This is because some members may feel that the requirements stipulated and "forced upon them" are unjust or unfair. An example is a parent who carries the notion, "Why do I have to be here? I didn't do the crime, so why do I have to do the time?" One of the first tasks of a group leader is to locate commonalities among group members that serve to bind them and provide a context of shared experience and collaboration.

The extent to which a group shares a belief that a problem exists determines the nature of group cohesion as well as the problem-resolution tactics. Parents who believe they should not be in the group that but other parents should be in the group might affect the pace at which groups become cohesive. One parent may not own a problem but exclaim in body language, if not verbally, "Hey, I'm just fine, but you (a child or other parent) have a problem." A youth who views him- or herself as "not delinquent" may view another as "delinquent" because the crime the other committed was more severe. Thus the level of motivation among group members and the stake each has in the success of the group varies greatly across group members.

The extent to which perspectives related to the reason for being present in a group and the nature of the problem overlap initially or as the group process unfolds contributes to group cohesion. The group leader advances the notion in the early stages of group formation that the group has a reason to gather, interact, and remain together. A sense of purpose must be visible and a regard for the progress towards achieving a goal must be formed.

This does not mean that group members must agree, only that they hear accounts of other members that are persuasive in remaining included in the group. Sometimes a member of the group may not view great commonality with other group members in life experience but feel a compelling need to remain part of the group because of the help that member thinks he or she can offer others. Many possibilities exist that pertain to overlap of life experiences across families that create a sense of connectedness. Some are:

- common experience;
- belief that something can be learned from someone else that will help a person;
- obligation to participate (e.g., youth offender mandated to attend);
- commitment to group well-being;
- observation that group members have skills (or attitudes) to learn;
- belief in the goals of the group existence shared by other members.

Peeling Off Labels

Often a part of the view of group members in a multiple family group intervention program (such as the Family Solutions Program [FSP], a drug abuse group, a school problems group) is that someone, either oneself or another, has deficits that require repair. Examples would be a family with a drug or alcohol problem, a youth offender, or a failing and truant student. One of the major goals of a multiple family group model is to expand the person's perspective by locating space that allows for a revision of the etiology. That is, a group leader will move away from the view that one person is defective, inadequate, or insolent, to one in which the family of the "targeted" group member (e.g., at-risk youth, truant student, juvenile first offender) comes to the discovery that they are all implicated in the circumstance in which they find themselves.

The engagement of multiple families aids in this process of expanding each person's view of him- or herself and the purpose of participation in a group. The possibilities for sharing among group members helps broaden awareness of oneself and one or more other family members. There are many illustrations based on case material previously presented. The following discoveries reflect some of the modifications families can make in their view of the problem and hence solution:

1. A mother hears her daughter read aloud the What We Like About You card at graduation with all the comments made by other group members about the daughter's characteristics ("you are a real leader," "you are fun to be around," "you are caring"). Mother has the opportunity to modify her view of her daughter to now include competencies.

2. A youth complains in the group that his father living elsewhere in town calls him every night to check on homework. When two other youth jump into the discussion with comments—"I can't believe you are mad about that. My father left home when I was 3; I wish he would call just one time"; and "my father left just before I got in trouble. He hasn't spoke to me since"—the first complaining youth begins to appreciate his father's calls, and the father no longer feels so uncertain about whether he should call. The complaining youth has the opportunity to realize that his "intrusive" father is not so demanding after all and is simply expressing concern or affection.

3. A youth much smaller than the others feels inadequate in the group; when the group becomes frustrated with its inability to solve the "traffic jam" activity, the smaller youth orchestrates the resolution of their dilemma, and the group begins to pay attention to him. Observing this, the parent begins to view the child as creative, competent, and valued by others.

The challenge in group work that is "remedial"—gathered around a symptom or problem—is that group members view themselves (possess a personal view of self) as having a pathology, a deficit, or serious fault. These can be long-standing self- and other-perceptions of these attributes which make revisions of these stories intractable. For example, a youth offender may be seen as a "deviant," an absent father may be seen as a "deadbeat dad," or an emotional mother who continually berates or goads her child may be seen as "a kid raising a kid" or an "immature adult."

If this view is comprehensive, in which all behaviors are judged by that label, and it is of long duration, the problem becomes reified and so does the perceived solution. The locus of responsibility for having the problem becomes hardened as well. In the examples given above, the predominate view of the problems is that the at-risk youth, such as a juvenile offender or problem youth, needs to be "fixed" and the absent father needs to be "educated." The "kid raising a kid" or the "immature mother" needs to "grow up" or develop self-worth.

Believing these labels and directing the group discussion accordingly by characterizing youth with these labels contributes to a limited and restrictive perspective of the youth. Instead, group leaders can attempt to influence group members by "peeling off the label," or expanding the frame of the problem to include the context. Hence, in the examples delineated above, an attempt would be made by the group leader to:

1. Explore how the "deviant" youth also does or could conform successfully to certain systems, such as school, church, or other families.
2. Recruit the "deadbeat dad" into the multiple family intervention program or discuss the custody and visitation arrangement.
3. Draw in a youth who is much smaller than the others or feeling inadequate in the group.
4. Help the "kid raising a kid" (the critical or negligent parent) to restrain herself from demanding obedience in ways that are developmentally inappropriate, such as incessant threats, scolding, or blaming. The parent can be taught to develop alternative methods such as encouragement and support and to provide the child with sufficient space to make decisions. In this way, the consequences require personal responsibility and the chance to make mistakes that require self-attribution ("I have nobody to blame but myself") is possible.

A major feature of the multiple family group process is the incorporation of an expanded view of the "other." For the parent, it means viewing the child in a broader way that includes not only the poor choices made or the limited skills exhibited but also the attributes that a child draws on to make progress and experience success. As Becvar et al. (1996) state, "Stories

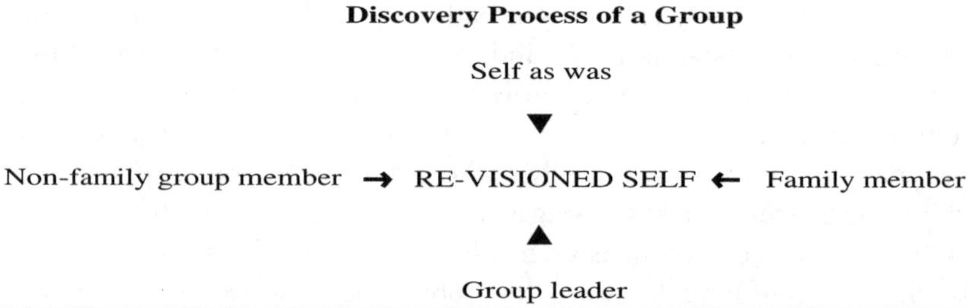

Discovery Process of a Group

Self as was

▼

Non-family group member ➜ RE-VISIONED SELF ⬅ Family member

▲

Group leader

Fig. 7.1 One way to map the goal of group process.

about other parts of a client's life that have not been told or have not been considered to be worth telling can be recounted" (p. 46). This recounting can be drawn from a wide range of sources, the self, a family member, a nonfamily group member, or the group leader(s). Many illustrations used previously in this volume are representations of this restorying process. Other scenarios follow in this chapter. The diagram in Figure 7.1 can serve as one map in conceptualizing the goal of group process.

The Discovery Process of a Group

There are many models of group work that have been developed in recent decades (Bion, 1961; Braaten, 1974; Jacobs & Spradlin, 1974; Yalom, 1975; LaCourseiere, 1980; Corey, Cory, Callahan, & Russell, 1992; Becvar et al. 1996; Gazda, Ginter, & Horne, 2001). The contents of these models will not be explicated here, but a professional interested in developing a group and serving as group leader would be advised to seek out these resources for guidance. In most of these models, however, there are similarities pertaining to stages of group work, although the terminology may vary and the emphasis placed on certain phases may differ. These commonly accepted phases are briefly delineated here to acquaint the reader with an overview or general structure that drives the multiple family group intervention program described in the text. Awareness of these stages has influenced decisions that group leaders make regarding structure, content, and procedures in planning and implementing the program.

1. The Planning Stage

Before the first session of a planned group, the leader(s) and facilitators, helpers, or interns gather to discuss appropriate structures, procedures, content, and pacing of the group experience. Previous group work is assessed to determine what worked effectively, and what did not, and whether what worked was due to the unique nature of the particular group or because of its value as a general group element that should be a common component. An example of the latter in our experience would be the crucial development of trust and cohesion in a group early in its formation. An example of the former would be a topic based on the particular offense or offenses committed, such as the need to include a focus on school truancy, theft by taking, or assault. More attention is directed in the group experience to these topics and related activities, such as removing impediments to school attendance. Some of these impediments are the disorganization of the early-morning schedule before school, transportation problems, and weak home–school partnerships in which parents have little contact with the school and a lack of understanding of the expectations and assignments. Other aims are promoting family cohesion and constructing conflict-resolution role-plays.

Specific roles can be delineated for group leaders. For example, in the first session of the FSP it must be decided who will role-play a parent, youth, and the leader in the first meeting. Another example is who should describe the overall program and outline the basic requirements such as attendance, punctuality, and participation. Each family that will be represented in the group can be described in the planning stage, such as family structure, particular information known about the family from their court hearing or risk assessment, and the nature and seriousness of the offense.

The planning stage is a time when strategies are formulated to recruit adults into the program who have some sort of meaningful relationship to the youth. For instance, a father living outside the home might be recruited to the program, provided the ex-wife is amenable to this strategy. A mother's sister who lives in the neighborhood and has regular contact with the youth should be invited and encouraged to attend. In the FSP we have had clergy participate who know the family well and want to fill the void of a parent who works an evening shift or is too ill to attend.

The planning stage is important to ensure that the most optimal environment for the group to bond exists from the very beginning of the program. In addition, such planning increases the probability that the most optimal support network can be recruited and that available personal resources will be present on behalf of the youth.

2. The Orientation Stage

The inception of this stage is the first meeting of the group participants. Sometimes it stretches into the second meeting, depending on attendance and success of the first night. In this stage a number of elements are incorporated to *jump-start* the group formation as a problem-solving entity. The stated purpose of the group is presented, group procedures are outlined, family members introduce and describe themselves, and exercises are offered to encourage trust and cohesion.

During this phase it can be determined which families and family members are open to the experience and anticipate it with optimism and hope and which are deeply embarrassed, angry, or confused about their presence and events leading up to a referral. This assessment helps determine where efforts are needed to support these skeptical or reluctant members and to "hear their story" (e.g., "I cannot take the time for this"; "Why am I coming? I didn't get in trouble"; and, "You can't possibly know what I have been through in my life") both during and after the first session. Logistical problems such as transportation or time allotment, can mask ambivalence or opposition to the group experience. Hence logistical problems are important to resolve in assertive ways so as to overcome ambivalence and increase motivation.

3. The Work Stage

In the multiple family group program described in this volume, the *work* stage begins in session 2 and develops throughout the program. This does not mean the end of the orientation stage, as the work stage and orientation stage overlap while family members grow more comfortable with each other in the group setting. Because family members come into the program with different experiences, attitudes, and circumstances, they integrate themselves into the program in various and unique ways and at different times. Some group members have more confidence or energy than others. Youth are sometimes reticent because they lack the experience to participate in shared activities with adults that require verbal interaction.

The work stage begins as the group members develop a shared sense of purpose and attribute meaning to the process and content of the group. Members find it easier to engage in activities and tasks that fit the purpose of the group for them. There is a human "shell" that begins to melt away as they feel more comfortable in the group. Group members find it easier to be more open without serious concern about the risks involved in doing so. They begin to express their needs and desires in making changes in their lives as well as the lives of other family members. Group members also begin to relate to others in ways to which the group responds congruently to help them be successful. For instance, a youth may have difficulty articulating his feelings, but another youth, or a sensitive adult and one who can identify with this predicament, may coax the reticent youth to use more words or may say the words for the shy youth to pull him out of his shell.

This melting away of the "shell" includes the youth, who must be attended to in unique ways because their group experience is limited. They may not be self-assured and ready to talk due to anger or embarrassment about attending the group. They may be fearful of the consequences of their participation because of their uncertainty of adult support and distrust of how others will use information they share. They also may lack confidence in their ability to represent themselves truthfully. Furthermore, they may be less capable than the adults of articulating their personal beliefs, feelings, and needs.

The group leader needs to search for group processes through relevant topics and activities that foster increased youth participation. The leader must be comfortable with silence in the beginning and respect the youth's apprehension or uncertainty. The group leader must work on refraining from rushing in too quickly to help the youth "open up," as each child has a particular temperament, unique circumstance, and reason to share or not to share one's life. To rush in too quickly can appear to some youth as prodding or intimidating and can thereby cause the youth to build up a harder shell and a greater determination to remain passive or silent.

4. The Termination Stage

The multiple family group model described here is finite in length. This is primarily due to logistical and legal reasons. State laws place conditions on length of probation for juvenile offenders. In addition, some states require that any obligation required by the court of a first-time offender, such as counseling or community service, be completed within a specified period of time, such as 90 days. If youth attend the FSP as a condition of probation, the program must end no later than the termination of probation. In a few cases, families express a desire to continue in a group like this even after termination, and recommendations are made. These include attending another multiple family group being planned, referral to other group experiences that exist in the community and relate to family issues, or family therapy.

When legal statutes are not relevant, as with behavior problems or families of truant students referred by a school, a set number of sessions can be contracted. Following the agreed-upon contract, the group can discuss whether it has met its goals or is committed to further group work. Then a new contract can be negotiated. In this way, group members can have the opportunity to sense completion and progress in meeting their goals. Without it, group members float in a nebulous space without a sense of direction.

An equally important dimension of the termination stage is that it provides for a feeling of achievement and closure. Many families who participate in a multiple family group program have had few experiences in their lives in which they have completed a program successfully. Hence family members have few opportunities to experience closure on an important challenge and problem they have overcome. Graduation night in the program provides an experience in which families are recognized for their achievements and are provided a time of reflection. Family members are requested to share anything they wish about the program and their involvement in the presence of other group members. Often they express their appreciation to group leaders, other families, and family members. They also proclaim the changes they have made since the inception of the program. For instance, Patti, Shay's mother, stated, "When I first had to come to this program I didn't think I could afford the time. Now I realize I can't afford *not* to spend time with my child." Brandon, Virginia's son, went to the front of the room during this time of sharing at graduation and said, "Thank you for letting me be your friend during this time. Now I don't ever want to see you here again!" (a joke about avoiding a reoffense). The families laughed because they understood what he meant and so did not take his comment personally. In fact, the families were pleased that he appeared to show more resolve to avoid trouble in the future.

Another important aspect of termination is the opportunity to generate the belief among group members that they do not have to continue to think of themselves as being in need of a support group. This dependence on a support group can arise if they continue to have a sense of their own victimization, a sense of blame, or a view of their own personal inadequacy.

Program termination provides a new metaphor. Families become equipped with a different story about themselves. They find group support in this experience, which can be integrated into their community involvement and support, such as with a church, social organization, school, or neighbors. The FSP is viewed as a vehicle for overcoming conflict and feelings of hopelessness, but it is not the only necessary agent for living life and raising a child, "staying out of trouble," or attaining success or personal well-being. They feel uplifted and affirmed as persons. This is not to assume that the problem areas of their lives end and that we "sugarcoat" their accomplishments. Instead, the notion conveyed at termination is that the story can be more fully told that their lives have meaning and can include more productive and satisfying ways of living.

The Group as a Laboratory

Group and family therapies do have similarities. Both can provide a social context for learning and behavior change through the interactional forces that create new meanings and self-reflections. In some cases, such as the multiple family group model, these approaches can involve several family members. Group and family therapies can be more complex than individual intervention. They can be more like everyday social reality, with each member and family having a unique story to tell with an obligation to listen or understand another's story. And participants must react to a number of people just as in the everyday world.

In the model explained in this book, for example, youth are required to react to other parents and adults as well as their own parents. This creates a network of relationships that simulates a community. For instance, conflict-resolution role-plays presented in front of the entire group elicit parental responses that affect one or more youth who are not of the same family. An example from our own program is a role-play in which Sam confronts Robert, who is wearing a "cool" jacket. Sam remains ruthless in his pursuit of the jacket, and Robert maintains his determination to keep the jacket. When it becomes clear that the two are about to reach a level in which the next step could be a scuffle, the role-play is halted. At this point, parents make comments about this confrontation. One parent, Virginia, says that a jacket or pair of shoes is not worth putting yourself at physical risk. She remarks that "a hundred dollars is a small price to pay to avoid serious injury." Joan, Robert's mother, announces that protecting your property is important: "Who knows what the kid would come after next time? It would never stop, the intimidation." Parents then interact as a "network of consultants" in the service of the youth. Thus, while parents are involved as in a family therapy setting, the multiple family group structure brings to light alternative views that can be expressed by members of other families that can affect both youth and parents in a given family. Debra remarks, "I agree that getting a reputation as an easy target needs to be avoided, but so too does being beat up or hurting someone else badly. They need to find ways to solve intimidating situations without harm." These interchanges among group members broaden the scope of the dilemmas that youth encounter. Some youth discover acceptable alternatives that defuse situations and garner parental support. In this case, Robert discovered that while his mother might be upset that an article of clothing was taken from him, giving up such clothing desperately wanted by someone else was a good option if it preserved his well-being.

One of the activities in our model, as described in the previous chapter, requires parents to write descriptions of each youth in the group on cards that are presented at graduation night. The youth read these What I Like About You cards aloud to the entire group as they are presented. This procedure allows for each youth to proclaim a level of "truth" that youth might not ascribe to on their own or up to that time. Youth read aloud to the group comments written about them such as "you are fun to be around," "you are a natural leader," and "you are sensitive and kind."

The therapeutic use of this interaction among participants allows the group leader to remain relatively inactive and *decentralized* so that family participants will relate to each other in a credible way. The uniqueness of the multiple family group model is that the source of the information presented (whether it be sensory, verbal, or emotional) is derived from members of other families. This process brings forth new ideas and beliefs that can affect self-perception and views of problems or difficulties and their solutions.

An explanation for the quality of a sporting contest given by coaches or broadcasters is that the best games or competitions are those in which the referee or umpire is unnoticeable—virtually invisible—by spectators. For instance, in a baseball game, the umpires might not be noticeable if calls of balls and strikes or base running judgments are conducted accurately and fairly. In a tennis match, the chair umpire who is not noticed is one who has a calm demeanor and rules on line calls with authority but without bias. If there is a contention by a player that something is objectionable, challenging a line call or rule, the umpire is clear and concise in responding with the goal of moving the match along in a smooth and purposeful manner.

This approach is similar for a group leader in a multiple family group model. A leader steers the group process of participants without being too busy or active. Yet the leader senses when a disjointed conversation or interpersonal exchange emerges. A disjointed element in group interaction is one that diverts the conversation away from the intended purpose of the group or one in which the group participants interact in such a way that the conversation is superficial, acrimonious, or irrelevant.

One important benefit of this process of being a "chair umpire" or "home-plate umpire" is that family members have the opportunity to develop compassion for others. With "patient" and therapist, or family and therapist, there is no abiding concern for the well-being of the therapist. Therefore patients do not develop compassion except within the context of family work through interaction and guidance from the therapist. That is, the family may develop an appreciation for the therapist who expresses genuine concern and acceptance of its members. Yet the therapist is perceived as mentally healthy and well adjusted (whether true or not) and therefore not in need of help from family members. The likelihood of parallel process or transference is remote when a network of group members is available to share life circumstances and a range of emotional responses.

In multiple family group work, each family is legitimately hurting or struggling in some way, and this is acknowledged by the group members; other families and family members are tapped for their help and support. Each story of a family member is shaped in some way so that it is defined as a certain level of struggle or pain. In this way the listener is called upon sometimes to privilege that story over his or her own, putting concerns in perspective and sometimes deferring to others as a simulation of life experience.

By being with other families, each family feels less alone and alienated. This is particularly important for disenfranchised families who have little inner peace but have no connections as a result of this hardened persona. In multiple family group intervention, a family experiencing isolation and despair can now see the group as a place where they can be helped and where they can be honest. As a result, things that are said can have a different outcome or ending. In group work, power is more equal among parents and, to some extent in a collaborative model, across generations represented by grandparents, parents, and youth.

Another basic element of groups is that they stimulate typical patterns of social interaction that can be captured and examined. In this way the group becomes a "laboratory" in which social change is possible. Distortions can be identified and corrected. For instance, a father may label an adolescent as incompetent; and the adolescent and entire family may believe this frame. However, in group situations the adolescent may be seen differently through group activities or discussions. Sam was seen as a "bully" as a result of the school fight, but in the group he became known as a "gentle giant" who rallied his peers to complete tasks assigned in each session. Robert was viewed as "quiet and devious" but became someone considered vulnerable and lonely as the group unfolded. In this way, the group helped Sam be a positive leader and Robert be receptive to support and friendship.

Interactions and experiences weave together in group process regularly that can rattle a cognitive frame. The jarring of rigid perceptions can be a process such as discoveries about a youth's qualities not observed before. This cognitive shift can expand another's thinking by softening the hard edge of seeming "callousness." The frame can even be reconstructed by dispelling myths created by or about the youth. In our "traffic jam" exercise, for instance, which frustrates so many families, it may be an adolescent who figures out the solution by suggesting a step forward or backward that unsticks the entire process. Or a wife might label her husband as a tyrant in the family. Yet in the group setting the husband may be demure or highly collaborative, providing the family with a different experience of one of their own members.

This different experience, or "discovery" (Quinn, 1996a), is possible when the conditions are optimal for openness and genuine verbal exchanges. This has been termed the "working stage" (Corey et al. 1992), in which "quick reassurance and advice do not facilitate self-examination, but respect and willingness to listen can encourage members to explore issues" (p. 115). There must be an invitation to family members to explore ideas and the depth of their feeling and belief systems. The intensity and complexity of these group dynamics become systems that are not necessarily accessed in the normal unfolding of everyday life.

Families are often too hard-pressed to meet the financial needs and task accomplishment of everyday living to reflect on their life's frustrations.

The group experience provides an opportunity to "wall off" some of the vast complexity of living to give proper attention to a focus on issues that have been neglected. These neglected issues that come to the forefront can be in the realm of interpersonal conflict, resentment and blame, hopelessness or embarrassment, rigid views of oneself, others, or situations, or a lack of coping skills. During this moment the families are suspended from the worries and frustrations of life tasks. Instead, they are asked to focus on what they are doing to help each other, including helping their children succeed in school, in relationships, and in personal confidence.

The Dimensions of Process and Content

There are two aspects to communication in any social interaction (Watzlawick, Weakland, & Fisch, 1967). There is the "report" dimension, in which the topic for conversation is selected and explored. In a parent–youth interchange, the topic could be chores, being picked up from school, helping with homework, or a sharing of an interesting experience one of them had during the day. There are myriad topics that could be discussed. There is also a "command" aspect to communication. This aspect pertains to the rules of interaction: Who chooses the topics for conversation, who must respond, in what way is a statement acceptable? In addition, over time, agreement is reached as to which nonverbal gestures can be expressed and what they mean. Command features of interaction describe the ways in which group atmosphere is created, as members and leaders attain influence and recognition as well as feel confirmed and validated.

In group process, both of these aspects of communication exist as well. The report reflects what is interesting or relevant to the group participants. A parent may want to discuss thoughts about the child or about him- or herself as a parent, including discipline or attitudes about the child. A child may want to discuss how to get permission to stay out later or go to a certain place. A group leader may have a selected topic to explore, such as instilling greater cooperation between the parent and youth, or increasing the skill level in a youth's management of interpersonal conflict.

It is important for the group leader to attend to topic selections because an acceptable or relevant topic is more likely to encourage conversation, attendance, and the potential for positive change. In multiple family group intervention, it is important for family members to have the opportunity to express their needs in the group, what they need help with, or what attitudes or behaviors they hope someone in the family changes through the group experiences. For instance, Joan hopes Robert will become more responsible for decision-making that will prevent further incidents of stealing bikes. Shay hopes Patti will "be nice" and not constantly criticize her in front of the group members during the sessions. Parents and youth are given the opportunity to examine the planned topics for the program and suggest new topics that might not have been planned. In this way, the group members become more invested in the group experience. The content dimension, then, in this case is a cocreated agenda established mutually among the group leaders, parents, and youth.

The "command" dimension in social interaction has to do with how group members relate to one another. Roles become defined in the group process as the shared experience unfolds. Group leaders define their position by the manner in which they participate; for instance, as the architects of topics or as negotiators or facilitators of topics. Do the topics (content) provide psychoeducation, new information, or teaching of skills? Or do they emphasize the management of conversation, allowing group members to select topics and pursue their own desired goals?

The process of a group is extremely vital as it pertains to the development of psychological safety in the group. The group must make progress over time in interactions that permit and encourage group members to express themselves freely and help one another attain their goals to satisfy their needs.

Family members in a group also take on roles. One, like Debra, may be a leader who is involved in the choice of topics or topic changes. Another member, like Virginia, might influence the affect or emotional climate of the group by being humorous, sad, or playful. Denise influenced the group on the night of a session in which she discovered earlier that day that Brittany had been caught shoplifting. Denise came into the session fuming, and it was clear that she would be preoccupied with her anger regardless of the topic. And the group would be preoccupied with noticing Denise being mad and wondering what they could do to help her. So the group leader had to make an adjustment to shift from the planned and scheduled topic momentarily to invite Denise to share her anger with the group.

Without achieving this element of group process, very little else can be accomplished that reflects the benefits of group work. That is, the aim of creating a shared experience so that family group members can help each other is unlikely to occur if members do not: (1) feel comfortable in the group; (2) feel supported to express themselves genuinely and fully; and (3) have a high regard for the well-being of the other group members. Because of the necessary group dynamic of trust and a sense of group connectedness, the initial stage of group work must focus on creating a group mentality—a shared focus of the group's intent and importance.

It is very important for group success that the leader have a sensitivity toward the effects of group work on the lives of individual members and those in relationships with those members. It is the intention of group work to stimulate new learning and encourage a context that includes new insights, attitudes, and behaviors. In this sense the group context is a laboratory in which to explore alternative ways of living in one or more aspects of members' lives. This could be in the domains of parenting, personal well-being, improved parent–youth relationships, and the identification of new opportunities.

When group members return to their natural environments—their homes and social contexts in which their interaction is required—they are likely to find themselves constrained in living out these alternative ways of living because others in these natural environments do not expect new behaviors and therefore become confused by them. These group members then experience role ambiguity or strain in these relationships if these changes are not accepted by others. It is important for group leaders to be aware of these possibilities so that meaningful change can be maintained and become durable over time.

One way to support changes in the family is to assign tasks between group sessions that fortify these changes. A group leader can devote a few minutes at the beginning of each session to ask families to report how their family contracts, or "pledges," are going. Homework assignments can be given to promote alternative family transactions and role changes. The group leader can ask individual families during informal time, such as before the group starts or after the session is over, about the status of changes the family agreed to make.

A major reason why family members of at-risk youth are invited to attend the multiple family group intervention program is to bolster the changes under way in a family. Desired changes can be supported instead of restrained by other group members. For example, a youth who participates in a conversation in the group in which peer group influences are examined and new peer choices are explored must have ongoing support. Support will be needed from parents or other group members, including the support of the leader, if the youth is to be successful in revising his or her peer group and extracting him- or herself from the "old" peer group to reduce the risk of further delinquent acts. Brittany had shoplifted twice with the same "friend." But Brittany was determined not to distance herself from her peer for fear of being viewed as "conformist" and controlled by her parents. The second shoplifting incident that occurred earlier on the day of a group session created a crisis that provided an opportunity for the group's influence to emerge. Not only was Brittany's mother, Denise, adamant about change, but the voices of Debra, Patti, and Mark spoke in support of Denise's demand that Brittany make new friends or spend more time with other friends who would not tempt her to theft. Denise's voice got stronger and her expectations of Brittany clearer as other adults expressed the position that Brittany must not associate with this "friend."

Another impediment to change might be a parent who decides that it is important to expect more in the parenting realm from a coparent who lives somewhere else. Potential problems can exist between coparents if the one living outside the home becomes agitated or confused about these changed expectations from the parent who revises a role via the group process. Of course, it is optimal for the coparents to attend the group sessions so that the opportunities to negotiate changes in coparental roles can be available with the help of group members. For instance, a noncustodial father who happens to have a high aptitude for math and science needs to be recruited into the intervention program as a resource for his teenage son's math and science struggles, as well as a father who was supportive of his son's athletic pursuits.

Parents' Views of Youth

A frequent presentation in multiple family group work with youth offenders or behavior problems is the parent's belief in the principle of having a "faulty" child. The faulty-child principle drives a parent's coping method, which evolves little by little to convince others that the youth is defective, deprived, or callous. Parents do not always view clearly their own role and conduct in the context of their child's life or recognize their influence. The way parents live their lives influences worldview, attitudes toward oneself or others, and emotional security. Some parents are blind to this notion and live in a manner that says: "I travel in my own orbit and my son travels in his own." We know this is not possible, and yet parents possess this myth in their approach to managing life for themselves.

Many parents overlook the power of their words as they speak to their children. They may cajole, criticize, or remind them of their obligations such as homework or chores. An event at one time is not converted to another subsequent event and interpreted as an outcome. Instead, each event is viewed as unrelated to any other event. A parent who labels a youth as "lazy" for not finishing chores sometimes does not anticipate that the child might construct a view of him- or herself, drawn from such parent input, as one who believes in his or her own laziness. This created myth then influences future situations in which initiative is needed. The "labeled" youth believes that mustering sufficient initiative is not possible. The end result is that the youth comes up short in mastering personal responsibilities or the ethic of hard work. For instance, if Robert believes his mother thinks of him as a "thief," he is not as likely to leave an item alone that tempts him when no one is looking. If Patti thinks Shay is "lazy" because she has excuses for not going to school, and receives calls from her teachers regularly about Shay's failure to hand in school assignments, Patti is not as likely to expect behavior that demonstrates high ambition. With low expectations for school success placed upon her, Shay is will have a tendency to "cut corners" with schoolwork and do the bare minimum.

Only when parents acknowledge their central involvement in the developing life of a young person does the process of behavior and belief system change occur. Hence, in multiple family group work, the process and content of group experience must cast out this belief of independent family members traveling in different orbits. Instead, this false and damaging belief must be replaced with a belief and level of participation in which the family members, including the parents, share in a journey in which they are all important to and influential upon each other. In the case of a parent who possesses the perception that her son is "lazy," creating situations to allow the son the show initiative and interest are vital to his future. A son who believes that he can accomplish tasks and achieve success is more likely to be productive, while a son who is convinced that he is lazy is likely to remain passive and grow in self-doubt. The child who constructs a view of self as "lazy" will search for ways to avoid the daily tasks of life as well as the work expected by others.

Fostering new perceptions of youth is more likely when certain communication pathways are actually blocked. Hoffman (1981) identified this as the "too-richly cross-joined system." Family members, due to the relative stability or permanence of the network of interactional processes, become rigid and predictable in the messages each family member sends to the others. As family members dutifully accept certain roles, the messages they convey reflect as well as organize certain roles of individuals in the family. Over time, each person's verbal exchanges become calculated and predictable. Under these circumstances, communication that is new and innovative is stifled. Family members become bored and unaffected by each other in ways that stifle their cognitive and emotional development.

It is not uncommon in families of adolescents that each person can predict what will come out of the mouth of the other (parent or adolescent) before it happens. Then responses are already formulated as if they are robotic. Brittany knows her mother will repeatedly criticize her for being "too easily led by her friends," and Shay knows Patti will spew out comments about Shay's laziness. In turn, Brittany will argue with her mother and refuse to distance herself from her friend, and Shay will employ Patti's label of laziness and continue to waste time and have little desire to impress or strive for great accomplishments. The goal of multiple family group intervention is to break up these rigid ideas about one another as well as their patterns of interaction.

A misunderstanding has crept into the social fabric about relationships in the form of communication problems. A parent or youth might say, "we just don't communicate" or "we can't get along." It is not possible not to communicate as long as two people are in the presence of each other (Watzlawick et al. 1967). If a wife returns home, sees that her husband is in the kitchen preparing food, and sits down to examine the mail without a word being spoken, a piece of communication has occurred. She might be saying, "I'm still mad at you for what you did this morning," or "Finding a check I have been waiting for in the mail is more important at the moment than checking in with you," or "I need a few moments of solitude after a stressful day," or a host of other messages. But what is actually occurring when someone says "we just don't communicate" is that what is being communicated is problematic, unpleasant, or hurtful. They have not discovered a way to communicate in such a way that they benefit by being in each other's lives.

This rigidity can be observed in groups when family members talk about each other in front of other families. For instance, in the group setting, when parents are encouraged to talk positively about their children, they cannot resort to the typical negative comments to which they are accustomed. Or, if parents are typically quiet or inattentive, they cannot resort to silence when the group leader or another family expects them to speak about themselves or their child.

> When Robert and Joan began the activity of building a tower with gumdrops and toothpicks, they are uncomfortable in a situation in which they are compelled to "play" together. It is not in mother's modus operandi—her range of interactional behaviors with Robert—to have fun together or enjoy the cooperative element of their assignment jointly to build a tower. Instead, Joan's resentment toward Robert and Robert's belief that his mother does not enjoy him blocks them, and they continue to interact in a derogatory or critical manner. However, if they are asked to build the tower without talking, they are asked to create a new way of relating that fosters mutual accomplishment. They are breaking the homeostatic manner of their communication pattern that is so suffocating. Instead, they create a new cooperative working relationship with each other. Robert and Joan end the activity feeling comforted by the knowledge that they can work together and enjoy it.

What can happen in group work is that ordinary pathways to communication can be blocked by altering the context of their interactions so that parents and youth can create and build new forms of communication. These forms can include play, encouragement, shared confidences, guidance, personal stories, and hopes and dreams. In Joan and Robert's case, it is hoped that the tower-building exercise becomes an extended interaction between the two that is uncommon but potentially productive. Their new style of communication must conform to the group setting. When Robert and Joan see other families enjoying each other, working together to build a tower, an opportunity presents itself to them to expand their view of each other as collaborators instead of combatants.

This attempt at blocking rigid pathways of communication can occur not only when group leaders facilitate discussion but also when parents and youth from other families participate in discussion. For instance, when the youth bring in their list of characteristics that they believe make an "ideal parent" in Session 4, the parents are not in position to defend previous behaviors that were less than ideal. For instance, Shay listed "be kind more" because Patti yelled at her a lot and ridiculed her in front of her friends. If the youth list "be kind more often" on their chart of qualities of the ideal parent and present it to the parents, the parents cannot discuss why they cannot be kind. The context of the information, coming in the form of a request or attitude of the youth, alters the dialogue in such a way that the parent is compelled to consider his or her own behavior as it pertains to "kindness."

Group discussions must facilitate the encouragement of each member's voice so that relevance is achieved. In turn, reaching a level of relevant discussion can be translated into common themes that the group can share and hence invest in and own. In the exercise involving families building a tower with gumdrops and toothpicks, family members cannot verbally communicate with each other. Rather, they must follow the lead of another action by a family member to construct the most stable and tallest tower. This exercise becomes enjoyable for the families as they "play together" in a simple, relaxed manner. Yet, despite the pleasure families derive from this experience, the subsequent group discussion is crucial to change. When the time limit for building the tower has expired, families come back together and discuss their experience.

Unfolding Group Process: A Case Illustration

The parents and youth break out as separate families and are given the task of building a tower out of gumdrops and toothpicks. Their goal is to build the tallest tower they can, and it must stand on its own. During the group discussion following the activity, one mother, Patti, who had constructed a rather short and unstable tower, complained that, "Shay and I didn't start the exercise with the same number of gumdrops and toothpicks as everybody else." This was not true, as one of the group facilitators disseminated the same number of toothpicks and gumdrops to each family. However, Ed, as group leader, refrained from commenting about this, hoping that Patti's explanation would be challenged. Debra responded, "Well, isn't that like life? I mean we don't all start off with the same advantages, but yet we're all supposed to make progress in life and get to a point of

making it." Then Ed asked what the secret was to building a tall tower. Joan
stated, "What I realized was that the base of the tower was the most important
part, if you have good foundation in the beginning it makes all the difference."
Virginia concluded, "Yeah, that's like raising kids, you gotta start them out with
the right experiences." Patti feels forced to respond: "Well, I just think we got a
bad start."

This chain of comments illustrates the potential of the group experience. The group episode raised awareness for family members about personal responsibility and their commitment to each other. This rich
interchange includes (1) honest expression of feeling ("we didn't have the
same number of toothpicks. That wasn't fair"); (2) interpretation or modest confrontation ("well isn't that like life—some start farther back than
others?"); (3) new learning ("I learned that the base of the tower is most
important to what happens after"); and (4) interpretation/analogy ("Isn't
that like raising children? You have to make sure they start out in life in a
good way.").

Change and Possibility

Group processes, like the one about towers, can generate new meanings for
individual family members. Interpretations among group members are
more likely to occur as group members develop a shared alliance together
so that honesty and personal belief can emerge. Of course, this process can
only occur subsequent to shared time in a context in which trust and cohesion have been built.

The question can be asked: How do we actually know that new meaning
has been constructed? In the case of the bitterness underlying Patti's remark that the exercise was unfair because fewer gumdrops and toothpicks
were available to them to build a high tower, will Patti actually alter the
problematic self-perception that "life is not fair to me?" Can she adopt the
view that it is important to accept her situation more freely and willingly?
Or will Patti continue to look for ways to explain a lack of success, ways
that may be unfounded? That is, will Patti blame outside factors not of her
own choosing as reasons why she is not successful in her life? After all, the
group facilitators make sure that all families receive the same number of
gumdrops and toothpicks.

There may be no sure way of knowing whether significant or meaningful change has occurred as a result of a given experience or observation.
Clinicians recognize that the effects of particular intervention experiences
may not be observable during the time of intervention. These latent effects
may never be measurable, although they can be accessed through follow-
up assessment and anecdotal data. However, why does the interchange

described among group members discussing the gumdrop and toothpick exercise seem to show promise for change? First, there seems to be a theme established within the group process. It might be labeled "attitude about fairness and success." Each comment closely built upon the previous one as responses were linked logically and sensibly. Second, there appears to be honesty here, as participants did not simply attempt to corroborate each other's experience. Instead, each comment was unique and not bound by social pressure to agree or "be nice." Third, there were "categorical jumps" in conversational domains within the discussion. If we return to this interchange, it might be represented by the following:

> Patti: "I didn't get the same number of gumdrops and toothpicks." Meaning: The game was set up so I couldn't win, so it was unfair. This is why I couldn't compete: somebody else is at fault.
> Debra: "But isn't that like life? We don't all have the same help or support." There is a sincere challenge and modest confrontation expressed, suggesting that the story of group member 1 might not be true (or at least accepted by others).
> Joan: "I noticed that building a strong base makes the difference." This represents a categorical jump—a new observation—and another comment about the conditions necessary to build a tall tower.
> Virginia: "Isn't that like raising children, they have to start out with the right conditions." This represents a shift in category again, drawing an analogy to the group's agenda (parent–child relationships) in building parenting skills and strengthening family relationships.
> Patti: "Well I just think we got a bad start." Patti may be referring to having fewer gumdrops than other families; but now there is the possibility that she is referring to having fewer resources to raise Shay or having misfortune early in their life together that made parenting difficult.

During this interchange and for the remainder of the discussion, Patti did not express defensiveness or hostility based on the subsequent comments from Debra, Joan, and Virginia. This suggests that Patti is listening and remaining open to other ideas. She could be in the beginning phase of developing a revised perspective about her situation and realizing that it might not be as hopeless as she thought. She might also be able to begin to accept her situation and expend more energy on improving and valuing her life rather than resenting it.

While it is important not to make too much of one interchange, a number of elements of potential change have been demonstrated in this case illustration. Trust has developed in the group that allows each person to feel valued. An openness has been exhibited as each member presented unique ideas. Interpretations of each group member's comment were constructed to build a common understanding of an important parenting goal—to develop a good foundation for children. The inclusion of analogies also helped to foster understanding.

Change and Group Leader Influence

Change often derives out of collaborative experience shared by those who struggle with similar life difficulties. The interchange depicted above was wholly shaped by group participants without facilitator intrusion or involvement. It is quite possible that group members can "breathe in" the meanings intended by statements made by other group members with openness. There can sometimes be "obstructions" in breathing processes in interchanges between the group leader, who does not share, or at least is not perceived by group members to share, the same experiences managing family or life difficulties. This would be the case particularly in regard to the populations addressed in this text—juvenile offenders, truant students and their families, and at-risk youth with behavior problems. These particular families may have a tendency to view their situations as quite separate and distinct from group leaders, who are professional and are perceived to be free of such struggles. This is so even though professionals can struggle with similar parenting difficulties or adversity that impedes their life satisfaction.

It can be difficult for group leaders to be silent during these times of group interchange. They may intrude, usually for one of two reasons: (1) because they think that their perspective that comes wrapped in professional training is almost certainly valid; or (2) because the facilitator becomes preoccupied with seeing to it that change occurs and must reiterate important group comments to "hammer the point home." However, when group leaders impulsively, prematurely, or too frequently offer observations or interpretations, the power of the group comments diminish. Group members may begin to feel marginalized, as if their life experience and opinions are not that important to the group. The openness to learning can shut down as the source of the message turns away from "one who knows what I am going through" and toward a professional (group leader) who may be perceived as "outside the shared experience of the group."

A group leader must attend to the context of discussions generated from group exercises or activities. The enjoyment of an activity must be seen as important, but often only as a precursor to change. Some inexperienced leaders become enamored with the fun or enjoyment experienced by the families. Such leaders draw the conclusion that such enjoyment will automatically produce bonding that will heal the wounds resulting from prolonged interpersonal confrontation or neglect. These inexperienced group leaders may have a naive sense of conditions necessary to produce family change as well as a belief that such an experience will generalize to similar family experiences in the natural environment.

The group leader's role is not simply to help people feel good or enjoy themselves, somewhat like a recreation director. Nor should the leader view his or her role as the problem-solver for the group. Too often the family members perceive such messages from group leaders as oversimplified advice, too limited in its range sufficiently to cover a given family experience. It is better that leaders "not go there" but instead promote deeper inquiry into the experience of the group participants. Some examples of initiating inquiry are openers such as:

- "Share with us what that must have been like."
- "What happened after that?"
- "How did you deal with that?"
- "As you think about what happened right now, how would you have handled it differently?"

This inquiry expands the space for further discussion among group participants who can overlay their own similar dilemmas or successful solutions. The group members remain energized and validated as significant members of the group.

The Potential of the Multiple Family Group Process

Specific leader characteristics in promoting success of a program have been delineated. The importance of these characteristics cannot be overemphasized. The challenges to forming, stimulating, and advancing group processes that culminate in behavior change are many. Coleaders can be important because of the many challenges in managing group process when several families comprised of several family members are present. It is extremely difficult for one leader to conduct a group discussion or activity and observe the tone and direction of the group process. For instance, one leader may be able to pay attention to "the focal person," such as a youth or parent talking, but cannot adequately track the responses of others in the group to the focal person. With coleaders, one leader can attend to content (the topic of the discussion), while the other attends to process (group atmosphere).

The primary building block of a multiple family group intervention model is the presence of collaborative elements of shared life experience across persons and families. When one asks the major question, "How does a multiple family group intervention model differ from other intervention models, including family therapy?" the answer is: "Persons in the multiple family group model are uniquely placed to draw on the life experiences, human emotions, and interpersonal affirmation of other persons in the group, which can result in a positive change." This process of immersion in shared life experience provides people with opportunities to modify behaviors, beliefs, and feelings because they have developed respect and compassion for each other.

Family group process offers unique advantages to the youth and parents. They share a commonality in a number of ways. Youth enter the program with the same presenting problem, for example, behavior problems such as truancy, juvenile offense, or behavior bothersome to others. And because there are common characteristics that can be associated with juvenile offenders or youth with behavior problems, family members share other elements in common. These include questions such as: "How could you do this to me?" "Haven't I taught you anything?" and "What has been so bad about your childhood that you would choose to do this?" As mentioned previously, characteristics of school failure, parent–child conflict, ineffective parental monitoring, poverty and/or unemployment, attributions of blame, negative peer influences, and father absence have been found to associate with offending behavior. As a result, families may find themselves having similar life challenges and struggles to others in the group. For instance, discussion of school failure and the worries and frustrations of parents who see their children fail in school can be broadly relevant to the group. Parents have a common interest in locating ideas that create advocacy roles for parents in support of their children's education. Or concern about the child's peer group can be shared by several parents who are open to ways to redirect a youth's social network. Parents may find shared frustration in unsuccessfully managing a child's time outside school, disagreeing about curfew, and negotiating acceptable places to go and activities for children.

Another domain of shared experience is within the emotional network of parents' lives. Parents may discover that they share feelings of anger about their child's disobedience or of embarrassment about a child's arrest. They may also feel sad or guilty as parents that they have not been effective in guiding their children towards success and responsible independence. They may feel general despondency and a sense of futility about their own effectiveness.

Larger in scope, parents may feel discouraged about the direction their lives are going in, the life circumstances they find themselves in, and failures in the past. Sharing these emotional aspects of their lives with other parents provides an opportunity to acknowledge their current life situation.

More important, it provides the context for them to claim their lives and reach again for their life goals. Responses to their plight might provide legitimate compassion and encouragement from the most important and legitimate source—other parents. Parents may be the most effective source of compassion for each other in the group, in that by sharing the emotions, they become linked with each other. When they are linked, there is not as much of a sense of urgency to fight against themselves or even to change too quickly.

Sometimes people simply want to share their struggle to receive validation. They are not expecting a suggested solution to the problem. We were recently reminded of this circumstance, in which expectations get crossed, by a client who stated that she felt misunderstood because the therapist wanted to resolve her child care situation when the client really just wanted to be heard and to have a "forum" for self-reflection through dialogue (Quinn & Nagirreddy, 2001).

Professional providers, however, are mandated by theory, health insurance, or simply self-definition as a member of a professional community to "fix" or eliminate the problem in the sufferer. In the case of multiple family group intervention, the parents' suffering is validated, not skipped over, ignored, or hurriedly pushed out of the way to get on with the change process and its demands—behavior change. This is not to say that behavior change is not a goal, but rather that it is an outcome of a strong interpersonal connection. This is borne out by research on therapeutic alliance (Bordin, 1978; Pinsof & Catherall, 1986; Quinn, Dotson, & Jordan, 1997; Duncan & Miller, 2000). Families participating in intervention have a stronger commitment to change when the therapist and the other families in group intervention care about them and exhibit a commitment to support them.

More important than an alliance with the group leader, however, are the feelings surrounding personal identity that are formed from the unfolding of the group process. Cultural bias that results in separation between family and professional can fall away when a group arising out of the "community"— the group of families—forms itself. An ownership of one's situation can emerge as defenses break down. Families can discuss the naked truth within their own or other family units. Family members are not confined to a role similar to a professional, in which formal academic theory, hierarchy between professional and client/patient, or accountability to a referral source or health care company is necessary. Too often a client is organized to remain sick, mad, or bad as diagnoses are assigned, medications are prescribed, and the language of pathology is employed in the therapeutic setting.

In multiple family group intervention with at-risk youth, the language of the social network is about "what *can* happen" instead of "what did happen."

Topics for discussion and the responsibility for change are disbursed among family members instead of being owned by the group leader. For instance, the first meeting of the FSP includes an invitation to the parents to examine the program contents and to recommend changes. A written schedule of dates and topics is distributed. These solicited changes are driven by the needs of the families in a particular group and the desire to be continually relevant and intense. Over time and the completion of 200 cycles of the FSP, certain topics and activities have always been included, as they are staples that serve to insure the success of the program. Feedback from families during and after each cycle of the FSP provides confirmation as well as opportunities for modifications and provides evidence of the effectiveness and relevance of session activities. While families have unique characteristics and histories, they also share many commonalities within the culture and share the challenges of facilitating their children's developmental demands and challenges. These overlapping experiences become the material for group discussion. Greater credibility is assumed within this context. Concepts like "advice" and "answers" are discarded in this framework (Quinn, 1996a). Instead "solutions" are generated from the cocreated meanings emerging from group process between and among family members and group facilitators.

Family members who share their own stories about their lives create an environment of empathy and emotional support. These participants are encouraged to voice their opinions, attitudes, and ideas for problem resolution. For example, when a parent defends spanking as a punitive intervention to change a conduct problem of his or her child, it is helpful to have other parents available who can express an alternate view. This alternative view can be considered by the parent advocating spanking because each parent appreciates the challenges faced by other parents; therefore solutions offered by other parents have legitimacy. This issue will receive further attention below.

Sometimes parenting values and strategies are culturally based. One example is the view of corporal punishment. One potential group characteristic is diversity, which serves to reflect different views of parenting practices that can be debated and, if appropriate, altered or ratified by parents focusing on dilemmas such as corporal punishment. The FSP has always retained group leaders and assistants (facilitators) who reflect the racial and class differences of the family groups. In this way the leaders have a broader credibility with the range of families who form a group.

While the youth were performing community service by preparing a meal at the homeless shelter, group discussion among parents focused on discipline. In one session on the topic of discipline strategies, one parent, Joan, remarked that "spanking was the only thing her child understood." Sometimes, she said, even "whipping" was necessary. The program leader invited a guest speaker trained in parent education to provide some alternative views of child behavior management and discipline. The guest speaker attempted to increase the parents' awareness of the use of logical consequences and praise when appropriate. However, the majority of the parents in the group in fact believed as Joan did: that spanking was often necessary and the most effective discipline strategy. The guest speaker continued to emphasize consequences and praise, while the parents continued to defend the use of spanking as a child management technique. The atmosphere became tense and adversarial. After just 15 minutes of discussion, the speaker actually had to ask for a brief break to regain composure and get a drink of water. When the group discussion resumed, Debra made a remark that shifted this conversation. She said, "Really, I don't use spanking until I use two other things first. The first is love, the second is talking." Denise followed by adding, "Well, I wish I could use spanking like I did, but Brittany is too big for it. It doesn't make sense."

Then Debra gave some examples. As she talked, the parents became more interested in her thoughts and open to the options she presented. The leader became more supportive of the parent as the leader became validated. The group session did not end with all parents planning to discard the method of spanking. However, they did grow in their appreciation for other methods to take the place of spanking in some situations that, to them, previously called for spanking. A group leader cannot completely penetrate the mind-set of the collective opinion of parents on the role of spanking. However, when one parent began to share her own experience with other options for discipline, thereby adding something new to the discussion, other parents in the group became receptive, and the adversarial relations diminished.

Family Group Formation

The families who participate in the FSP are varied in many respects. Some differences are structural, such as the number of parents in the home and the presence of extended family such as grandparents, aunts, and uncles in the lives of youth. At every opportunity leaders of the FSP invite any adults to attend the program who have some *interest and continual presence in the life of a youth.* Group members in a multiple family group intervention program can be family representatives who do not live in the home but regularly interact with the youth. Most common is the coparent who does not have custody. The identity of this person is sought and recruitment into the program is planned.

Several methods are used to recruit adult advocates of the youth in the program. It is the goal of the multiple family group program to recruit as many adults as possible who have some sort of ongoing contact with an at–risk youth to participate in the program. This is important for expanding alternatives toward change and to provide richer discussion for problem-solving. Furthermore, to remain passive in recruitment of adult members can, in some cases, unwittingly permit a youth and a reluctant adult who avoids the FSP to avoid dealing with their conflict. In fact, sometimes it is the very adult with whom the youth has the most conflict who avoids the intervention program. The program cannot be as effective if family members who are in extreme conflict with the at-risk youth do not attend.

At the risk-assessment phase, in which a family is referred, say from the juvenile justice system or school, we ask for a description of family composition. This inquiry includes information on who lives in the home and who are the other adults important to the youth, such as grandparents, aunts, uncles, and friends of the parents. If the family is a single-parent structure, we ask for information pertaining to the other parent. In particular, we are interested in the whereabouts of the other parent, the level of involvement of the other parent in the youth's life, and the level of possibility that exists to recruit that parent to the program. We are sensitive to the relationship between the two parents if they do not live together. It is important to make sure that the inclusion of both parents in the FSP will not create overwhelming tension both for them and within the group process. When it is learned that a noncustodial parent lives in the same community as the youth and custodial parent, permission is requested by the program representative of the custodial parent to contact the noncustodial parent. In most cases it is acceptable. In some cases, it is more than acceptable—it is welcomed. One custodial parent responded to the question, "Oh please contact him. I have felt for a long time he needed to get more involved with his son. I haven't been able to do it; maybe you can."

Where the attendance of ex-spouses would not create anxiety, both parents attend, and attention can be given to the triadic problems that may exist. Some problematic interchanges can include unresolved issues pertaining to parental monitoring of the youth, blame that keeps the ex-spouse connected but paralyzes the child, and prior injustices that keep them from cooperating to meet the needs of their child. At graduation night, which is largely festive and joyous, parents who both participate feel a sense of accomplishment in sharing a valuable family experience. This experience that the divorced parents share allows both to feel a sense of success and closure. Often this successful experience together provides momentum for the ex-spouses to form a more collaborative parenting team in the future to provide a more satisfactory life for their child.

Families also vary in characteristics pertaining to how they function. This is learned at the risk-assessment stage, in which the family is asked to complete self-report measures related to parent-adolescent communication and family functioning. In addition, parents are asked to assess their level of parental monitoring and supervision. Drug and alcohol screening occurs, as well as determination of academic status of the youth (attendance, grades, suspensions). This information provides: (1) an opportunity to screen out any youth and families who may not be appropriate for a multiple family group intervention program at that time; (2) an opportunity to learn more about each family to help group leaders plan a relevant schedule of topics; and (3) a baseline of data that can be used to compare changes in parent-adolescent communication, family functioning, delinquent behavior, and school status at the postintervention stage.

CHAPTER 8

Group Process Challenges and Resolutions

Over the course of the Family Solutions Program (FSP), further assessment is made by leaders who observe the group process. Concerns that surface for leaders or family members are acknowledged, and attempts are made to address youth and family difficulties. The following illustrations provide a glimpse into the nature of group processes that can surface from family concerns and problems during the intervention program. Included in these scenarios are possible approaches to resolve these group process challenges, with the goal of helping a family member develop a skill or resolve a family problem.

Challenge 1

Some youth have difficulty speaking in a group setting as a result of a sense of inadequacy or apathy. These youth may want to be skipped when a group leader goes around the circle and asks each group member to comment. Responses that a group leader may request can be based on questions the leader may ask, such as:

- "Before we adjourn for the evening, I would like to go around the circle and ask every person what they learned from this activity (or discussion)."
- "I would like to hear from the young people here right now. What did you think about this video. What did you learn?"
- "I would like everyone to think of one thing that might help Brittany and Denise bury their anger, at least for a short time, and be cooperative or positive with each other"

Resolution 1

The leader looks for opportunities to elicit a comment from a youth who may be silent and passive. One mechanism is to ask a question and give the instruction that each person in the group will make a response. For instance, during the session on resources, each family member would be asked to provide one illustration for the group of how a certain resource was helpful in his or her life. Examples might be: a special teacher, a camp counselor, a Boys or Girls Club volunteer, an aunt or grandmother. Youth are asked to describe how that person contributed to their life. This exercise might be somewhat easier for each youth to comply with as it provides an opportunity to identify someone who cares about them.

If a video is presented, one question by the group leader can be formulated following the video, and each person is asked to make a comment. For example, an award-winning video on youth who are in incarcerated settings and narrated by youth provides a provocative picture of the consequences of the criminal behavior of youth. Some questions that can be posed specifically to youth include:

- "What is your reaction to what you saw?"
- "Did you know you could go to jail for [referring to specific scenes in the video that correlate with certain crimes]? What did you learn?"
- "What needs to happen in your life so that this doesn't happen to you?"

Following an exercise on peer pressure and peer influence, a group leader might ask:

- "Describe an experience or situation when you were with friends, or people who were not really your friends but were about your age, that led to a negative or bad outcome."
- "Before we finish our discussion on peer pressure, I would like each young person in the circle to share one thing with the rest of us that you will do to resist peer pressure to do something that could lead to a bad result for you."

A part of one session of the FSP focuses on the importance of resources and how everyone must seek out help occasionally or often. A discussion ensues about the specific resources available in the community, such as certain churches for some, specific people who can be relied upon, agencies that provide help, and neighbors and friends who can be trusted. Subsequent to this group discussion, each person is asked to describe a time when a resource was beneficial to resolving a difficulty or engaging in a desired opportunity or experience. The leaders usually begin with an example from their own lives, and then family members respond. In some cases, youth might begin initially by saying, "I don't know, or I don't know what you mean." Then further examples might be given that youth could choose from or use for clues, such as "When have you asked a teacher for help, or a friend, or a neighbor?" And "What help did you receive? How was it meaningful?"

No youth is allowed to opt not to answer. Occasionally, if a youth has become angry or extremely self-conscious about being the focus, a group leader may offer to skip past the youth and return at the end. The leader must always remember to return to that youth so that the youth does not begin to believe that silence will be permitted. In one group, Ed, as group leader, said, "Would someone in the group remind me to come back to Shay if I forget after we get around the circle?" In this way the group shares in the responsibility with the group leader of complying with the rule of participation in the group.

Although a group leader will patiently wait for a shy or passive youth to take a turn and respond to the leader's question, long silences should be avoided because they can turn into power plays used by youth. Long silences can be used by youth to frustrate the leader. The youth may hope the leader moves on, and in effect tries to make a statement: "You can't make me do anything." We ask the group to help the youth as well, so that the ownership for the success or meaningfulness of an activity is dependent upon the families.

> *During one session in which Robert would not respond, Joan announced to the group, "You remember, now, that my son is shy." Joan's intent, an honorable one for any mother, was to "shield" her son Robert from embarrassment and the perception that other group members might develop that he was incompetent. The group leader responded: "We do not want to embarrass Robert, we want to help him. And it is for this reason that the group thinks it is important that he develop the skill to verbalize his thoughts and experience the benefits and possibly enjoyment of group discussion. Sometimes learning by doing is the best way." Ed, as group leader, was aiming to help Robert build a skill—a bolstered confidence—by encouraging a behavior not typically exhibited—talking in a group. Eliciting new or underutilized behaviors is a very effective way to alter attitudes and perceptions of self. In the end, the goal is to help a youth like Robert believe in his/her own competence, worth, and value to others. Maybe then Robert can speak in the presence of adults at church, at home, or in a class presentation.*

Challenge 2

Parents who have difficulty managing their children's behavior in an acceptable manner can often be found using physical threats, spanking, or scolding. Parents who use methods of discipline that are narrowly employed, such as the continual use of spanking or physical threats, are likely to have continuous communication problems with their children including a harsh tone, interruptions, and negative attributions, including that a child is "lazy" or "hateful."

Response 2

Several options have been used. One is to invite a guest speaker from a child abuse council or an agency sponsoring parenting programs to discuss effective ways to maintain discipline. If corporal punishment issues are raised that are controversial or invite debate among the parents, the guest speaker who has training in these topics can utilize skills to manage the controversy. In this way, no FSP leader or facilitator is co-opted to be the spokesperson for a given side of the debate. Thus trust and credibility between leaders and families are preserved.

Another option is to invite the group to discuss alternative methods of discipline that they have used effectively. A group leader could ask, "What methods have you as parents found effective in helping your children follow the rules?" Or "What have you found to work when your child has not followed a rule that helps get him (her) back on track?"

A third method is to take on a particular parenting problem mentioned by a group participant and encourage the group to examine the problem and construct an alternative solution. You can begin by identifying a discipline situation and asking, "What would you do if . . . ?" or "How do you react when . . . ?" Again, allow the alternatives to emerge from the range of parenting experiences and beliefs represented in the group.

> *When Denise came to the session on the night when Brittany had been caught shoplifting that very day, she was fuming. Ed said: "I think the group can help you come up with a sensible plan, Denise. Because they are parents they understand your frustration and anger, but they can help balance it because they are not you and they might be able to help you do the reasonable and sensible thing. I would like to ask the group, what would you do if you were Denise right now, tonight, knowing that you have to help Brittany learn from this and understand that she cannot continue doing this one more time? She is already in serious trouble because, as a repeat offender, the court could implement some very severe penalties." The following sequence of interactions occurred: (1) Debra helped comfort Denise; (2) Patti suggested that Denise work with the schools and be notified immediately of any absence from a class; (3) Joan urged Denise to not allow Brittany to go out at night for at least two weeks; and (4) Mark told Denise that she should require Brittany to repay the retail store for the value of the items Brittany stole and write a letter of apology. Denise began to see her way out of her predicament with the help of the group.*

Challenge 3

Domination of certain members of the group can occur, usually by a parent. There are parents who possess a high level of emotion and who have difficulty being calm or patient when a group convenes. Yet each individual under optimal group conditions (e.g., trust, honesty, empathy) in the group desires an opportunity to speak and receive help from others to strengthen their family.

Response 3

It is important for the group leader to establish rules for turn-taking in the group. A group leader's options in establishing rules to counter this tendency of talking over others or not giving up the "podium" can be initiated either at the outset of the group's formation or at a time during the group program in which this problem might surface. Some examples of rules to encourage turn-taking include: (1) setting time limits of 1 to 2 minutes; (2) no more than 3 comments per topic; and (3) only the one holding the designated object such as a tennis ball or wearing the hat can speak. But most important is fostering group bonds that encourage a shared sense of fairness in the group and a regard for each other's challenges and difficulties. In this way, artificial rules are unnecessary as the group process unfolds over time and subsequent sessions.

A direct intervention by a group leader when such dominance prevails is to request others to speak and inform the dominating participant that it is time to "share the floor with those that might also have important ideas or solutions." Do not shy away from controversy that might exist in the group. It may be that there is a dissenting view in the group against the view expressed by the dominating group member. These dissenting views are solicited to counter the dominance of that member and promote balance in group discussion. A group leader can identify a group member who is familiar and would be known to add weight to the side that challenges the view of the dominant speaker to maintain the controversy. By expanding the space for controversy, the group leader is promoting discussion that can help clarify certain positions on parenting or life situations of group members. Depending on the issue, the group leader may step out of the neutral position to advance a position deserving of consideration.

> Debra expressed her view in a session one evening that she thought the school was wrong in punishing her son, Sam, for fighting because he did not instigate it. She was convinced that he was simply defending himself and, being a large boy, hurt the perpetrator without malicious intent. Debra had been a thoughtful and courteous group member throughout the program, and no parent really wanted to challenge her because she was respected by the group. However, Joan forthrightly responded to Debra's stated position by pointing out that she thought Sam needed to learn how to manage confrontations such as the fracas he was in at school, because he was large and he could hurt someone very badly even if the fracas was not his fault. There was a moment of quiet in the group, because other group members were initially surprised by Joan's boldness in disagreeing with Debra, the most universally liked parent in the group. But Joan

found this occasion to be an opportunity to challenge. She had been feeling badly about being perceived so far in the group as the mother who could not control her child's stealing behavior. Her son Robert, being small, quiet, and somewhat "sneaky," found stealing bikes to be a way to get things without confrontation with others. So this was Joan's opportunity to "shine" by challenging the behavior of someone else's child. After a pause, Virginia stated, "I think Joan may have a point, Debra. It would probably help Sam to learn other ways to react to confrontations." Debra responded with, "Well maybe so, but I still think the school was wrong." Mark, Brandon's father, then added, "You may be right, Debra, but Sam will forever think that he did nothing wrong if you keep blaming the school for Sam's behavior and the punishment they gave out." While Debra was not ready to give in after these three group members' comments, she began to think more about helping Sam deal with confrontations differently and accept some of the responsibility for his actions.

The group leader should not expect immediate results from controversial discussions that unfold in group discussions. Some of the opinions or views of parents have been firmly held for a long time, partly fueled in many cases by experiences in their own families of origin as children themselves. In time, group members may change their views about situations and what they need to do differently as they consider varied opinions expressed by different parents. Sometimes, the changes that parents make can happen rather quickly, even though these parents do not announce these changes to the group by saying, "I guess you're right," or "You helped me change my mind for the better." Group leaders need to be patient and hopeful that parents will be affected by group discussions in which controversy is present.

Challenge 4

Lack of participation by a parent can occur because of shyness, sense of inadequacy, apathy, or perceived inability to communicate. Group leaders will be challenged by the reticence of a particular group member. How does a group leader elicit the "voice" of a quiet parent?

Response 4

A group leader can look for an opportunity during a group activity to request a quiet or withdrawn parent to be a leader in a group activity. An example could be serving as recorder reporting on group comments from the parent group. A group leader could identify the shy or reluctant group member as someone called upon first when a question to the group has been posed. This makes particularly good sense when the leader knows the parent well enough to justify the appropriateness of this request. For instance, a reticent parent may have a particular knowledge about a subject that is the focus of the discussion or have an experience similar to the one being described by another parent. Search for the strengths of the person when the opportunity arises. Or ask the parent to describe an ability or situation in which that competency can be utilized. For example, if the subject of spiritual need is mentioned by a member of the group and there is some knowledge that the shy parent possess spiritual resources, that parent can be asked to describe how such a resource is utilized.

> *Ed, the group leader, tried to find ways to encourage Jackie, David's mother, to participate more. He realized, knowing that Jackie organized each day around her spiritual and religious life, that when Patti expressed her frustration that she had no where to turn for help, this was the moment to ask Jackie to discuss her spiritual and religious orientation. ("Jackie, you have shared with us your faith in God. When you feel discouraged how do you connect with God?" (One could say "the Church," or "a spiritual being.") Jackie perked up and slowly began to describe her faith in God and the ways she draws on this power to manage some of her frustrations and direct her behavior.*

Ten Principles of Multiple Family Group Process

After implementation of over 200 cycles of 10-week-session programs of the FSP, it is clear that there are basic elements of multiple family group process vital to the success of the group experience for youth and families.

Principle 1

Balance the needs of youth with the needs of parents. Or involve children to avoid an atmosphere of boredom for them or feelings of being ganged up on.

1. Implement an activity in which children praise their parents.
2. Ask for only youth comments in a group discussion.
   a. "OK, we have heard from the parents, now let's have the youth share."
   b. "We usually hear from the parents when a topic of discussion is raised, let's reverse it, and ask the youth to go first, what do you all think about this?"
   c. "You know, Brandon had a good idea about that earlier (or last session), remember? Brandon, could you share that with the group again?"
   d. "Youth, Robert, Sam, Brandon, David, Brittany, and Shay, what did you learn from this discussion?"
   e. "Youth, if you had to draw (act out, role-play), what does your picture of [e.g., a good friend, a good student, a good parent, after-school time, etc.] look like? Each go to a separate piece of poster paper I have placed on the wall and draw it." (Parents can watch, get a snack, carry on a discussion of their own during this time, or even draw pictures of their own to level the playing field.)

3. Search for opportunities to encourage movement, such as "What would this look like in real life [at home, in his bedroom, etc.]? Sam and Robert, would you come up and show us?

4. Move yourself as group leader to be in the direct vision of the youth so you can make eye contact with them. "Denise, would you change seats with me? Thanks."

5. Organize a room that is not too school-oriented (avoid rows of desks or a group of tables if group members would have their backs to others).

Principle 2

Spread the wealth—promote interfamily strengths:

1. Convert weekly phone calls to a family group discussion in the next session (after getting permission from the family to use them as an example): "I talked with the Johnsons on the phone this past week and we talked about how they were doing on the family pledge that each family developed last week in our session. I wanted to share with you what they did that made it work so well for them. Actually, Mrs. Johnson, would you and David share with the group what you did to get the homework done?"

2. When you, as a group leader, feel cornered or spotlighted when a family (or families) looks to you for an answer/solution, elicit responses from group members *before* adding your own thoughts or experience. You can say: "These are difficult challenges. Has anyone else dealt with this problem? How have you handled it?"

3. Encourage families successful at implementing tasks at home that were planned in the previous group session to help others get it done by asking, "How were you able to get that school conference scheduled that we talked about last week?" or "What did you have to do to pull off the plan of getting all the chores done at home?"

Principle 3

Pace a group discussion or activity properly so that it is meaningful yet avoids being dragging or boring:

1. Family self-disclosure/enthusiasm
   Example: A group member might say, "I don't like doing this!" or look bored.
   a. Go around a circle and ask each family member to describe what they plan to do this week to make the task (e.g., eat together, keep the house clean) work.

    b. Ask each group member for an opinion (e.g., how much time should be spent on homework, how much allowance should be given, what should the curfew time be).

2. Content dissemination

   As a discussion or activity unfolds, stop and check with group members what they have learned so far or whether there are any questions. "Let's stop for a moment. Are there any questions [or comments] so far? Patti, you seem to have a handle on this. How did you make progress on it?"

3. Exercises

   a. Do not belabor an exercise—end it while energy and enthusiasm are high, not low, but only after the goal of the exercise has been met or the exercise has been saturated so that the goal can be met in the subsequent group discussion about the exercise.

   b. Explain instructions clearly and move around the room to facilitate, so that time is not lost as a family tries to understand and initiate the exercise. Point out what a particular family may be doing well so that other families can catch on. Assist a family that is having trouble because their emotions (i.e., anger towards each other, frustration about the confusion in the instructions) are blocking their progress.

Principle 4

Structure the rules. Rules for group organization must be emphasized early so that deviations outside the parameters of the rules can be legitimately identified and used for socializing norms of the group.

1. The group leader can say at the outset, "Rules are important for things to get done by any group. Your family would be a good example; you have set rules in your family to get things done and to reach your goals like raising children successfully."

2. When a youth leaves the room, avoid the temptation to rescue or retrieve the youth yourself. Instead, ask the parent of the youth to retrieve the child. "Jeff, did you give permission to Brandon to leave the room? No? I didn't think so. Would you go get Brandon for us?"

3. With talking or interrupting, ask yourself, "Is Joan taking responsibility for Robert's talking inappropriately?"

   a. If so, track it and stay removed.

   b. If not, wait, then as a group leader state that you really want to hear from Robert because the group will benefit, but ask Robert to wait for his turn.

4. If some participants come late to sessions on a regular basis, do not respond punitively at first but take action to avoid a slippery

slope, before other families start coming late as they see the first family come late regularly.

   a. "Patti, is there anything I can do to help you and Shay get here on time?"

   b. "Denise, I want to keep the meeting interesting to everyone, and for that to happen, it is important to reduce the distractions of people coming and going at different times, so is there anything I can do to help you and Brittany get here on time?"

   c. "I know we have tried on several occasions to start promptly, but we seem to have late arrivals each week, and it interferes with making progress in helping your family. Should we start at a different time?"

   d. Finally (for mandated groups), "I think we have talked a number of times about the importance of starting on time, and we still don't have everybody on board with this rule. So I think we will have to do the following: if you are more than 15 minutes late, I will have to count you absent and it will decrease your chances of finishing this program successfully."

Principle 5

Resist temptations to be mechanistic. There are usually multiple responses that are appropriate in responding to questions from group members seeking advice. It is best to explore options that capture the range of group perspectives, finally adding your own as group leader only if it expands the perspectives reflected in the group's comments.

1. A parent may say, "What is parental monitoring? What does that term mean?" asking for help in monitoring a youth's out-of-home behavior. The monitoring assignment given to parents during a session may have multiple meanings based on the definition of the word "monitoring" and the position a parent has about the extent of control he or she has or wants.

   a. "See if you can monitor in a new way," or "Really, that's what you think it means? Well I think it means. . . ."

   b. "Can we think of some other ways that you can [monitor your child, have fun together, get homework done, etc.]?

2. How families spend time together is not as crucial as that they *do* spend time together. Tell families, "I would like to go around the circle and ask each person to describe one of their best times together as a family and why it was the best time."

3. While there are parents who rely on one form of discipline, which may be corporal punishment, there are many alternative discipline

```
                Checkout Receipt
                 Eagle Library
               04/20/06  12:08PM

PATRON: WILLIAMS, TORI LASHAUN
_____

 Family solutions for youth at risk : appl
CALL NO: 616.89156 QUI
       31978059681171        DUE: 05/11/06
_____

 White oleander
CALL NO: CD FIC FIT
       31978059763847        DUE: 05/11/06

               TOTAL ITEMS: 2
**********************************************

For your convenience we offer:
   WEB RENEWAL at http://www.imcpl.org
      PHONE RENEWAL at 317-269-5222

   SIGN UP TODAY FOR EMAIL REMINDERS!
```

strategies that parents use. Before identifying and explaining the most appropriate ones for promoting child well-being and preparation for adulthood, ask group members which discipline strategies they find most effective and why. Also ask them which discipline strategies they use or have used in the past that are *not* effective, and why.

Principle 6

Search for a high probability of success. A group leader should promote parenting strategies or youth decisions described in group discussions that improve the parent–child relationship or competence of the youth.

1. In discussing school problems, a parent may complain that the reason his or her child is failing is that "The school [or teacher] has it out for my child." Instead of explaining that this is probably not true or asking other parents to discuss how the school or teacher has it out for their children too (which fosters negative talk ill-suited for problem resolution), ask whether there are any parents who have had to overcome this concern in the past. Ask, "Has anyone here felt in the past that the school or a teacher didn't treat your child fairly? How did you overcome it?" Get some positive talk started that accelerates so that different group members discuss problems they have overcome to be successful in school.

2. Begin the process of improving school life for youth by asking them to identify a teacher they like or think will take a special interest in helping them succeed. Plan a strategy that creates a partnership with a teacher, much as youth need mentors, grandparents, neighbors, or coaches to take a special interest. "Which teacher do you sense has a desire to help your child succeed, who teaches a class in which you want your child to improve?"

3. When planning strategies with teachers to build school success, whether it be academic or behavioral-oriented, devise a plan that is challenging but "doable." A strategy is not likely to be productive if it is unrealistic or perceived as too difficult. It is easier to reach a difficult goal if it is divided up into parts that insure success at each step along the way.
    a. Choose one subject to improve in at a time instead of all subjects.
    b. Specify the behavior to be changed, such that it is focused and realistic.
    Examples include scheduling a designated homework time in the evening, getting through math class without getting up from the seat, or carrying an agenda book with assignments in it in a pocket so that it does not get left in a school locker.

Principle 7

Reverse negative talk in group discussion. Parents may be angry at their children for their misdeeds or disobedience and hence want to get on a soapbox or go on a tirade when given a chance in front of a group. This release may be helpful to the frustrated parent but create a perception of blame in the group which is not conducive to problem resolution. Such toxic words can also damage a youth's self-esteem.

1. To respond to a parent who says, "He is always . . ." or "He never [cleans his room, does his homework, takes out the trash, treats his sister nicely, etc.]" the group leader should ask the parent, in an attempt to reverse the negative talk: "What would you like to happen more?" or "What obstacles need to be removed so he will comply?" And "How can you help?"
2. The leader can ask the entire group, "Does anyone have an idea that would help Patti and Shay get out of this mess?" Or "Let's hear from the youth—can you give some suggestions to Shay about how she could get this [homework, chores, anger] changed that would get her off the hook or help her mother out? I am guessing that some of you have been in this situation and have some ideas about how to handle it?"

Principle 8

Make the program "boy-friendly." Boys need to be active in order to accommodate their high energy and desire to express themselves physically. Interactions with boys are more productive when there is a mutual engagement in a task or activity.

1. Encourage movement. Ask a boy who is trying to explain a situation, "How would that look?" (get him to draw a picture on the board or act it out); "Can you show me how that happened?" (again, invite movement). "Who do you need from the group to play other parts to re-create the situation?" "Let's move our chairs back so that Robert can have enough room to enact his situation?"
2. Be patient with verbal limitations (head down, long pause). Do not get impatient; encourage the group to be sensitive to a boy's silent pause, and be nonevaluative of the boy's limited vocabulary. Enlist other youth to fill in words to the boy's sentence or story to make it complete. When Robert had difficulty explaining his feelings of rejection when he was left out of the peer group activity, Ed, the leader, asked Robert to choose some youth who could represent his peer group as well as the people involved with Robert after he had left with hurt feelings.

3. Encourage parents to be patient when a boy has a turn to speak. Make sure in a family discussion that a boy has a chance to speak. Block others from helping the boy, even though they mean well. In the case of Robert, who had trouble responding verbally to a question, Debra wanted to "rescue" him by helping him come up with an answer. Ed, as group leader, blocked Debra from continuing by saying, "Hold on Debra, I think it's great that you want to help Robert, but he needs to work a little harder at this—you and his mother will not always be around to be his mouthpiece."

4. Some boys are often quiet and do not volunteer as a coping mechanism to protect their anxiety about speaking. Make sure you directly invite a reluctant boy to speak.

5. Affirm a boy's discomfort about "being put on the spot." When David was asked whether he had anything on his schedule during after-school hours that reflected school-related activities, he was silent and nonresponsive, indicating his discomfort with being the focus of attention. Ed asked, "David, you probably are doing what you think you should be doing or what you like to do after school, so it is understandable that you don't have anything on your schedule about school. Let's think about how you could schedule an activity after school that would help you improve in school."

6. Request help from boys when setting up or tearing down the group circle, refreshments, and so on. Boys like to help lift, carry, or move furniture or equipment. They can carry audiovisual equipment, bring in refreshments, and move chairs. Set up a plan in which each youth, especially the boys, are assigned a task in getting the room ready each week for the family session. This will foster their enthusiasm for the program and provide a sense of belonging.

Principle 9

Change or redirect the tone/speaker/focus of the child. There are times when the behavior of a youth deters group process from unfolding. Sometimes youth are not listening to the discussion. They may get up and move around, such as getting a refreshment or using the restroom, while a group discussion or activity is ongoing. As a group leader, ask:

1. "What would you do if a child began walking around the room?" The group leader in this instance should consider whether a youth's behavior is legitimate and conforms to rules of the group. For instance, if there is a rule that a youth can get up at any time and use the restroom or get a drink, then the group discussion or activity should continue without interruption. The leader can

continue facilitating a group discussion and encourage group interaction. If, however, a youth getting up during a group discussion or activity has just sat down from a similar trip to a restroom or refreshment table, then the group leader needs to stop the discussion and remind the youth of the rule. If the youth leaves without the group leader noticing or before the group leader can stop the group process, the group leader should ask the parent of the youth who left the room for help in retrieving the youth. A group leader should avoid taking responsibility for a youth's behavior that interrupts the group but instead ask the parent of the youth to take responsibility for monitoring the youth and guiding the youth back to the group. If a youth gets up routinely and consistently over several sessions, the group leader may wish to talk with the family after a session and conduct a problem-solving discussion. Finally, another option when a youth fails to remain seated for an appropriate period of time, is that the leader may ask the group for help: "What shall we do to help Brittany stay in her chair?" When the group is involved, more influence can be directed toward the behavior that detracts from optimal group discussion.

2. "What would you do if a child talked nonstop?" Initially it is of benefit to the group for youth to be involved in group discussions and activities. Typically youth as a group are not as vocal as their parents in the early stages of multiple family intervention. Some youth are uncomfortable talking in the presence of adults. As the group becomes cohesive and group members become comfortable with each other, youth should be expected and encouraged to speak during discussions. Sometimes a group leader may need to ask a question and request that only youth can answer, as a way to involve more youth. If a youth becomes a spokesperson for his or her peers and does most of the talking for the youth, then the group leader must intervene to enlist more peer involvement. Youth can be asked to meet together with a group facilitator and prepare a presentation or role play. Also, a group leader can follow a youth who talks for an extended period of time, construct another question, and pose it to the group with this caveat: "I would like Shay to take a rest (a vacation) and see who can answer this question besides Shay." A leader could also have an object that serves as the "baton" for permission to talk; the orange, stuffed animal, or apple squeeze, for example, is passed around, and only the youth holding the object can speak.

3. "What would you do if a child said something embarrassing about a parent?" The leader can ask the parent to explain to the child

why his or her comment is embarrassing. This attempt to help the youth understand the power and harm from words provides an opportunity for youth to encounter conflict or injustice and resolve it peacefully. In some cases it can be appropriate to include other parents in the discussion when a child says something embarrassing or hurtful about a parent in the group. In this way, a child is afforded an opportunity to gain respect for adults.

4. "What would you do if a child said something indicating a possible parent abuse incident?" Initially, a group leader should ask the youth to provide details of the incident. A parent may also explain or provide further details of the incident identified by the child. The leader can ask the group members to respond to the situation to add other perspectives. If the group leader concludes from these steps in the discussion that more needs to be known and that a clear decision cannot be reached about whether abuse occurred, then the group leader should ask the family to remain after the session to discuss the possible abuse incident in more detail. At that time, a group leader may determine that no follow-through is necessary or may believe that abuse occurred. In this latter case, a group leader can discuss the situation with a supervisor for guidance and consider reporting the incident if the law in their state requires it. If a report is made, the group leader needs to meet with the family to inform them that a report was made and to discuss the appropriateness for their continued involvement in the group. A group leader should take steps to work with an agency that investigates abuse reports and help to insure that the family receives professional help to prevent any further abuse.

Principle 10

Change or redirect the tone/speaker/focus of the parent. Even more common is a parent who dominates a group discussion. Denise often came to group meetings angry at Brittany and wanted to start each session with a complaint or story about Brittany's latest problem behavior. Ed had to be prepared at the beginning of each session to plan an activity immediately so that Denise would not have an opportunity to begin talking about Brittany. As a group leader, ask:

1. "What would you do if a parent started telling a story that was embarrassing a child?" A group leader should immediately halt this story even if the parent has not had a chance to finish. If the parent objects, the leader needs to explain the reason for halting the story. The leader can also ask group members whether they think the telling of this story is harmful to the child, thereby helping the

parent get confirmation of the appropriateness of the group leader's judgment to end the story. Sometimes parents report behavior of their children that is not only embarrassing but critical. A youth can feel devastated by such criticism because it is leveled in front of a large group of peers and other parents. Again, a group leader should interrupt a parent's statement that is excessively critical and lacking of any attempt to translate the criticism into a problem-solving discussion. When Denise spoke at length about Brittany's "bad attitude," skipping school, and associating with someone who was a juvenile offender, Brittany fumed. To avoid an escalating sequence that might result in Brittany getting up and walking out or yelling at her mother, Ed stopped Denise by saying: "Denise, I know you are frustrated and angry at Brittany, and she hasn't proven her willingness to cooperate, but we're going to do something tonight in this session that might help the two of you. So if you could hold off for now and maybe what we do can help the two of you. And at the end of the session, I'll give you an opportunity to let us all know if things are any better. And if they aren't, we'll discuss some options as a group about what to do." In this way, Denise has an opportunity to experience a different way of fostering a better relationship with her daughter, and the group members are not deprived of their own opportunity to work on strengthening their own families.

2. "What would you do if a parent sermonizes?" Some parents feel that their problems are worse than problems of other parents. These parents may also possess substantial anxiety and have difficulty managing it without "venting." A group leader needs to permit long statements by parents in the early stages of a group program so that these parents feel acknowledged that their problems are serious and that they carry large burdens, whether it be job stress, feeling disrespected by a child, or having marital problems. Sometimes parents cover up their sense of inadequacy as parents by acting aggressively to disguise this inadequacy. They may talk loudly, provide rigid solutions to problems ("He needs a good talking to"; "She's not going out for a month!"; "Kids need to learn respect"), and intimidate other group members. A group leader must buffer a parent's gruffness by framing discussion in a way that allows others to speak. Examples might be: "Let's hear from the mothers here," or "I think it's time we shifted gears and did an activity." A leader can also offer a different perspective with a sound rationale as a counter to the sermonizing parent, so that the parent does not start "running the group" and the leader's

credibility is not reduced. If group members perceive that the group leader cannot handle or control the sermonizing parent, the group begins to lose confidence and motivation to believe that changes can occur. In some cases, a leader may choose to foster counterarguments by members of the group. For instance, Ed remembered that in an earlier session Debra had spoken of her determination to stay positive with Sam despite his mistakes. Debra was a teacher and she knew the importance of giving encouragement to students and believing in them. During one session in which Denise once again talked about Brittany and concluded that "Since she is the daughter from hell, a parent has to take matters in her own hands and break her down," Ed felt compelled to break in and ask Debra to counter Denise's tirade. Ed turned to Debra and asked, "Debra, I think, being a teacher, you have totally different ideas about how to relate to Brittany. And I can see your different ways in the manner in which you guide Sam. Would you talk to Brittany now?" Debra jumped at the opportunity. She criticized Denise for her callous demeanor. Debra told Denise that she did not see any way that she was going to help Brittany with this approach and that her style was only leading to a downward spiral that was very destructive. Debra said, "Frankly, I would not be surprised to hear that Brittany had run away. I hate to say that Denise, but I think that's how awful Brittany feels and how discouraged she is that she can get any help from you. I'm not saying it is all your fault, but I think this mess you and Brittany have can only change if you change your attitude. After all, you're the adult!" It just took one statement from Ed to unleash the torrent of "honest appraisal" by Debra that Denise needed to hear in order for her to consider changing her attitude.

3. "What would you do if a parent delves into minute details of an incident that bores the group?" It is important to curb stories or accounts parents provide about their lives that bore the group because the effect is a depletion of enthusiasm or energy. In today's world there are many choices people can make about how they spend their time. A multiple family group intervention program must compete with television, the computer, leisure activities, and many other choices for a family's time. Therefore the group leader must use time wisely, create enthusiasm and fun, and provide learning experiences that are relevant to the lives of the participants. A parent who has little enthusiasm or dominates discussion but does not contribute to learning or building family strengths diminishes the intensity of the program. In these cases a leader may choose to plan

more activities so that families are busy working on tasks rather than having discussions. Also, group discussions can be more carefully controlled. For instance, a group leader could ask questions with the restriction that responses must be one word or one sentence. Or, the leader could require nonverbal responses such as drawings, role-plays, or gestures. Finally, a parent who expands a story by making a short story long can be prompted by the group leader with a specific question asked during the story. The leader could say, "Let me stop you there, Mark, because I think there was something important there that you just said." Or "So, Virginia, what would you like the group to know, if you could whittle it down to a few words?" A group leader sometimes has to be a traffic cop—conducting the sequence of speakers or the time they speak in a co-ordinated fashion that allows each traveler to reach the destination.

4. "What would you do if a parent reports a possible abusive interaction with a child?' A similar procedure needs to be followed as delineated in the fourth point of Principle 9. One additional factor in a parent comment that hints of abuse, which can suggest a possible abuse incident not typically detected when a child hints of an abuse incident, is a parent's defensiveness. This reticence by the parent to explain his or her improper behavior can alienate him or her from the group. The leader needs to urge group members, particularly parents, to help the parent of focus acknowledge the facts of the referenced incident and be accepting of the parent so that they can be supportive of the parent's need to change behavior. Otherwise the target parent may quit the program to avoid recrimination. One additional obligation of a group leader is to speak with the parent about not blaming or punishing the child who reported the incident in the group discussion. A child needs to be protected and the leader needs to garner assurance from the parent that no punitive action will be taken by the parent against the child in the coming weeks as punishment for revealing such an incident.

Utilizing the Strengths of the Group

There can be vast differences among group members and between families based on values, family-of-origin influences, and current life circumstances. One of the tasks of the leader is to acknowledge the unique situation and set of circumstances of each member. Yet it is crucial to create elements of the group process that will allow the group to experience commonality, a feeling of belonging and unity of purpose. The activities outlined in chapter 6 are intended to accomplish this objective.

A common concern or question in working with groups is how to unify a group that experiences a sense of differences. It is sometimes a challenge to establish the important place of each family member's participation. Family members may feel inadequate compared to other families. Sometimes certain family members feel more competent than others and believe that either they or the other family members do not belong in the group. These differences need to be acknowledged and not hidden or anxiously avoided. Differences can be utilized for the welfare of the group. One way to do this is to draw out the group members who have strengths that can enhance the group process and the experiences of others. The scenario described earlier in this book of the contagious effect of Virginia's tendencies to be a nurturer to others illustrates the balance of group similarities and differences. Many responses to these challenges are possible beyond the number that can be delineated here. Each group and leader will know his or her group the best and be able to motivate or facilitate discussion based on these individual characteristics of the group.

The purpose of building on strengths of families is to utilize the group's presence to help one family help another family. The focus of a group leader is to draw on the utility of a client or family's characteristics that can promote change. In a multiple family group model, the potential exists to utilize a given group member's or family's characteristic that can be drawn into group process and can contribute something to another group member's or family's dilemma or difficulty. Virginia's exuberance and nurturing tendencies "rubbed off" on other group members. In addition, her generosity contributed to their feelings of validation and enjoyment about being there.

There is an almost infinite array of these sorts of possibilities within a group. Some examples of identifying and sharing strengths include:

- One family's story about how they maintain the ritual of eating together each evening strengthened another family's commitment to do the same.
- One youth's sense of humor became contagious and other youth began to end their silence in the group and join in the fun.
- Finally, one father's belief in tolerating his son's hairstyle was evident when the boy came in with a head full of tight curls, which led to a discussion of acceptable dress and appearance, ownership of the human body, and what is tolerable. This lead another father, who was embarrassed about his son's appearance, to become less rigid in demanding a particular physical appearance of his own son, knowing that another father was not opposed to his son's unique look. This led into a discussion by the group of how

important it is "to pick the battles one chooses to fight," because differences across the generations are inevitable.

The value of group process cannot be truly discerned because it is not easy to measure its full effects on group members. Yet the enthusiasm and focus within the context of group interaction is often apparent, and such relevance provides opportunities for learning and change. There are three facets to successful group process that a group leader must shape: (1) the common notion of the group's purpose—why the families are together (e.g., the presence of a youth offense or problem behavior); (2) the unique value of each member's participation and contribution; and (3) the common goal of personal and relational change. The group leader who holds these elements as being crucial to success can not only permit but also expect the families to share in the responsibility for change.

CHAPTER 9

Profiles of Youth and Outcomes of the Family Solutions Program

In over a decade of implementation of the Family Solutions Program (FSP) approximately 1,200 families have been referred to the program. Since 1993, almost 1,000 juvenile first offenders and their families have completed a risk assessment at the time of their adjudication. The juvenile courts have enthusiastically recognized and collaborated with this program since its inception (see Quinn, 1999; and chapter 10 for discussion on collaboration and "mainstreaming" a program). Collaboration is an essential ingredient in successful implementation of a youth intervention program. The juvenile courts in the geographic location in which the FSP began have increasingly referred youth to the FSP.

This collaboration has reached a milestone in service delivery as an example of a program that began as an alternative approach with a "trial run" to one that is a mainstay of the juvenile courts. It has reached its goal of serving all at-risk youth who are first-time offenders with early intervention. This result is largely due to the promising results based on recidivism outcomes as well as testimonials from families who complete the program. In addition, juvenile court staff have observed the changes in the families as they follow them in the context of their caseload responsibilities. Agency staff also notice a difference in the families who are referred to the FSP who happen to have a youth who reoffends. The regional administrator of juvenile justice reports that these families are more cooperative with juvenile justice staff as their cases are reviewed again, compared to families who were referred to the FSP but never attended (Conkle, 2001).

The juvenile court has allocated space for the administration of risk assessments and an office for the liaison staff member of the FSP who coordinates referrals. Supplies and copying privileges are granted the FSP, and staff are welcome at case reviews of first offenders. Hence data are routinely gathered on youth and families, and the referral process from court to FSP has been streamlined.

The risk assessment is used for a number of reasons. First, the data generated at the risk assessment help familiarize the intervention program staff with youth and family characteristics, problems, and risk and protective factors. Data collected include:

1. *Demographic* information such as sex, race, income, and age;
2. *Family* information on the level of relationship and family conflict, overall family functioning, presence of substance-abuse problems, school difficulties (grades, unexcused absences, suspensions); family composition (number of parents in the home, location of an absent parent, presence of extended family such as grandparents, number and ages of siblings, presence of a stepparent); number of transitions in the family in the last 12 months (gain or loss of family member and its effect); curfew/parental monitoring; frequency of family routines such as dinners together and shared holidays/vacations; and
3. *Youth* data such as level of involvement in school, community, and church activities; peer relationships, delinquent behavior of friends, and the availability of family members to participate in the FSP.

There are additional strategic purposes of the risk assessment prior to the inception of intervention once referral by the court is made to the FSP. Information from the risk assessment can provide important information to group leaders and help plan the program. This information insures relevance of program content to the families and focuses on skills that need development. For example, if several of the youth have exhibited behavior such as assaults or hostile incidents such as school fights, more conflict-resolution skills can be integrated into the program and topics pertaining to interpersonal skill development can be designed.

In addition, *maybe more crucial to the success of the program implementation is the opportunity for the family to meet a representative of the FSP and become familiar with the benefits of the program for the family*. This is important since some families are ambivalent or opposed to the initial referral to the program.

The FSP representative, possibly the group leader who will lead the group the family is assigned to, can develop rapport with the family at the referral meeting and emphasize the positive aspects of the program (e.g., its record of successful outcomes for youth; the opportunity to meet other families and develop a wider support network; accumulating family experiences that promote greater cohesion). Families can view a 12-minute video that provides an overview of the program, shows the program in action, and presents participating families describing their positive experiences. The logistical details of the program are shared with the family at this time, including the date of the first session, place, and time. All family members are invited to attend, and the parents are told that they are required to attend regularly in order for their child who was referred to have his or her case expunged. Over 85% of families who are referred to the FSP and complete the risk assessment attend the first session, and over 75% of those who were initially referred by the court complete the program.

Profile of First-Offender Youth Based on the Standard Administration of the FSP Assessment

It is important to describe the youth population that have participated in the FSP to provide a rationale for the treatment approach and a context for reporting treatment outcome. The following data provide a summary of youth and family characteristics among youth who have completed the standard risk assessment subsequent to referral to the FSP:

- mean age is 13.6 years;
- 69% are African-American;
- 62% live in one-parent homes, with 24% of these single parents having never married and only 33% being married and living with a spouse;
- 34% of mothers report that another family member has been involved in criminal activity;
- 45% of youth participate in church activities;
- 38% of youth participate in school activities;
- 26% of youth participate in community activities; and
- 46% of families make less than $20,000 per year and only 20% of the families make $40,000 per year or more.

Hence this sample has a majority of African-American families, largely single-parent family structures, and many who are poor.

Peer Group Affiliation

Many studies have confirmed the association between negative peer group interaction and problem behavior or juvenile delinquency. Peer affiliation is a major influence on the likelihood of delinquent behavior. One of the

Table 9.1 Age Difference between Juvenile First Offenders and Friends ($n = 583$)

	n	**Percent**
All friends are no more than 2 years older	289	50
One friend is more than 2 years older	80	14
Two friends are more than 2 years older	42	7
Three or more friends are more than 2 years older	172	29

factors in assessing negative peer group influence is the age difference between an identified youth and his or her peers. In our data only half of the youth (50%) identified their friends as about the same age as they are (less than 2 years older) (see Table 9.1). Conversely, almost one third of the youth (29%) reported that 3 or more of their friends were more than 2 years older than their age. In addition, over half of the youth (54%) reported that they had friends who were involved in the juvenile justice system.

When youth were asked if any of their friends were involved in a gang, 12% of youth reported that they had at least one friend involved in a gang. Given that the geographic area in which these youth live is not from a major metropolitan area, this finding suggests that even in middle- and small-sized communities, gangs are present. Also, given that the mean age of these youth is 13.6 years, indicating that many are in junior high or middle school, the number who report that they have friends in gangs is substantial. It might be expected that older youth who are repeat juvenile offenders would have a higher frequency of friends engaged in gangs, and gang involvement is a potential risk for some delinquent youth.

As reported by parents, almost one third of the youth have friends who have been in trouble with the law (Table 9.2). The fact that almost half of the parents report that they do not know whether their children have friends who have been involved with law enforcement may suggest that many of parents do not know enough about their children's friends to know whether they have been arrested. Finally, about 43% of parents report that their children's friends were largely responsible for getting their own child in trouble

Table 9.2 Friends of Juvenile First Offenders Who Have Been in Trouble* ($n = 601$)

	n	**Percent**
Yes, arrested	104	17.2
Yes, appeared in court	86	14.2
No	131	21.7
Do not know	280	46.4

* Reported by parent.

Table 9.3 Friends of Juvenile First Offenders Got Child in Trouble* ($n = 605$)

	n	**Percent**
Yes, definitely	87	14.4
Had some influence	170	28.1
Very little influence	54	8.9
No	192	31.7
Do not know	102	16.9

* Reported by parent.

(Table 9.3). Again, a large number of parents report that they do not know whether their children's friends were responsible for the trouble. This suggests that the majority of parents, if they knew all their child's friends, would report that friends were involved in their own children's trouble.

Three conclusions can be drawn. First, friends are involved in many youth arrests, indicating that peer influence is a strong predictor of youth crimes. Second, parental monitoring is weak for many juvenile first-time offenders, given that many parents report not knowing the identity or characteristics of their child's friends. Third, an emphasis on parental monitoring, its importance, and the skills associated with it, should be incorporated into family intervention programs for at-risk youth.

Parental Monitoring

One of the strongest predictors of delinquency as well as the likelihood of a youth engaging in high-risk behaviors is the level of parental monitoring in the family. In our sample, parents were asked whether they knew what their children were doing during nonschool hours. Among 732 parents, slightly over one half (56%) of them reported that they "have clear knowledge of his/her activities" (Table 9.4). Almost half of the parents had either "some knowledge" or "little or no knowledge" of his or her child's activities during nonschool hours. FSP activities include schedule-keeping that is shared between parents and children, as well as attention to peer group networks and the presence of negative influences.

Table 9.4 Parental Monitoring of Juvenile First Offenders ($n = 732$)

Knowledge of child's activities during nonschool hours	Frequency	Percent
Have clear or knowledge	410	56
Have some knowledge	255	35
Have little or no knowledge	67	9

Table 9.5 Failing Classes This School Year* ($n = 651$)

	n	Percent
None	273	41.9
One or two	208	32.0
Three or four	55	8.4
More than four	63	9.7
Do not know	52	8.0

* Reported by parent.

School Problems

School success is a strong predictor of successful child outcomes and preparation for adulthood. The data in this study regarding school grades, absences, and suspensions suggest that academic difficulty and school behavior problems contribute to youth engagement in juvenile delinquency. As reported by the parents, *less than half of the youth* were passing every subject, and close to *1 in 5 youth* were failing three or more subjects in the current year in which they were assessed (Table 9.5). In reporting on the previous school year, almost half of the youth failed at least one subject for the school year (Table 9.6). The educational debate about passing or promoting to the next grade a student who fails subjects is an important but unsettled issue. Among the youth in FSP, given that retention rates are a function of individual school district policies, it is likely that many of the youth who failed at least one subject still moved onto the next grade. While this might be considered a successful event, there are two potential problems. First, a youth is not prepared for the next level of academic skills due to his or her failure to comprehend basic or fundamental skills. This leads to increased academic problems and a greater likelihood of failure as youth advance to the next grade level. Second, the youth may not associate any penalty or problem with failing a subject if he or she is promoted to the next grade and hence does not garner any increased motivation to do better in school.

Table 9.6 Classes Failed Last Year* ($n = 631$)

	n	Percent
None	318	50.3
One to two	183	29.0
Three to four	48	7.6
More than four	44	7.0
Do not know	38	6.0

* Reported by parent.

Table 9.7 School Attendance of Juvenile First Offenders*
($n = 688$)

	n	**Percent**
Everyday	443	64.3
Most days	172	25.0
Only sometimes	50	7.2
Not at all	23	3.3

* Reported by mother.

Further evidence of school challenges for youth offenders is provided by an examination of retention rates. Among 874 first-time offenders in the sample, 349 (40%) of the youth had been held back a grade in school. This presents a different problem for youth, parents, and schools. There are a number of consequences to the event of being held back in school. A child may feel discouraged and lose interest, confidence, or ambition in school endeavors. Also, a child becomes separated from friends and is subsequently placed in a school setting with children who are younger. This result may put distance between himself or herself and classmates, or create developmental challenges as the retained child fits in less well with the classroom culture. While the debate rages, it is important for FSP, and any intervention program for youth at risk, to place academic progress at the forefront of programmatic considerations.

About two thirds of youth attended school every day, according to their mothers (Table 9.7). About 1 in 4 parents reported that their children attended school most days, and 10% of youth attended only sporadically. Given that the mean age in this sample is 13.6 years, this indicates that 1 in 10 middle or junior high school students attended school sporadically, if at all. Given that the source of the data is mothers, it is possible that figures for irregular attendance are higher, given that some mothers may worry about punitive action taken against them or do not want to admit responsibility for their role in insuring school attendance of their children.

Data were gathered from schools regarding suspensions and unexcused absences. The sample for these two categories is lower than the other categories because the source of these data is the schools, and some schools did not respond to requests for this information despite the fact that parental consent was given. Nevertheless, the sample size is large enough to be useful. First, *less than one third of the youth* who were juvenile first-time offenders had *no* record of school suspension (Table 9.8). *In fact, there were almost as many youth who had been suspended 4 or more times from school as those never suspended from school.* This is an indication of the difficulty that youth have within the school setting, which suggests that they are not

Table 9.8 Juvenile First Offenders Suspended from School* ($n = 180$)

	n	Percent
None	55	30.6
One	36	20.0
Two	22	12.2
Three	21	11.7
Four or more	46	25.5

* Reported by school.

adequately performing academically and have interpersonal problems and skill deficits that interfere with their school life.

There can be two conclusions drawn from these data. First, school difficulty is a primary influence on juvenile delinquency. Second, family intervention programs must address school-related problems, particularly in the realm of helping parents become more effective advocates and resources for their child's education. In the FSP much time is devoted to this topic.

While school suspensions are a common occurrence for at-risk youth and juvenile offenders, so too is the problem of unexcused absences. In fact, being absent from school could be a direct reason that youth become juvenile first-time offenders as schools refer these youth to the juvenile court. *Less than 1 in 10 youth* had *no* unexcused absences as reported by the school (Table 9.9). *One in 5 youth* had missed over 20 days of school *without* a legitimate reason. And these data are often collected during the school year, depending on when a youth is referred to the FSP. This means that for both school suspensions and unexcused absences, these numbers would be higher if data were collected at the end of the school year.

Again, these results provide a rationale for the inclusion of school-related topics in a family intervention program for at-risk youth. In fact, given that parents attend the FSP, more opportunities and approaches to

Table 9.9 Unexcused Absences of Juvenile First Offenders* ($n = 235$)

	n	Percent
None	19	8.1
1–5	64	27.3
6–10	49	20.9
11–15	40	17.1
16–20	18	7.8
More than 20	45	18.8

*Reported by school.

Table 9.10 Participation in Non-Schoolday Activities ($n = 861$)

	Yes	Percent
Church	392	46
School	337	39
Community	225	26

address school problems are possible. For instance, in the FSP, parents are asked to assess and revise their own schedules to see how they can be more involved in supporting their children's academic needs and activities. Parents role-play a teacher-parent conference to improve their skills in establishing a good rapport with the school. The aim of this role-play is to create problem-solving strategies that culminate in parents and teachers working as a team on behalf of the child. Parents and youth also learn about successful people who have had to overcome obstacles to complete an education, and how educational success allowed for a rich, rewarding, and successful life. In addition, parents are encouraged to create a home environment for learning in the evening, including quiet time with parent involvement.

Community Activities

Youth were asked whether they participated in church, school, and/or community activities such as volunteer organizations, Scouts, arts, or music. Of the three categories, more youth reported that they participated in church activities (46%) than the other two categories (Table 9.10). However, this was still less than half of the youth. A little over one third reported that they participated in school activities and about 1 in 4 participated in community activities. One conclusion drawn from these data is that there is a high proportion of youth who are not involved in structured and age-appropriate activities after school and on weekends. There is a greater chance that in these cases youth are not in the presence of adults and are not developing skills or commitments to a meaningful community life.

Family Activities

Families in contemporary society have more activities than ever before and more opportunities to engage in a multitude of pursuits, including leisure activities, sports, and job responsibilities. Some parents create schedules that require incessant transportation of their children to various after school and weekend activities. Some parents work more than one job and some may work odd hours. As many families have schedules that require daily adjustments, time together has shrunk. Research has consistently

Table 9.11 Family Rituals (How often does your family have dinner together?) ($n = 694$)

In a week:	Child		Parent	
	N	**%**	**N**	**%**
Never	96	14	33	6
1–3 times	198	29	225	38
4–6 times	82	12	94	16
Every day	318	46	247	41

shown the relationship between families who spend time together and healthy child outcomes (Fiese, Tomocho, & Douglas, 2002; Imber-Black, 2002). Family rituals provide a sense of security and stability, help protect children from risks associated with child rearing in single-parent, divorced, and stepparent households, allow for open emotional exchange between family members, improve academic achievement, and increase children's feelings of acceptance and worthiness.

One of the characteristics of family cohesion is eating dinner together. While this is not possible in some homes due to work demands, it is nonetheless the most likely and practical strategy in a family for being together. Having dinner together provides the opportunity to participate in conversation that bonds family members. Children feel affirmed when their parents ask them about their day or listen to the day's highlights or "lowlights" and generally enjoy each other's company. Mealtime can also be a good opportunity for children to learn important lessons from their parents as parents talk about their work, their own relationships in the outside world, and their attitudes about life and people. Mealtime can be an opportunity to laugh and tease in a friendly way. In our data *less than half of the 694 families ate dinner together every day* (Table 9.11). Almost one third of the youth and over one third of the parents report that they ate together 3 or fewer days in a week. About 1 in 7 (14%) youth report that they *never* ate dinner as a family.

A family with three small children made a decision to not have any television in the home. They organized their evening to have dinner together and then have reading time afterwards. During dinner each night, each member of the family was expected to share with the family two things: (1) "What's the bad thing that happened during your day?" and (2) "What's the good thing that happened during your day?" The bad thing was always the first thing in the sequence so that each person could end their story of their day on a good note. After dinner, they participated in silent reading time and time when the mother or father would read a story to the family. As the children became proficient in reading, each of the children began to read a story to the family.

Table 9.12 Percent of Friends Engaged in Delinquent Behavior*

	All	Most	Some	Few	None	Do not know
Cheated on tests	3	6	13	22	38	18
Damaged/destroyed property	3	4	13	16	49	15
Used marijuana	3	7	9	12	53	16
Stole an item worth less than $5	4	6	10	18	46	16
Threatened to hit someone without reason	5	5	11	14	52	13
Used alcohol	3	6	9	15	53	15
Broke into a house or car to steal	1	2	3	6	72	17
Sold hard drugs—heroin, coke, or LSD	1	1	3	6	73	17
Stole something worth more than $5	2	4	9	12	54	19
Suggested you do something illegal	4	4	6	15	64	7
Got drunk once in a while	4	4	8	13	55	17
Used drugs such as speed/barbiturates	1	2	4	5	67	21
Sold or gave alcohol to kids under 18	2	2	3	6	69	18

* Number of youth responding to each item ranges between 471 and 493. Note: Total percentages for each item may not always equal 100 due to rounding.

Delinquent Behavior

Asking youth to report their own juvenile offenses is a questionable tactic because they are not likely to be forthcoming about crimes they may have committed or trouble they have been in. Like most people, the idea of self-recrimination is repugnant or ill-advised in youth as well as adults for fear of punitive consequences or negative perceptions by others. Hence the youth were asked about behaviors of their friends as a proxy for their own problem behaviors. The assumption can be made that youth whose friends exhibit problem behaviors are likely to be exhibiting such behavior themselves. One way to examine the data in Table 9.12 is to add the percentages of youth who reported that at least a few, some, most, or all of their friends engaged in that particular behavior. Stealing an item worth less than $5 (38%), cheating on tests (44%), and damaging or destroying property (36%) were the illegal or unethical behaviors that at least a few, if not more, of the youth reported their friends engaging in (Table 9.12). *Over one third (35%) reported that their friends had threatened to hit someone without reason, a third had friends who use alcohol (33%), and almost one third (31%) reported that their friends used marijuana.* Given that the average age youth is between 13 and 14, a large number of middle school and junior high students are involved in destructive behavior. About 1 in 8 (12%) had friends who had broken into a house or car to steal.

Table 9.13 Parent–Adolescent Communication Prior to Intervention

Group	Mean
Juvenile first-time offenders ($n = 473$)	61.92
Parents of juvenile first-time offenders ($n = 419$)	64.03
"Normal" families (youth)*	66.58
"Normal" families (parents)	75.63

* The term "normal" families was used by the authors of this scale to describe a subgroup of a larger, randomly stratified sample of 1,140 intact families from across the nation (Barnes & Olson, 1985).

These findings suggest that juvenile first offenders are embedded in social peer networks that engage in delinquent activities. Many of these youth encourage or legitimize this behavior as a way to overcome their boredom, express their anger, or provide a means of getting basic needs met such as food, clothes, or spending money.

Parent–Adolescent Communication

Prior to intervention, the families were asked to complete a 20-item parent–adolescent communication scale (Barnes & Olson, 1982). Families with good parent–adolescent communication viewed themselves, according to the Circumplex model, as scoring higher on family cohesion, family adaptability, and family satisfaction (Barnes & Olson, 1985). Sample statements that the youth responded to included: "I find it easy to discuss problems with my mother," "Sometimes I have trouble believing everything my mother tells me," "My mother tries to understand my point of view." Statements parents responded to included: "My child nags/bothers me," "My child is a good listener," and "I openly show my affection to my child." Among 426 "normal" families in this study, the group mean for mothers regarding their adolescent was 75.63. The group mean for adolescents regarding their mothers was 66.58.

In a study using the Parent–Adolescent Communication Scale to examine juvenile delinquency among high school students, having an open communication with either of one's parents was significantly associated with less serious forms of delinquency, based on a self-report delinquency scale (Clark & Shields, 1997). The same pattern holds for problem communication with parents and delinquency reports. In Table 9.13 you will note that the means for parent–adolescent communication in the "normal" sample are substantially higher than for parents and youth in our sample of families. The difference in means is even more widespread between the two groups of parents than between the two groups of youth. The importance of family communication is emphasized throughout the FSP. Promoting family cohesion by virtue of their shared participation in the program provides the impetus for improving family communication. Some specific activities that focus on communication include exercises to improve speaking and listening skills, problem-solving, family games, making family pledges (negotiation), and sharing affection with each other.

Family Functioning

A family-functioning scale has been administered at intake since the inception of the FSP. The Family Apgar (Smilkstein, 1978) is a 5-item scale tapping dimensions of family life that are known to contribute to child well-being. It is based on a systems model incorporating stress and change/adaptation in one or more family members. The conceptual view of this measure is that of an assessment of the family functioning as a supportive and nurturing social unit for individuals in the family. The instrument was found to be useful as a psychiatric screening measure in a family physician's clinic, the General Health Questionnaire (McNabb, 1983), particularly for depression, and has demonstrated accuracy in screening patients in a family practice clinic who have psychological distress (Hilliard, Gjerde, & Parker, 1986), as well as patients in a family practice clinic. The Family Apgar was used to assess teens, some of whom were seen in an adolescent health center, with mental, physical, and family problems, as well as those living in residential settings (Shapiro, Neinstein, & Rabinovitz, 1987). Results indicated the measure to be a valid screening tool for teen population. The Family Apgar as a measure of low social support has been correlated with child psychosocial problems in a pediatric clinic (Murphey, Kellher, Pagano, Stulp, Nutting, Jellinek, Gardner, & Childs, 1998). The total scores range from 0 to 10 for the Family Apgar. Individual scores are assigned a value of 0 (hardly ever), 1 (some of the time), or 2 (almost always).

The mean score on the Family Apgar in the sample of youth referred to the FSP at the pretest prior to intervention was for the youth 6.42, for the mothers, 7.40, and for the fathers, 7.52. These means are lower than for some other populations, and higher than for a reported clinical sample. A sample of married graduate students had a mean of 8.24, a sample of 527 college undergraduate students had a mean of 7.6, and a group of 133 patients at a medical center had a mean of 8.22, while a group of 158 community mental health clinic patients had a mean of 5.89 (Smilkstein, Ashworth, & Montalvo, 1982). Hence the first-time youth offenders had a mean substantially lower than college students and patients at a medical setting, but slightly higher than a group of psychiatric patients. Interestingly, for each of the 5 items, a higher percentage of youth reported "hardly

Table 9.14 Family Functioning Prior to Intervention in Families of Juvenile First Offenders

Can turn to family when something is troubling me	Percent of Youth*	Percent of Mothers**	Percent of Fathers***
Hardly ever	11	9	8
Some of the time	33	33	30
Almost always	56	58	62
My family talks over things with me			
Hardly ever	20	10	10
Some of the time	39	43	44
Almost always	41	47	46
My family accepts and supports me			
Hardly ever	11	9	4
Some of the time	33	34	36
Almost always	56	57	60
My family shows affection and notices feelings			
Hardly ever	11	7	4
Some of the time	30	27	32
Almost always	59	66	64
My family and I share time together			
Hardly ever	12	6	7
Some of the time	38	35	39
Almost always	50	58	53

* The number of youth who responded to each item ranged between 839 and 846.
** The number of mothers who responded to each item was between 722 and 729.
*** The number of fathers who responded to each item was between 159 and 161.

ever" than did mothers or fathers (see Table 9.14). This indicates that the youth rated their family functioning substantially lower than their mothers or fathers did.

A score of less than 6 on the Family Apgar has been considered an indication of family dysfunction (Mengel, 1987). Among 832 juvenile first offenders in our sample, 29% had scores on the Family Apgar below 6. Among 709 of their mothers, 24% had scores below 6. Among 158 of their fathers, 23% had scores below 6 on the Family Apgar (Table 9.14). Hence at least 1 out of 4 families had scores indicating serious family dysfunction.

Youth reporting lower scores than parents on views of family functioning should be a cause for concern, because youth do not have a voice that is heard among professionals as loudly as that of adults. There may be a punitive effect for youth who speak out and express their discontent. In addition, given that youth report their communication with parents to be lower than parents do with their youth, youth may not be understood or appreciated by their parents for expressing their dissatisfaction in the family. One benefit of a multiple family group program is that family functioning difficulties perceived by youth can be addressed without punishment or retribution. Since program activities are relational and activity-based, strengthening the family is possible and provides the potential for improved family functioning. This can be done without requiring children to express their discontent before family intervention is initiated; yet these data on family functioning scores provide a rationale to include family involvement in intervention with at-risk youth.

These data on youth and families of juvenile first-time offenders document the difficulties that youth and families have in achieving family satisfaction in relationships. The data also indicate that for parents who are expected to provide support to their children, many parents are not succeeding in helping to build competence in their children to achieve in school and establish positive peer influences.

Studies on Recidivism of Juvenile Offenders

The total cost of a violent-crime career is estimated to be well over $1 million, while the yearly cost of incarcerating a juvenile for one year is approximately $34,000 (Office of Juvenile Justice and Delinquency Prevention, 1995). The question needs to be asked often: Are there interventions existing or that can be developed to interrupt a violent-crime career that can not only better the life of an offender but also reduce the high costs of incarceration and court costs?

Custodial institutions and traditional training schools have been suspected for some time to be havens for becoming better criminals (Jensen & Rojek, 1998). Over 30 years ago, Schur proposed that: "There is now widespread recognition that the legal processing of juveniles, whatever it is called and however it is described, is in fact significantly punitive and potentially stigmatizing. This first became clear in the commitment to institutions, which function as 'schools for crime'" (1973, p. 127). Jensen and Rojek offer a direct challenge for those accountable for the case dispositions of juvenile first offenders and budget allocations: "Billions of dollars are spent annually on the juvenile justice system but a basic recidivism rate is not computed" (1998, p. 408).

One of the first studies to address recidivism in a systematic manner was conducted in the late 1980s and looked at young adult offenders who were paroled in 1978 and followed for 6 years. Their rearrest, reconviction, and reincarceration rates were computed. While these young adults were not all juvenile offenders, the FBI found that after 6 years, 68% of these offenders were rearrested, 52% were reconvicted, and nearly 50%

were reincarcerated (Jensen & Rojek, 1998). Jensen and Rojek summarize their assessment of imprisonment and alternatives by stating that "programs that attempt to alter the offender's environment, group life, or social relationships while minimizing barriers between the youth and the community show promise of reducing recidivism relative to training schools but may do no better than routine probation" (p. 425).

The work of the Oregon Social Learning Center has demonstrated success in curbing recidivism through emphasizing stronger bonds between parents and children, improving parental monitoring, and insuring appropriate reactions to approved and disapproved behavior in youth who have committed theft (Patterson & Fleischman, 1979). In a review of the literature on alternative approaches, such as diversion and restitution, mixed results were found. In fact, Scared Straight and boot-camp programs appear to be ineffective and may have iatrogenic effects (Jensen & Rojek, 1998). Jensen and Rojek contend that while recidivism has been found to be lower when juveniles agree or are ordered to pay restitution to their victims directly or through earnings derived from community service (Butts & Snyder, 1992), restitution effects such as mediation are not well known as there are sparse results on this approach.

Outcomes of the FSP on Recidivism

Since the youth and family data presented in this study pertain to juvenile first-time offenders, one marker to determine whether family intervention is effective is to examine whether the recidivism rate for FSP graduates is lower than for alternative case dispositions of juvenile first-time offenders. Whether a second juvenile offense has been committed following an intervention program is an important index of program effectiveness. It is an index that is of great interest to judges and court personnel as well as community and government leaders. Judges and court personnel are interested in serving youth effectively and reducing the caseloads of their staff. The community is interested in reducing crime to provide a positive business climate and insure public safety. Government leaders are interested in these issues as well as fiscal responsibility in controlling spending costs for government agencies and services.

In studies examining FSP effectiveness, there are two comparison groups available to examine any differences in recidivism. One is the youth who are referred to the FSP but fail to complete the program. The other comparison group is youth placed on probation, a standard and traditional case disposition for a juvenile first offense in most juvenile courts. Recidivism was recorded by tracking juvenile court records from 1993 to 2002 for those youth who were referred to the FSP between 1993 and 2001.

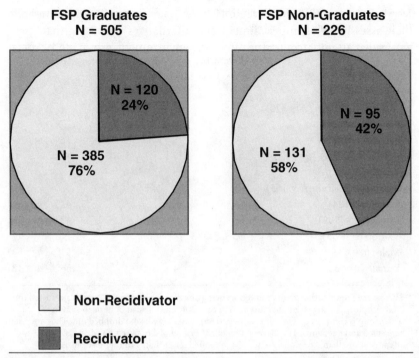

Fig. 9.1 Comparison between Family Solutions Program graduates (completers) and non-graduates on recidivism.

A master list of all referred youth was matched with court dockets at regular intervals. Hence any youth who was referred was tracked throughout this time period until the termination of his or her minor status. There were 505 FSP graduates and 226 FSP dropouts between 1993 and 2001 (Fig. 9.1).

Of the 226 youth who did not complete the FSP, 41% never attended and another 36% attended 1 to 3 sessions. Only 23% of the dropouts attended 4 to 8 sessions; hence the dropouts were exposed to very little of the FSP. In comparing the FSP graduates to nongraduates, the overall recidivism rate for FSP graduates was 24% (120/505), whereas FSP youth who dropped out of the FSP recidivated at a 42% (95/226) rate (Table 9.15). The differences between the two groups of FSP graduates and dropouts hold for African-American and white youth and for both male and female youth. Recidivism rates are higher for males and for African-Americans in the FSP graduates group than for females and white youth, and for African-American youth in the FSP dropout group. The recidivism rate for FSP dropouts was the same for both males and females.

Table 9.15 Recidivism Rates for Juvenile First Offenders: Comparisons between FSP Graduates, FSP Dropouts, and Youth Placed on Probation

	Overall	Race	Gender
FSP Graduates ($n = 505$)*	24% ($n = 120$)		
White ($n = 166$)		10% ($n = 16$)	
African-American ($n = 320$)		32% ($n = 103$)	
Male ($n = 302$)			27% ($n = 82$)
Female ($n = 203$)			16% ($n = 32$)
FSP Noncompleters ($n = 226$)**	42% ($n = 95$)		
White ($n = 52$)		31% ($n = 16$)	
African-American ($n = 165$)		46% ($n = 75$)	
Male ($n = 124$)			42% ($n = 52$)
Female ($n = 102$)			42% ($n = 43$)
Probation ($n = 95$)	55% ($n = 95$)		
Male ($n = 63$)			54% ($n = 34$)
Female ($n = 32$)			56% ($n = 18$)

* There were a few youth who did not report being either white or African-American, and so the total sample is slightly larger than the sum of the white and African-American samples.
**This group is comprised of youth who were referred to the FSP who dropped out. They attended between 0 and 8 sessions; 41% never attended, 36% attended between 1 and 3 sessions, 23% attended more than 3 sessions. Hence 77% attended fewer than 4 of the 10 sessions.

The probation comparison group of comparable juvenile first-time offenders was from a different but adjacent juvenile court. Like the FSP groups, the mean age of the probation group was between 13 and 14. The sample was largely white, whereas the FSP groups in the adjacent county are composed of a majority of African-American youth. The probation group recidivated at an even higher rate (55%) than the FSP dropouts and substantially higher than the FSP graduates. This rate is comparable to the national average for juvenile first-time offenders. The high recidivism rates found in this study for the probation group were similar for male and female juvenile first-offenders. Hence, in this case, the traditional use of probation could be viewed as much less effective, if not ineffective, in curbing recidivism rates. Overall, then, the rate of repeat offenses for juvenile first-time offenders was substantially lower for graduates of the FSP than for either the dropouts from the FSP or juvenile first-time offenders placed on probation. Furthermore, these differences held up for white and African-American youth and for both males and females.

Figure 9.2 provides a pictorial view of these results on recidivism, comparing the three intervention groups: FSP graduates, FSP dropouts, and youth placed on probation. This view indicates that youth placed on probation (and who complete probation successfully) recidivate at a much

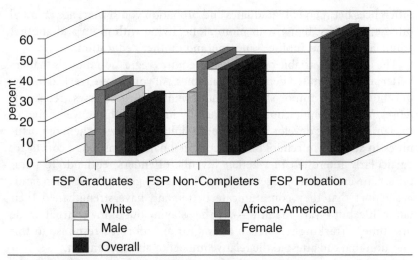

Fig. 9.2 Recidivism comparisons for three groups of juvenile first offenders.

higher rate than youth who complete the FSP. This difference holds up for both males and females. Somewhere between these two groups are the rates for male and female and African-American and white youth who are dropouts from the FSP. The vast majority of these dropouts attended fewer than 4 of the 10 sessions of the program.

Comparisons of Odds of Reoffending Among
Interventions on Recidivism

There are statistical techniques available to assess the likelihood of a reoffense given alternative explanations for each of the three interventions—FSP graduates, FSP dropouts, and youth placed on probation. When a study lacks random assignment to treatment, procedures must be implemented that deal with data artifacts. A quasi-experimental design was employed and addressed two specific data artifacts: (1) unequal effects of outside influences; and (2); a priori difference between groups (Fortune & Hutson, 1984). Preintervention variables were used as covariates to deal with possible differences across the three groups. T-tests were calculated to learn whether or not the covariates considered most correlated in the literature (age of youth, age of parent, ethnicity of youth, education of parent, number of siblings, socioeconomic status [SES], seriousness of offense, and family crime) significantly differed across groups. The variables selected as covariates were determined by these t-tests (Family Solutions graduates/dropouts; Family Solutions graduates/probation) and by the literature on recidivism of juvenile offenders. Mean differences between FSP graduates and dropouts were ethnicity and mother's income. Mean differences between FSP graduates and probation youth were: age at initial offense, ethnicity, living with mom alone, living with mom and another adult, family crime, mother's income, and mother's education.

The outcome variable of recidivism requires regression models that are better suited to limited dependent variables. All youth were tracked for the duration of their minor status in the juvenile courts to assess repeat offenses. While juvenile courts are generally interested in the well-being of the family and the development of youth skills that provide them opportunities to succeed in school and accept personal responsibility, courts are particularly interested in whether juvenile offenders reoffend. To paraphrase, juvenile court judges may say, "I'm really glad to hear when families report that they communicate better and have strengthened their family life, but I want to know—are they staying out of my court after the first time?" Tracking recidivism allows for an informed response to this question that can attest to the relative impact of an intervention.

By asking the question of whether a juvenile offender reoffends, a dichotomous variable is created in which a youth is given a value of 0 or 1. Logistic regression modeling is more effective than linear regression in modeling probability with dichotomous variables. The results can be interpreted in two ways: as odds or as probability. Odds ratios provide the likelihood of reoffense compared to another variable, similar to the odds in sporting events. Probability predicts the likelihood of a certain result occurring, given a number of characteristics.

The *odds ratios* estimating the probability of a reoffense for a youth who is referred and finishes FSP, a youth who is referred to the FSP but does not graduate, and a youth placed on probation, are reported in the *Journal of Community Psychology* (Quinn & VanDyke, 2004). In this article, results are reported indicating the effectiveness of the FSP when first-time juvenile offenders complete the program compared to youth who drop out and youth who are placed on probation. In addition, *when graduates and dropouts of the FSP are combined (an intent-to-treat analysis), results still indicate that youth even assigned to the FSP (even if they do not complete the program) has a better chance of avoiding a repeat offense compared to a youth placed on probation.* Hence, even if there are differences in youth or family characteristics between the graduates and dropouts of Family Solutions that influence recidivism outcomes, *these differences are not so substantial that they negate the effectiveness of the program compared to probation.* Simply *assigning* a juvenile first-time offender to the FSP improves the odds of a lower likelihood of reoffense compared to placing a juvenile first-time offender on probation.

The results in this chapter are reported as the odds ratio providing the likelihood of reoffense compared to another variable, in this case, another

Table 9.16 Comparison of Three Groups: Odds of a Youth Reoffending ($n = 455$)*

FSP graduates are:
9.3 **times** less likely to reoffend than **all** youth placed on probation
9.5 **times** less likely to reoffend than **males** placed on probation
10.9 **times** less likely to reoffend than **females** placed on probation
4.4 **times** less likely to reoffend than **all** youth who dropped out of FSP
2.5 **times** less likely to reoffend than **males** who dropped out of FSP
1.9 **times** less likely to reoffend than **females** who dropped out of FSP

---

* FSP graduates: $n = 267$; FSP dropouts: $n = 93$; youth placed on probation: $n = 95$; males: $n = 264$; females: $n = 191$.

intervention. As you will note in the following table (Table 9.16), FSP graduates ($n = 267$) are *9.3 times* less likely to reoffend than youth placed on probation (95), and *4.4 times* less likely to reoffend than a youth who is referred to the FSP but drops out ($n = 93$). The majority of youth who drop out do so very early and hence are not receiving a concentrated dose of intervention. Table 9.16 also reports that FSP male graduates are 2.5 times less likely to reoffend than males who drop out of FSP, and 9.5 times less likely to reoffend than male youth referred to probation. In addition, an even higher probability of not reoffending is indicated for females: female FSP graduates are 1.9 times less likely to reoffend than female dropouts and *10.9 times* less likely to reoffend than female youth placed on probation. Hence, when the juvenile court judge, juvenile court program administrator, or probation officer asks: "Is an FSP keeping more youth from coming back to court later for another offense than if they were placed on probation, the answer is, "Yes!"

To address the possibility that these dramatic differences are due to self-selection into program participation, we examined varied factors that might indicate such selectivity. In comparing the two groups of FSP referrals, completers versus dropouts, we found no significant differences on any demographic variable (age, family structure, income), family variable (family members involved with the legal system, parental attitudes, family functioning self-report, parent–adolescent communication), or social patterns (level of community activities, church attendance, or education—school grades in math and English, school absences and suspensions, school activities).

The importance of tracking recidivism is well documented in this project. Reporting recidivism rates has helped legitimize the program with juvenile court judges, youth service agency administrators, and funding sources. Not to be overlooked, many of the public have a heightened sensitivity to youth crime because they have been victimized or know someone who has been from burglary, car theft, assault, and the like. Hence the public is committed to controlling crime rates, which can be observed in many ways: supporting prison construction funding, lobbying for new laws treating juvenile offenders as adults, and purchasing their own security equipment such as alarm systems and gates. If funding for intervention to address juvenile crime is provided, the sources of funding want to know whether their commitment is a good investment in reducing crime and experiences of victimization.

At the same time, it is important to see recidivism as only one criterion for success. For one, recidivism has a wide variety of meanings, such as police contacts, arrests, convictions, parole violation, and reimprisonment (Farrington, Ohlin, & Wilson, 1986). In addition, official records reflect behavior of agencies as well as offenders. Changes in police patrolling patterns, changeover in the police forces, or new developments in the community such as new laws (such as violations for loitering or curfew), or the implementation of educational programs in the schools that make a difference—all can affect rearrest rates. And rearrests do not necessarily indicate ineffective treatment. Treatment might have caused reduction in the frequency or seriousness of offending or the length of a criminal career. For example, as we presented from our own data, juvenile offenders who complete the FSP who repeat offend only on average less than once, whereas juveniles who do not complete the program average more than two repeat offenses.

But the FSP should not be evaluated only by statistics. Parents can benefit from the program as well as youth in ways other than the youth not committing a reoffense. Therefore the families themselves have been asked about their experience in the FSP.

Feedback from Families

One of the most uplifting experiences in the program is the time devoted at graduation to family testimonials. This time is designated to offer families an opportunity to share their experiences of the program. Many families stand up to express their appreciation for the program and how it has made a difference to them. When the leader asks families at graduation to share what the experience in the FSP has meant to them, the initial response from the group can be reticence. They look around to see who is going to go first. But once the first person begins, usually a parent, "the door opens" and every group member—parents and youth—volunteers to make a statement. Some stand up, occasionally one will go to the front of the room to see everyone and be seen while they make their statement.

One parent remarked, "Before I came, I didn't think that I could afford the time to come to the program, now I realize I cannot afford *not* to come to the program." Several families have asked if they can go through the program a second time. And these are some of the same parents who attended the very first night of the program and made comments like, "Why do I have to be here? It's my kid that messed up, not me." Or they were embarrassed about having others in the community see them at the program. They say, "It sure was nice to feel that I wasn't the only one who had a child that did something wrong. I learned so much from the other parents and what they do to make things better." One parent said:

> You know, when I was asked in the grocery store by someone who knew I was having trouble with my daughter how things were going, I "bragged on" my son. I said I had signed up for a parenting class and everything is working out. When that person asked me how she could do that, I realized I was caught—I had to claim ignorance by saying I don't know if they are taking any more parents, because I didn't want that person to know the program was actually for youth who had been in the juvenile court.

Parents have repeatedly expressed their appreciation for the experience that has culminated in their graduation. They often acknowledge the new realization that they can have much more influence in their families in a positive manner than they imagined. They express new hope and a newly created vision. One said, "I am so sad that this program is over because it has taught me so much. How can we continue to meet?" A father, speaking for other parents, stated, "This is a good example of how important we are to one another. We can't run and hide and think we can work out everything ourselves. We must stick together." Other parents called out "that's right," and "we really do." His use of the word "we" no doubt had two meanings. He was talking about the group of families in front of him present at graduation. Yet he was referring also to humanity—that people are social creatures and need to reach out and share experiences to help each other.

The following comments were said at graduation by the group members who have been featured in the stories in this book:

> One mother, Jackie, told a story during one session of a situation that she confronted at home while participating in the FSP. She described the situation in which her son, David, and friends had "trashed" the house. This included putting a hole through the living room wall. Jackie talked in the group about this and described her response—that David was grounded for a month. Ed, the group leader, asked, "just to be sure, how old is your son?" Ed knew how old David was, but wanted this fact to be known to the group to emphasize a point he wanted to make. Jackie stated that David was 15. Ed asked, "Is it possible that a boy of this age would be capable of repairing the wall that he and his friends damaged? Could he get piece of Sheetrock or patch it if possible?" Jackie said that the hole was too big to patch, but that she thought he was capable of getting the Sheetrock (which he would pay for) and recruiting someone who had the skill of installing it, and for them to repair the wall. Jackie said she had not thought about this, but that, yes, he

was capable. Jackie recounted this story at graduation night and stated, "You know, you all made me realize that I had been treating David like he was 10. It was eye-opening to think about how I had been interacting with him like he was a child, rather than a young man becoming an adult. The question from Ed about whether David could repair the damage he had done made a big impact on me and it changed my way of relating to my son."

The following comments were made at graduation by some of Jackie's comembers of the group:

Patti: "I really enjoyed it and I met a lot of nice people I made friends with who can help me."

Debra: "I enjoyed the group and although I don't want to come back under these circumstances, I believe it has changed Sam's life. Ed and the facilitators for the group would talk to him and he would think about what they would say, I could tell on the ride home, and he really listened."

Sam: "I will think the next time before I get into a fight. Mom, I hope some day I can do for you like you have done for me."

Jackie: "This is the most wonderful thing I have participated in. The first night in this program I asked, 'God, why am I here?' And he has answered me. I have learned many things. God has helped me listen, not to be so quick to judge, and to be more loving."

David: "I'll miss Brittany's big mouth!" (laughter from the group). "Really, I know now why I need to go to school. I don't want to make what a high school dropout makes."

Joan: "I liked the discussions we had after the activities, and I learned to listen to my kids and respect them—not be so hard on them."

Brandon: "I liked all of the activities, especially since my dad (Mark) came to some of them. The program made me remember to think before I do stuff."

Mark: "My son got a second chance and we met great people too."

Denise: "It helped teach us about teamwork and working together with the people working with us."

Robert: "It's fun to be in because there are a lot of fun games to play and fun activities."

Virginia: "This program has changed the way my household works. Now we can talk to each other about anything. I will miss everybody here."

Brittany: "It made me realize that my mother's views mainly aren't to punish me but to tell me right from wrong in life. I really appreciate my mother coming to this class with me."

Jeff: "I enjoyed meeting the other families and listening to what they had to say. It was nice to know we weren't the only family with problems."

At the second-to-last session of the program, a homework assignment is given by the group leader to the youth. The assignment is to prepare at least a half-page description of what the FSP meant to them. The youth are asked to be prepared to stand in front of the group and read their prepared written statement: The statements from Brittany, Robert, Sam, Brandon, David, and Shay delineated above were embedded in their graduation statements.

It is often difficult for youth (and sometimes parents) to leave graduation and return home. There is a sense of loss of group cohesion that many are not quite willing to release. Many family members stay to visit with each other and with group leaders and facilitators until they can begin to accept the termination. Of course, the group leaders make clear their availability in the future to anyone who needs help or referral to other resources. Just the offer to call and check in—let a leader or facilitator know how life is going—is relief to certain family members.

CHAPTER 10

Collaboration between the Family Solutions Program and Juvenile Courts, Youth Service Agencies, and Schools

Man cannot discover new oceans unless he has the courage to lose sight of the shore.
—André Gide.

Ernie Banks, the Chicago Cubs Hall of Famer (and my baseball hero growing up), always remembers the way his father worked and sacrificed to give him the chance to play baseball. Every day his father left the house before dawn and got home after dark. He worked so many hours that he hardly ever saw sunlight. Ernie was known during his playing days as both a graceful shortstop and a home-run hitter. He was known for his great attitude, and when he arrived at the baseball park, he would look to the sky and say, "It's a beautiful day; let's play two!" When Ernie signed his first contract with the Cubs, he sent a three-word telegram to his dad: "We did it!"

The Process of Institutional Change

Juvenile justice courts, schools, youth service agencies, and faith-based organizations all share a commitment to promoting child and youth well-being. Of particular importance is utilizing resources expeditiously and possessing confidence that programs implemented have a reasonable chance to benefit children. In over 10 years the Family Solutions Program (FSP) has grown from being an "alternative" case disposition to "try with some youth," to a mainstream intervention used for the vast majority of juvenile first offenders in same communities in Georgia. Surrounding counties covering a large geographic area of the state of Georgia have incorporated the program, and numerous youth services agencies, schools, and juvenile courts from around the state and nation have been trained to implement the FSP in their communities. The FSP curriculum manual has been developed to facilitate this training and provide guidance to group leaders to deliver the program. An additional benefit of the FSP manual is in standardizing the program so that it is implemented consistently by all group leaders and in different communities.

While an element of standardization is highly beneficial, a community must have its own local leadership and purpose to internalize a new program. This chapter describes our observations about the process of adoption of a new program by an institution. The purpose of describing this process of programmatic change is to provide other communities with the knowledge of this experience to facilitate the development of a multiple family group model in their own human services delivery systems.

There is a substantial body of evidence, some of which has been compiled in this text, that context factors, such as family, school, and community influences, play a role in youth at-risk behavior, truancy, behavioral problems, and delinquency. Yet intervention modalities which recognized these influences and incorporate their salience into intervention have not kept pace. Many interventions fall short of adequately developing the means by which youth, family, and community problems can be resolved or reduced. Instead, institutional forces and traditional views of youth as individuals who comprise the entity of pathology or incompetency still maintain a stronghold in human services delivery. Schools, juvenile courts, and counseling services remain cultures that stigmatize youth with labels and conveniently ignore the social influences of the family and community.

Some efforts have been made to develop intervention programs with family involvement. For example, a multisystemic approach has been empirically demonstrated to curb recidivism rates for serious and chronic offenders significantly (Henggeler, Melton, & Smith, 1992). Treating the family system of at-risk youth, including adolescent drug users, has been shown to be effective (McDonald & Frey, 1999; Liddle, 1996, 1999; Joanning, Quinn, Thomas, & Mullen, 1992). Family approaches to treating conduct disorders of adolescents show promise (Dishion & Kavanagh, 2003; Chamberlain & Rosicky, 1995). In addition, various states have developed model demonstration programs that show promise (see the Office of Juvenile Justice and Delinquency Prevention Blueprints series 2003, Book Three). Some successful programs have been replicated, and a few evaluated, in other communities. These interventions may have an impact on larger institutions such as juvenile justice agencies and drug treatment centers for adolescents.

Currently intervention sites such as juvenile justice, youth service agencies, and schools often underutilize the family. Even less likely is the deployment of multiple family groups, such as the one described in this volume, to serve at-risk youth.

The question might be: Why are intervention models using the family not considered or consistently implemented for meeting the needs of youth? One is the problem of tradition ("it's the way we've always done it") that allows program administrators and interventionists to stay in their comfort zone. Another reason is the theoretical biases of agencies and professionals who privilege certain ideas about the individual (e.g., the family is toxic; privacy of the individual; psychiatric diagnoses).

A somewhat neglected dynamic operating in the culture of human services delivery that results in program limitations and a lack of data on program effectiveness is the perception held by community leaders, professionals, and even the public that each community is unique and therefore not amenable to replication of programs. A logical question that has been neglected and yet important to answer is: "What is the process of institutional change (e.g., of juvenile courts) that can allow for an innovative program to emerge?" And if there are identifiable facets (phases, events) that foster institutional change, could they be organized to reveal patterns that would be translatable (generalizable) to other institutional entities (juvenile courts in other communities)? The hypothesis here is that instead of the old adage in human services delivery—let's not reinvent the wheel—the opposite idea may be more true—the wheel must be reinvented so that those traveling can invest something of themselves in the journey. In other words, institutional change may require a process inclusive of system involvement in which the system reinvents itself (Smale, 1995).

The project using a multiple family group intervention model described in this text has been in operation for several years (initiated in 1992). Initially the program was given birth due to a grant solicited by the author and colleagues. The acceptance level of the program was low. While some juvenile court personnel were eager for more effective programs and services, others were skeptical. Those embedded in the institution in which the program would operate, that being the juvenile court, had a desire to reach youth, but were hesitant to support an unproven program.

The FSP has moved from being an "alternative" experimental service to youth and families to being a mainstream juvenile court program with recognition by juvenile court judges, probation officers, and families. We have actually received requests from families themselves to the juvenile court or an FSP staff member to be referred to the FSP, a self-referral phenomenon that substantiates the credibility the program has gained in the community. The juvenile court in Georgia has decided to assign virtually all juvenile first offenders to the FSP. In addition, the Georgia Council of Juvenile Court Judges has allotted funds for its continuation, as well as funds used for services in which great autonomy exists by judges to determine their use. The FSP hovers at the top of the list of priorities. Infrastructure resources are also available, such as space, clerical help, and cooperation by staff. These elements substantiate the central value of the FSP as a vital part of the juvenile court mission as a preventive and early-intervention program. Inquiries from all parts of the nation are made about adopting the program. As such, it is timely to ask the following questions:

1. What processes have occurred since the inception of the program that have led to the evolution of the FSP, initially an alternative program, to its current status as a legitimate and central program of the juvenile court and its everyday functioning?
2. What is the process of program implementation that can allow for an innovative program to emerge?
3. Are there identifiable facets (phases, events) that foster institutional inclusion and growth of a program as opposed to the program languishing or terminating?

If these questions could be answered, they could reveal patterns that might be translatable (generalizable) to other institutional entities, such as juvenile courts and children's services in other communities. The intent of this chapter is to provide the reader with insight and a methodology for pursuing innovative programmatic changes within a traditional human services delivery setting. Our observations of this process of creating and developing the FSP have led us to formulate several notions about how program emergence and mainstreaming occur.

Growth vs. Stagnation/Termination

We have been guided in over a decade of program development by a set of fundamentals regarding successful implementation. We find these program features to be essential.

1. Initiators of a new program or institutional practice must cultivate and tend to the collegial relationships that are necessary between those who represent the "new" intervention program and those who represent the institution. Communication difficulties exist when telephone conversations and personal exchanges dissipate. We have found that regular telephone conversations with the judges and probation officers help clarify the FSP and the shared expectations that exist regarding the operation

of the program. These conversations include issues pertaining to the budget, family attendance, referral process, and programmatic details such as when the next cycle of the FSP should begin. Certain families may present special difficulties that require careful professional planning. These difficulties can include transportation problems in getting to the sessions, an unexpected loss or health problem in the family, a school suspension, or a criminal offense. If the offense occurs during the FSP, this second offense is not considered as recidivism in our outcome data, since the program was not completed at the time.

It is important for commitments made by personnel representing either the program or the institution to be met. For instance, there were initial difficulties when the FSP began with how to handle cases in which families did not attend the program. Whose responsibility was it to follow up with the absentee families? Was it the court's responsibility, since it has the legal leverage to invoke and maintain obligations to the court, or was it the FSP leader's responsibility, since the cases were assigned to the program?

This ambiguity in case management among the referral sources and FSP representatives can be handled in different ways. Court personnel and FSP leaders needed to devise a plan to address this scenario. The plan that was devised for the FSP included the following: (1) a list of families both present and absent for each session was faxed to the court by the FSP leaders, so that court workers were kept abreast of a family's status; (2) the FSP group leader would telephone a family that was absent sometime prior to the next session to remind the family of its obligation and the rule that only one absence is acceptable to qualify for graduation; (3) a family that was absent more than once was formally referred back to the juvenile court for case review; and (4) the court worker would meet with any family which had been absent more than once to implement another obligation (such as a formal and lengthier probation) or a referral back to the FSP for the next cycle of the program, if acceptable to the FSP coordinator.

The success of this plan hinged on each professional adhering to the plan and maintaining communication on issues pertaining to the status of each family case. FSP leaders must maintain records of attendance and provide weekly attendance reports to the court; and court workers must check these reports and follow up with any families that have lost their eligibility to complete the program. Adherence to the attendance monitoring protocol is vital so that FSP leaders can avoid threatened absences of other families who might assume that missed sessions do not result in any consequence. The FSP wanted to guard against the consequence that if vigilance in maintaining attendance and court follow-up was not exercised, families over time would spread the word: "Oh, you don't have to go to that program they told you about—nothing will happen if you don't go." In addition, the court can confidently assume that families referred to the program are receiving treatment unless it is informed of absences. In this way, the missions of the court and the FSP are preserved and responsibilities for case management are clear.

When the mission of an entity such as a court or an intervention program is being threatened, major problems within and between entities emerge. The court has a legal and professional obligation to adhere to legal sanctions and community expectations. The FSP has an obligation to preserve its integrity, such as the necessary inclusion of parents and the expectation that families will be present to help each other. When a plan such as the one delineated above is not implemented as agreed upon, then the mission is threatened. When this happens, professionals involved lose confidence in the collaboration and "pull out" of the program. Sometimes this breaking up is formal and decisive. Funds to support the program are cut off or contacts between the collaborators end or fade out. Yet on many occasions the collaboration weakens slowly as various components break apart. A professional may refer youth and families less and less often to the program, attendance lists are not routinely established and disseminated, families requiring attention are contacted less often, and group cohesion either never becomes realized or dissipates gradually.

2. Goal congruence must be established and maintained. The perceived reason(s) for the establishment and existence of a multiple family group program must be accepted and understood. In the case of a program for juvenile first offenders, there must be agreement that early intervention can potentially prevent further penetration in the court by a youth. And the value of parental involvement must be seen as crucial to this end. Early on in the evolution of the FSP, a court worker might have been tempted to urge the FSP leaders to accept a youth into the program without a parent who either refused to attend or was employed or had other commitments in conflict with the time of the program. While a youth could benefit from the program, the FSP leaders were concerned that a situation in which youth who could attend the FSP without their parents would encourage other families to send their youth alone, violating the theoretical underpinnings and mission of the FSP. Understandably, the court workers in these cases would view youth attendance as potentially helpful to them. In some cases, such referrals served the purpose of successfully handling a case disposition that might require minimal further involvement of the court and thereby reduce the caseload of a court worker. FSP leaders must be resolute in requiring parental attendance and clarify the goal of the FSP with court personnel. If a parent does not attend, the family does not

receive credit, and the likelihood of completing the program successfully is jeopardized. Hence the FSP representatives must be resolute in their commitment to family involvement.

Conversely, there are times when the FSP must acknowledge the goals of the court in its consideration of its operation. For instance, there might be regulations in a given state outlining the parameters of case disposition, such as the length of time a youth can be obligated to a court action such as a referral to the FSP. For instance, in the state of Georgia the maximum time that a youth can be obligated to an intervention is 90 days. This does not mean there are no avenues for extending youth commitments; however, the clerical work to do so becomes overwhelming. Therefore the FSP leaders have designed a program of 10 weekly sessions, even though there are some families who may benefit from extended intervention. And there are other families who actually desire to extend the program after they discover its value to them.

Another adjustment made by the FSP to accommodate the juvenile court was the selection of the site for the family meeting following a referral by the court. The FSP risk assessment was originally conducted at a site other than the juvenile court, with the assumption that this procedure would convey to the families that the FSP was not an arm of the juvenile court and was not interested in taking punitive action. However, about half of the families referred to the FSP after their court adjudication hearing did not show for their risk assessment scheduled at a later date at a site different from the court. As a result, these families were not adequately informed of the FSP and the details of their responsibility (such as attendance). Inefficiency increased as FSP staff attempted to make a second appointment with families. Even then, some families did not present themselves at these times. Therefore the FSP reviewed its operation and altered its referral procedures. Instead of the FSP referral intake and risk assessment being located at an alternate site, the FSP representative was present in the court during the family's initial meeting for the adjudication hearing. The court worker or judge informed the FSP representative of the possible referral to the FSP being planned so that he or she could be present. The risk assessment was then conducted at the same time as the hearing, and a linkage was made for the families to the FSP.

Adjustments were made by the collaborators to make the referral process more convenient and the family's attendance in the FSP more likely. Sometimes these meetings occur in the late afternoon or early evening for the convenience of the family, taking into account school commitments of the youth and job responsibilities of the parents. While this can present a hardship to professional staff, the likelihood of a smooth referral process that culminates in a family's attendance is a priority.

The perceived reason for the existence of a multiple family group model must be clearly and regularly stated. In our experience, bulletins or newsletters are written, published, and disseminated to community leaders, program staff, and referral sources. These newsletters feature current activities of the program and typically highlight a feature of the program. These features could include:

- the valuable contributions that parents are making to the program;
- illustrations of recent situations that have contributed to positive change (as long as they do not reveal a family's identity) such as transactions of group process;
- new components or content in the program;
- summaries of evaluation data such as parent and youth testimonials (anonymously);
- recidivism data indicating patterns of reoffenses or reactions to particular FSP activities such as the family auction, the money and education story, or conflict-resolution role-plays.

3. The current climate of managed care, health care crisis and reform, economic downturns, and emphasis on benchmarks in program development has fostered greater need for accountability. Budget directors and program administrators as well as local and state civic leaders and politicians are increasingly asking whether programs receiving funding can document results that justify support. A multiple family group program as described in this book is designed to address at-risk youth who present certain problematic behaviors that cause concern to parents, schools, courts, and the larger community, such as juvenile crime, truancy, or behavior problems. Program administrators and budget officers will ask: Is the program reducing these behaviors?

This question was formulated at the initial stage of program development for the FSP. It was clear that judges, court workers, school social workers, and the community would be asking: Does the FSP reduce repeat offenses by youth? Therefore criteria for evaluation were discussed and established. This was a challenge, because recidivism data can produce results that lead to conclusions that can be due to a host of variables. Some of these are: (1) the level of efficiency in data collection; (2) potential changes in law enforcement (increase or decrease in personnel or rearrangement of priorities); and (3) changes in community laws (such as curfew violations). Record-keeping of juvenile court cases must be understood. A computer system or a careful organization of documents must exist to develop and maintain reliable data. For instance, in the FSP, a computer program was developed to track all juvenile first offenders. A master list of offenders is maintained. Recent offender cases from court dockets are then matched against this master list to identify repeat offenders. These data are then used to provide some comparisons in recidivism rates between program completers and noncompleters. Risk assessment data are used to assess whether there are differences between these groups that could explain recidivism outcome other than the experience of the FSP. That is, if the groups differed on school problems, percentage of single-parent homes, family crime, income, or seriousness of offense, then these differences could explain differences in recidivism between the program completers and noncompleters. In addition, risk assessment data provide the FSP coordinator with information that helps formulate a recruitment plan to secure a family's participation and expand the support system to adults who live outside the home of the youth but have regular contact. Risk assessments also provide information to the group leader to ascertain the most appropriate session topics based on relevance and need.

Without evaluation, speculation grows about the utility of a program. A program becomes even more vulnerable if a major criticism is raised about the program, particularly if it is from someone in a strategic professional position, such as a judge, respected community leader, or budget officer. If a youth who completes intervention, such as a multiple family group program, comes to the attention of the community due to subsequent behavior problems, such as a major crime, a school incident, or the emergence of local knowledge about a youth's conduct, the program can be quickly circumspect. As a result, confidence wanes in the program.

Efforts to maintain the program may also dissipate, leaving the program more vulnerable. Therefore gathering data on program effectiveness not only helps establish the credibility of a multiple family group intervention program, but data are particularly crucial to offset theoretical biases or negative opinions by influential community leaders or professionals about the program that can periodically surface. For instance, an FSP cycle offered to truant students should have built-in data collection plans to gather school attendance and suspensions. Procedures for evaluation of the multiple family group program must be built into the program from its inception and be adopted and valued. Reports of outcomes must be in the language of the institutional leaders who have responsibility for that constituency. School personnel, such as principals and school social workers, need data on truancy improvements and behavior changes of students. They are responsible for insuring school attendance and fostering academic growth that produces the greatest chance for upward movement in test scores or individual improvement in school grades. The partnership, those collaborators that form to serve youth and families, then must ask itself how the initiative will be evaluated so as to be deemed valuable and deserving of continuation by the collaborators.

Using Evaluation and Collaboration to Build the Family Solutions Program

Continual openness to modification of a program is crucial to its long-term survival. The central theme of a multiple family group intervention program has remained intact. The focus on youth and family change in the service of productive behavior and healthy development has not diminished. The goal of the FSP is the enhancement of youth well-being and the participation of the family to influence youth and parents in a more productive manner. In fact, one of the reasons—maybe the key reason—that a family program sustains itself is due to the mutual agreement among agencies and their varied personnel that the central purpose of a program is the focus on family change. All decisions among collaborators, whether they be courts, schools, or youth service agencies, in tandem with the FSP, are made as a consequence of the shared view that youth and families will be better served as a result.

An ongoing recursive process among key "point people" in the FSP has contributed to its success. There must be an ongoing flow of communication among agency personnel (e.g., juvenile court, youth services agency), school program leaders, including administrative representatives, FSP group leaders and facilitators, and families. The potential gain is the opportunity for all collaborators to appreciate the value of the challenges of family intervention, the politics within the work environment, and staffing limitations of all concerned. As a result of this recursive process, modifications have occurred that have strengthened the program. Four examples are offered that reflect the recursive process among personnel and institutional structures.

1. In the early phase of the FSP, the referral process felt cumbersome and often resulted in an unacceptably high rate of absentee families. These were families that did not attend the scheduled appointment with the FSP representative after referral from the court. The families were asked to come to a site away from the juvenile court for a risk-assessment screening and information on the details of the FSP. It was the belief of the FSP leaders that scheduling such a meeting in a site separate from the court would convey to the families that the FSP was not a punitive program and that attitudes held by the court were necessarily those held by the FSP. Moreover,

the FSP might be seen as a benevolent program interested in the well-being of the family.

However, over 50% of the families did not attend this scheduled appointment, using explanations such as "I forgot about it"; "I didn't have transportation"; and "I wasn't sure of the location." Other reasons can be assumed but not stated, such as the hope that their case would be overlooked in time and that the court would reconsider its decision and require only the youth and not the parents to meet the obligation of the court. Sometimes a second risk-assessment meeting was scheduled if a family missed the first. However, this too often led to a no-show result.

A reconsideration was undertaken in which this problematic circumstance was examined. A decision was reached with the court that the risk assessment would occur in the juvenile court and that the court would notify the FSP representative administering the risk assessment when the family's adjudication hearing was scheduled. In this way, the probability of completing the risk assessment increased as families were more likely to attend their hearing in the court than to attend a risk assessment at another, sometimes unfamiliar location. The court personnel notified the FSP representative of a scheduled hearing of a youth and family who met the criteria for referral to the FSP. The family was then informed at the court that a referral to the FSP was recommended. During that time, the FSP representative established a protocol in which the risk assessment would be administered and the details of the FSP would be explained. The FSP representative could clarify any misunderstandings, emphasize the necessity of parent involvement, inform the family of the date, time, and location of the first session, and distribute a brochure describing the FSP. The FSP representative could also share successes of families who participated in the FSP in order to increase the family's positive expectations and interest. The FSP video in which youth and parents discuss their successful experiences in the FSP could be presented. Since this change of location for the risk assessment, the show rate for families referred to the FSP for risk-assessment screening has substantially increased.

2. We also found about a 25% rate of absences for the first FSP session, with another 20% dropping out after attending at least one session. Several concerns surfaced as a result of this no-show rate. The FSP representative had to devote more time to engaging the family via telephone calls, letters, and further explanation of the family's responsibility. If some families did not attend, the planned size of the group of about six families shrunk, which resulted in diminished group process. When a small group of families attends, fewer strengths are represented in the group, the range of ideas and problem-solving solutions narrows, and interest is diminished because the family learning curve flattens out.

In turn, group morale was threatened as participants thought, "If family x and family y don't have to come, why should family z and our family have to come?" When attendance lists reporting on family involvement were sent promptly to the court, the court did not initially follow up by contacting the families or reviewing the case to determine an alternative obligation such as a lengthier probation.

The FSP was faced at this time with a threat to its integrity. If referred families who did not attend spread the word in their neighborhoods that sidestepping the program was easy, other families would consider doing the same thing. The anticipated result was continued declining attendance and an increase in the workload of the FSP representative in charge of referrals and participation.

At this juncture, discussions occurred between the FSP leadership and the juvenile court in which the FSP concerns were registered. An explanation was provided to the court pertaining to concerns by the FSP about families not showing up and then not facing consequences for their refusal. Subsequently, the court willingly became more involved in checking attendance rates at the FSP. This was due to the first impression by the court that the FSP was useful to families. The court staff developed a plan to contact families that did not attend. These families were reminded of their obligation, and consequences for their failure to complete the program were delineated again. And the court was more determined to review cases of families that did not participate. They levied an alternative obligation or referral back to the FSP for the next cycle.

Court staff point out to families that the consequence of not attending the program results in: (1) a supervision fee being assessed; (2) probation; (3) weekly visits to the court; and (4) a longer time before court obligations are complete, which increases the chances of any future juvenile offense resulting in more serious consequences. Our experience has resulted in a greater appreciation for the court's demands. We have concluded that increasing physical accessibility between court personnel and FSP leadership, primarily increasing the time the FSP representative spends at the court, closes loopholes that allow families to drop out without consequence.

3. As the FSP evolved, it became evident that families referred to the program shifted in characteristics in ways that narrowed the potential value of the FSP. Court referrals were made by caseworkers in which the basis for referral varied from person to person. These referrals were done from the perspective of the best interest of the youth. Yet different reasons might be given for these referrals. One caseworker might refer a youth based on the nature of the crime (such as shoplifting or unruly behavior), another caseworker might refer based on the perception of whether the

parent would come, and a third might refer based on whether the next cycle of the FSP was about to begin. The program began to suffer from an identity problem in which its mission was in conflict with court expectations. For a time the program became a program "for shoplifters," at another time it became a program for "more motivated parents," and for a time it became a program for "unruly" children who needed more parental supervision.

Again, discussions among court personnel and FSP leaders occurred to resolve the issue, since the FSP had an original goal of including families regardless of offense (except those that a judge ruled met criteria for youth to be tried as adults), initial parental motivation, time since offense, or parent neglect. The result was a clarification of the FSP mission and a burgeoning of attendance by families with a variety of difficulties. In addition, the FSP became more responsive to the court's desire to have a program operating at all times. The FSP developed more family programs that overlapped, so that a new program could begin whenever a sufficient number of families were referred rather than when one FSP had ended.

4. Evaluation has been used to modify the content of the FSP by utilizing family feedback. The families are requested to share their expectations for the FSP—what issues will be addressed and what they hope to accomplish. The procedure for conducting this evaluation involves several parts. First, time is allotted for an open discussion during the first session. Second, in Session 2, after the proposed contents of the program have been distributed to the families and examined after Session 1, the group leader asks for feedback. Third, at the close of Session 5 and prior to the week of Session 6, topics are outlined by the group leader from a range of choices in the curriculum manual. The families reach consensus on the appropriate topics for Session 6, and the group leader plans for Session 6 accordingly.

The important aspect to modification based on evaluation is for the FSP leadership to be open to input from parents and to value their opinions and requests. One example is the previously described suggestion that parents made to the FSP group leader about shoplifting and arranging for the youth to seek retribution and closure with the store owners. Parents and youth can resolve matters more successfully when families believe there is value in the effort and activity. The leadership places equal importance on the recommendations of the families regarding content of the program. At the same time the FSP is a culmination of successful family experiences rated highly across cycles of the multiple family group model. The FSP manual is based on parent and youth feedback about each session in each group cycle of the program. However, the leaders must always be aware that particular characteristics, needs, and desires of the families should determine FSP content.

The collaborators, such as agencies providing referrals and treatment centers or units providing intervention, must share a set of common goals. In the case of juvenile offenders, the goals might be enhanced well-being of youth and families coupled with a decrease in juvenile offenses; for truant students, the goals would be regular attendance with punctuality and personal responsibility. There must be a sense that decision-making among collaborators is conducted within the parameters that any decisions are in the service of reaching these goals.

It is also important for each part of the professional network to have a respect for the unique goals of each other part. For instance, the court must respect the importance in emphasizing families as advocated by the leaders of the multiple family group leaders. And the intervention staff must respect the expectation of the referral source that the at-risk behavior of the youth will decrease or be absolved. For instance, the court has a desire for youth to increase their functional behavior and avoid reoffenses; a school has a desire for children to demonstrate daily school attendance and punctuality.

Several developments in the FSP have occurred as a result of its evolution as a viable program within the juvenile court system and schools. We attribute these developments to the cultivation of two forces: (1) reliable and trusting workable relationships within and across professional systems; and (2) the demonstrated effectiveness of the program as measured by outcomes such as recidivism and family reports of their positive experiences.

An Early Victory

Once initiated, the impetus for a successful collaboration is often dependent on a successful short-term outcome. This has been termed an "early victory" (Fitzgerald & Abrams, 1998). Progress in collaboration early on provides sustaining energy and commitment by staff who are strategically located in the partnership organization. In addition, early success breeds confidence in the plan, thereby providing motivation for continued involvement and a shared vision.

The FSP's early victory came in the form of family testimonials, which are routinely shared at graduation night. At graduation night, a potluck supper is held in which each family brings food. An inspirational speaker is invited and cards (What We Like About You) and certificates of completion are presented. The juvenile court judge is invited to graduation and says a few words of congratulations. The judge also provides some words of inspiration—a story of someone who has overcome great adversity or a lesson with a moral. Then the family testimonials usually begin, with the parents expressing their gratitude to the leaders for their compassion, patience, and understanding. Parents also describe how the program has specifically benefited them. For example, a parent may comment on his or her own realization that he or she needs to be more involved in their child's life. Another may admit to possessing a sense of futility about the family before the FSP, whereas now a heartfelt enthusiasm and concern is present; hope for the future has been rekindled. Another parent may admit to contributing to some of the family's problems and apologize for behavior during the first night that was hostile and interfered with building group support. Finally, one parent shared that she had made some new friends and that the accomplishment had made her feel more worthy.

A youth stands and thanks his mother for coming to the program with him. Another says that he has learned to "think before I act," and a third youth says she appreciated the stories told by some parents about how some of their friends when they were young led them "down the wrong path." As a result, she realizes that she needs to choose her friends more carefully.

As the judge hears these remarks, he constructs the idea that the FSP has been a valuable endeavor for many families. Their personal stories contribute to his appreciation for the program, which conforms to his mission of providing help to families that potentially alters a youth's developmental trajectory. Hearing individuals and families express heartfelt gratitude and depict the changes that have occurred in their lives incrementally builds value even more. The judge's presence to hear these family testimonials became the "early victory" for the FSP necessary to build the impetus for growth. As he noticed that these families were slow to depart after the final session, as parents talked to other parents and youth talked to the program leaders, he realized that these families had found affirmation and hope.

References

Achenbach, T. M., Edelbrock, C. S., Lynam, D., Moffitt, T., & Stouthamer-Loeber, M. (1993). Explaining the relation between IQ and delinquency: Class, race, test motivation, school failure, or self control? *Journal of Abnormal Psychology, 102,* 187–196.

Adams, C. D., Hillman, N., & Gaydos, G. R. (1994). Behavioral difficulties in toddlers: Impact of sociocultural and biological risk factors. *Journal of Clinical Child Psychology, 23,* 373–381.

Alexander, J. F., Barton, C., Schiavo, R. S., & Parsons, B. V. (1976). Systems-behavioral intervention with families of delinquents: Therapist characteristics, family behavior, and outcome. *Journal of Consulting and Clinical Psychology, 44,* 656–664.

Alexander, J. F., Pugh, C., Parsons, B. V., & Sexton, T. L. (2000). Functional family therapy. In D. S. Elliott (Ed.), *Blueprints for violence prevention* (Book 3). Boulder, CO: Center for the Study and Prevention of Violence, Institute of Behavioral Science, University of Colorado.

Ansbacher, H. L., & Ansbacher, R. (1956). *The individual psychology of Alfred Adler.* New York: Harper & Row.

Arcus, M. (1987). A framework for life-span family life education. *Family Relations, 36,* 5–10.

Arcus, M. (1992). Family life education: Toward the 21st century. *Family Relations, 44*(4), 390–394.

Atlanta Journal-Constitution (1999, June 13). Can we stop the violence? Only if we learn which programs work, and fast, experts say.

Barnes, G. M., & Farrell, M. P. (1992). Parental support and control as predictors of adolescent drinking, delinquency, and related problem behaviors. *Journal of Marriage and the Family, 54,* 763–776.

Barnes, H. L., & Olson, D. H. (1982). Parent–adolescent communication scale. In D. H. Olson, H. I. McCubbin, H. L. Barnes, A. Larsen, M. J. Muxen, & M. Wilson. *Family inventories: Inventories used in a national survey of families across the family life cycle* (pp. 33–48). St. Paul: Family Social Science, University of Minnesota.

Barnes, H. L., & Olson, D. H. (1985). Parent–adolescent communication and the circumplex model. *Child Development, 56,* 438–447.

Bateson, G. (1972). *Steps to an ecology of mind.* New York: Ballantine Books.

Becvar, R. J., Canfield, B. S., & Becvar, D. S. (1997). *Groupwork and social constructionist perspectives.* Denver, CO: Love Publishing Co.

Bion, R. W. (1961). *Experience in groups.* New York: Basic Books.

Bits and Pieces (2003, September) (p. 5). Chicago, IL: Lawrence Ragan Communications.

Bor, W., Najman, J. M., Anderson, J., O'Callaghan, M., Williams, G. M., & Behrens, B. C. (1997). The relationship between low family income and psychological disturbance in young children:

An Australian longitudinal study. *Australian and New Zealand Journal of Psychiatry, 31*(5), 664–675.

Bowen, M. (1965). Family psychotherapy with schizophrenia in the hospital and in private practice. In I. Boszormenyi-Nagy & J. T. Framo (Eds.), *Intensive family therapy* (pp. 213–243). Hagerstown, MD: Harper & Row.

Braaten, L. J. (1974). Development phases of encounter groups: A critical review of models and a new proposal. *Interpersonal Development, 75,* 112–129.

Brofenbrenner, U. (1986). Ecology of the family as a context for human development. *Developmental Psychology, 22,* 723–742.

Brown, B. (1995). *Who are America's disconnected youth?* Paper presented at the conference America's Disconnected Youth: Towards a Preventive Strategy. Washington, DC.

Brown, W. K., Zimmerman, B., Jenkins, R. L., & Rhodes, W. A. (1991). Recognizing delinquents who may need special help to avoid criminal conviction in adult life. *Juvenile and Family Court Journal, 42*(4), 35–40.

Buehler, R. E., & Patterson, G. R. (1996). The reinforcement of behavior in institutional settings. *Behaviour Research and Therapy, 4,* 157–167.

Butts, J. A., & Snyder, H. N. (1992, September). Restitution and juvenile recidivism. *Juvenile Justice Bulletin,* Washington, DC: Office of Juvenile Justice and Delinquency Prevention.

Caplan, N., Choy, M. H., & Whitmore, J. K. (1992). Indochinese refugee families and academic achievement. *Scientific American, 266*(2), 36–42.

Carr, M. B. (2001, Fall). Risk and protective factors among youth offenders. *Adolescence,* 1–13.

Carter, J. (2003). Personal communication.

Chamberlain, P., & Rosicky, J. G. (1995). The effectiveness of family therapy in the treatment of adolescents with conduct disorders and delinquency. *Journal of Marital and Family Therapy, 21,* 441–459.

Clark, D. (1997). *Puppies for sale.* Deerfield Beach, FL: Health Communications.

Clark, R. D., & Shields, G. (1997). Family communication and delinquency. *Adolescence, 32,* 81–93.

Cohen, M. A. (1998). The monetary value of saving a high-risk youth. *Journal of Quantitative Criminology, 14,* 5–33.

Coie, J. D., Dodge, K. A., & Coppotelli, H. (1982). Dimensions and types of social status: A cross-age perspective. *Developmental Psychology, 18,* 557–570.

Coleman, J. S. (1988). Social capital in the creation of human capital. *American Journal of Sociology, 94,* (Suppl. 95), S95–S120.

Comer, J. (1998, July). Keynote address at the U.S. Department of Education, Office of Special Education and Rehabilitation Services Annual Conference. Washington, DC.

Conkle, K. (2001). Personal communication.

Corbitt, W. A. (2000). Violent crimes among juveniles. In *The FBI Law Enforcement Bulletin.* Washington, DC: Federal Bureau of Investigation in association with the Gale Group and Look Smart.

Cowen, P. S. (2001). Effectiveness of a parent education intervention for at risk families. *Journal of the Society of Pediatric Nurses, 6*(2), 73–82.

Crime in the United States 2000 (2001). Washington, DC: U.S. Government Printing Office.

Davidson, W. S., & Redner, R. (1988). The prevention of juvenile delinquency: Diversion from the juvenile justice system. In E. L. Cowen, R. P. Lorion, & J. Ramos-McKay (Eds.), *Fourteen ounces of prevention: A handbook for practitioners* (pp. 123–137). Washington, DC: American Psychological Association.

Dembo, R., Williams, L., Wothke, W., Schmeidler, J. & Brown, C. H. (1992). Role of family factors, physical abuse, and sexual victimization experiences in high-risk youths' alcohol and other drug use and delinquency: A longitudinal model. *Violence and Victims, 7*(3), 245–266.

Derzon, J. H., & Lipsey, M. W. (2000). *The correspondence of family features with problem, aggressive, criminal, and violent behavior.* Unpublished manuscript, Institute for Public Policy Studies, Vanderbilt University.

Dishion, T. J., & Andrews, D. W. (1995). Preventing escalation in problem behaviors with high-risk young adolescents: Immediate and 1-year outcomes. *Journal of Consulting and Clinical Psychology, 63,* 538–548.

Dishion, T. J., Andrews, D. W., Kavanagh, K., & Soberman, L. H. (1996). Preventive interventions for high risk youth: The Adolescent Transitions Program. In B. McMahon & R. D. Peters

(Ed.), *Conduct disorders, substance abuse and delinquency: Prevention and early intervention approaches* (pp. 184–214). Newbury Park, CA: Sage.

Dishion, T. J., & Kavanagh, K. (2003). *Intervening in adolescent problem behavior: A family-centered approach.* New York: Guilford.

Dishion, T. J., McCord, J., & Poulin, F. (1999). When intervention harms: Peer groups and problem behavior. *American Psychologist, 54,* 1–10.

Doherty, W. (1995). *Soul searching: Why psychotherapy must promote moral development.* New York: Basic Books.

Doherty, W. (2000). Family therapists, community, and civic renewal. *Family Process, 39.*

Dornfield, M., & Kruttschnitt, C. (1992). Do the stereotypes fit? Mapping gender-specific outcomes and risk factors. *Criminology, 30*(3), 397–419.

Duncan, B. L., & Miller, S. D. (2000). *The heroic client: Doing client directed, outcome-informed therapy.* San Francisco: Jossey-Bass.

Eccles, J. S., Midgley, C., Wigfield, A., Buchanan, C. M., Reuman, D., Flanagan, C., & MacIver, D. (1993). Development during adolescence: The impact of stage-environment fit on young adolescents' experiences in schools and in families. *American Psychologist, 48,* 90–101.

Egeland, B., & Farber, E. A. (1984). Infant-mother attachment: Factors related to its development and changes over time. *Child Development, 55,* 753–771.

Elizur, J., & Minuchin, S. (1989). *Institutionalizing madness: Families, therapy, and society.* New York: Basic Books.

Elliott, D. S., Huizinga, D., & Menard, S. (1989). *Multiple problem youth: Delinquency, substance use, and mental health problems.* New York: Springer-Verlag.

Emens, E. F., Hall, N. W., Ross, C., & Zigler, E. F. (1996). Preventing juvenile delinquency: An ecological, developmental approach. In E. F. Zigler, S. L. Kagan, & N. W. Hall (Eds.), *Children, families & government: Preparing for the twenty-first century.* Cambridge, MA: Cambridge University Press.

Empey, L. T., & Erickson, M. L. (1972). *The Provo experiment: Evaluating community control of delinquency.* Lexington, MA: Lexington Books.

Epstein, J. L. (1983). Longitudinal effects of family–school-person interactions on student outcomes. *Research in Sociology of Education and Socialization, 4,* 101–127.

Estes, W. K., Koch, S., MacCorquodale, K., Meehl, P. E., Mueller, C. G., Schoenfeld, W. N., & Verplanck, W. S. (1954). *Modern learning theory: A critical analysis of five examples.* New York: Appleton-Century-Crofts.

Farrington, D. P. (1987). Early precursors of frequent offending. In J. Q. Wilson & G. C. Loury (Eds.), *From children to citizens: Vol. 3. Families, schools, and delinquency prevention* (pp. 27–50). New York: Springer-Verlag.

Farrington, D. P., Ohlin, L. E., & Wilson, J. Q. (1986). *Understanding and controlling crime.* New York: Springer-Verlag.

Federal Bureau of Investigation (1997). Unpublished data from 1980–97. Reported in the Office of Juvenile Justice and Delinquency Prevention Statistical Briefing Book. Retrieved from http://ojjdp.ncjrs.org.

Fiese, B., Tomocho, T., & Douglas, M. (2002). A review of 50 years of research on naturally occurring family routines and rituals: Cause for celebration? *Journal of Family Psychology, 16,* 381–390.

Fitzgerald, H. E., & Abrams, L. A. (1998, February 26). Applied developmental science: A scholarship based approach to university-community collaborations. Paper presented at the biennial meeting of the Society for Research on Adolescence, San Diego, CA.

Forgatch, M. (1991, June). Parent practices: Mediators of risk for antisocial behavior. In J. B. Reid (Chair), *A social interactional model of the development and prevention of antisocial behavior and conduct disorder.* Symposium conducted at the Third Biennial Conference on Community Research and Action, Tempe, AZ.

Fortune, J. C., & Hutson, B. A. (1984). Selecting models for measuring change when true experimental conditions do not exist. *Journal of Educational Research, 77,* 187–206.

Garbarino, J. (1999). *Lost boys: Why our sons turn violent and how we can save them.* New York: The Free Press.

Garmezy, N. (1985). Stress resistant children: The search for protective factors. In J. Stevensen, Jr. (Ed.), *Recent research in developmental psychopathology.* Oxford: Pergamon Press.

Gazda, G. M., Ginter, E. J., & Horne, A. M. (2001) *Group counseling and group psychotherapy: Theory and application.* Boston: Allyn and Bacon.

Geismar, L. L., & Wood, K. (1986). *Family and delinquency: Resocializing the young offender.* New York: Human Sciences Press.

Georgia Children and Youth Coordinating Council Report (1997). Atlanta, GA.

Glasser, W. (1985). *Control theory in the classroom.* New York: Harper and Row.

Godwin, C. D., & Helms, J. L. (2002). Statistics and trends in juvenile justice and forensic psychology. In Ribner, N. G. (Ed.), *The California school of professional psychology: Handbook of juvenile forensic psychology* (pp. 3–28). San Francisco: John Wiley & Sons, Inc.

Goldstein, A. P., Glick, B., Irwin, M. J., Pask-McCartney, C., & Rubama, I. (1989). *Reducing delinquency: Intervention in the community.* New York: Pergamon Press.

Goldstein, A. P., Sprafkin, R. P., Gershaw, N. J., & Klein, P. (1980). *Skill-streaming the adolescent.* Champaign, IL: Research Press.

Gordon, D. A., Arbuthnot, J., Gustafson, K. E., McGree, P., & Farrington, D. P. (1987). Early precursors of frequent offending. In J. Q. Wilson & G. C. Loury (Eds.), *From children to citizens: Vol. 3. Families, schools, and delinquency prevention* (pp. 27–50). New York: Springer-Verlag.

Gray-Ray, P., & Ray, M. C. (1990). Juvenile delinquency in the black community. *Youth and Society, 22*(1), 67–84.

Greenwood, P. W. (1996). Responding to juvenile crime: Lessons learned. *The Future of Children, 6*(3), 75–85.

Hawkins, J. D., Herrenkohl, T. I., Farrington, D. P., Brewer, D., Catalano, R. F., Harachi, T. W., & Cothern, L. (2000). Predictors of youth violence [Juvenile Justice Bulletin & Office of Juvenile Justice and Delinquency Prevention]. Washington, DC.

Henderson, A. (1989). *The evidence continues to grow: Parent involvement improves school achievement.* Columbia, MD: National Committee for Citizens in Education.

Henggeler, S. W., Melton, G. B., & Smith, L. A. (1992). Family preservation using multisystemic therapy: An effective alternative to incarcerating serious juvenile offenders. *Journal of Consulting & Clinical Psychology, 60,* 953–961.

Henggeler, S., Pickrel, S. G., & Brondino, M. (1999). Multisystemic treatment of substance-abusing and dependent delinquents: Outcomes, treatment fidelity, and transportability. *Mental Health Services Research, 1,* 171–184.

Henry, J. (1971). *Pathways to madness.* New York: Random House.

Hewlett, S., and West, C. (1998). *The war against parents: What we can do for America's moms and dads.* Boston, MA: Houghton Mifflin.

Hilliard, R., Gjerde, C., & Parker, L. (1986). Validity of two psychological screening measures in family practice: Personal inventory and family APGAR. *Journal of Family Practice, 23*(4), 345–349.

Hillman, J., & Ventura, M. (1992). *We've had a hundred years of psychotherapy—and the world's getting worse.* San Francisco: Harper.

Hill-Riley, J. (1994). Teachers' perceptions of families of difficult children as they affect contact with families. Doctoral dissertation.

Hoffman, L. (1981). *Foundations of family therapy.* New York: Basic Books.

Hoffman, L. (1990). Constructing realities: An art of lenses. *Family Process,* 1–2.

Hogansen, J., & Dishion, T. J. (2001). *Promoting change in parent group interventions for adolescent problem behavior.* Poster session presented at the 10th Scientific Meeting of the International Society for Research in Child and Adolescent Psychopathology, Vancouver, BC, Canada.

Howing, P. T., Wodarski, J. S., Kurtz, D., Gaudin, J. M., & Herbst. (1990). Child abuse and delinquency: The empirical and theoretical links. *Social Work, 35*(3), 244–249.

Hughes, R. (1994). A framework for developing family life education programs. *Family Relations, 43,* 74–80.

Huizienga, D., Loeber, R., Thornberry, T. P., & Cothern, L. (2000, November). *Co-occurrence of delinquency and other problem behaviors.* Washington, DC: Office of Juvenile Justice and Delinquency Prevention.

Imber-Black, E. (2002). Family rituals—From research to the consulting room and back again: Comment on the special section. *Journal of Family Psychology, 16,* 445–446.

Institute of Medicine. (1989). *Research on children and adolescents with mental/behavioral, and developmental disorders: Mobilizing a national initiative* (Contract N. 278-88-0025). Washington, DC: Department of Health and Human Services, National Institute of Mental Health.

Irvine, A. B., Biglan, A., Metzler, C. W., Smolkowski, K., & Ary, D. V. (1999). The effectiveness of a parenting skills program for parents of middle school students in small communities. *Journal of Consulting and Clinical Psychology, 67,* 811–825.

Jacobs, A., & Spradlin, W. (1974). *The group as agent of change.* New York: Behavioral Publications.

Jensen, G. F., & Rojek, D. G. (1998). *Delinquency and youth crime* (3rd ed.). Prospect Heights, IL: Waveland Press.

Jessor, R. (1991). Behavioral science: An emerging paradigm for social inquiry? In R. Jessor (Ed.), *Perspectives on behavioral science: The Colorado lectures* (pp. 309–316). Boulder, CO: Westview Press.

Jessor, R. (1993). Successful adolescent development among youth in high-risk settings. *American Psychologist, 48,* 117–126.

Joanning, H., Quinn, W., Thomas, F., & Mullen, R. (1992). Treating adolescent drug abuse: A comparison of family systems therapy, group therapy, and family drug education. *Journal of Marital and Family Therapy, 18*(4), 345–356.

Johnson, V., & Pandina, R. J. (1991). Effects of the family environment on adolescent substance use, delinquency, and coping styles. *American Journal of Drug and Alcohol Abuse, 17*(1), 71–88.

Kassenbaum, G., Ward, D., & Wilner, D. (1972). *Prison treatment and its outcome.* New York: Wiley.

Kelley, B. T., Loeber, R., Keenan, K., & DeLamatre, M. (1997). *Developmental pathways in boys' disruptive and delinquent behavior.* Washington, DC: Office of Juvenile Justice and Delinquency Prevention, December.

Koch, S. (1959). Epilogue. In S. Koch (Ed.), *Psychology: A study of a science* (Vol. 3, pp. 729–788). New York: McGraw-Hill.

Krisberg, B., & Howell, J. C. (1998). The impact of the juvenile justice system and prospects for graduated sanctions in a comprehensive strategy. In R. Loeber & D. Farrington (Eds.), *Serious and violent juvenile offenders: Risk factors and successful interventions.* Thousand Oaks, CA: Sage.

Kumpfer, K. L., & Tait, C. M. (2000). *Family skills training for parents and children.* Washington, DC: US Dept. of Justice, Office of Juvenile Justice and Delinquency Prevention.

LaCourseiere, R. (1980). *The life cycle of groups: Group development and stage theory.* New York: Human Sciences.

Laqueur, H. P. (1966). General systems theory and multiple family therapy. In J. Maserman (Ed.), *Handbook of psychiatric therapies.* New York: Grune & Stratton.

Laqueur, H. P. (1976). Multiple family therapy. In P. J. Guerin (Ed.), *Family therapy: Theory and practice.* New York: Gardner Press.

Larzelere, R., & Patterson, G. R. (1990). Parental management: Mediator of the effect of socioeconomic status on early delinquency. *Criminology, 28*(2), 301–324.

Lasch, C. (1979). *Haven in a heartless world: The family besieged.* New York: Basic Books.

Lawson, G., Lawson, A., & Rivers, P. C. *Essentials of chemical dependency counseling* (3rd ed.). Gaithersburg, MD: Aspen Publishers.

Liddle, H. A. (1996). Family based treatment for adolescent problem behaviors. *Journal of Family Psychology, 10,* 3–11.

Liddle, H. A. (1999). Theory in a family-based therapy for adolescent drug abuse. *Journal of Clinical Child Psychology, 28,* 521–532.

Lipsey, M. W. (1992). Juvenile delinquency treatment: A meta-analytic inquiry into the variability of effects (pp. 83–126). In T. Cook, H. Cooper, D. S. Cordray, et al. (Eds.), *Meta-analysis for explanation.* New York: Russell Sage Foundation.

Loeber, R., & Dishion, T. (1983). Early predictors of male delinquency: A review. *Psychological Bulletin, 94,* 68–69.

Loeber, R., Dishion, T. J., & Patterson, G. R. (1984). Multiple gating: A multistage assessment procedure for identifying youths at risk for delinquency. *Journal of Research in Crime and Delinquency, 21,* 7–32.

Loeber, R., Farrington, D. P., & Petechuk, D. (2003, May 1–19). *Child delinquency: Early intervention and prevention.* Child Delinquency Bulletin Series. Washington, DC: U.S. Department of Justice.

MacGregor, R. (1967). Progress in multiple impact theory. In N. W. Ackerman, F. L. Beatman, & S. N. Sherman (Eds.), *Expanding theory and practice in family therapy.* New York: Family Service Association.

MacGregor, R. (1972). Multiple impact psychotherapy with families. In G. D. Erickson & T. P. Hogan (Eds.), *Family therapy: An introduction to therapy and technique.* Monterey, CA: Brooks/Cole.

Mann, J. H. (1956). Experimental evaluations of role playing. *Psychological Bulletin, 53,* 227–234.

Martinson, R. (1974). What works? Questions and answers about prison reform. *The Public Interest,* 22–54.

McCord, J. (1978). A thirty-year follow-up of treatment effects. *American Psychologist, 33,* 284–289.

McCord, J. (1992). The Cambridge-Somerville study: A pioneering longitudinal-experimental study for delinquency prevention. In J. McCord & R. E. Tremblay (Eds.), *Preventing antisocial behavior: Interventions from birth through adolescence* (pp. 196–206). New York: Guilford Press.

McCord, J. (April 1997). Some unanticipated consequences of summer camps. Paper presented at the Biennial Meeting of the Society for Research in Child Development. Washington, DC.

McDonald, L., & Frey, H. E. (1999, November). *Families and schools together: Building relationships.* Washington, DC: U.S. Department of Justice, Office of Juvenile Justice and Delinquency Prevention.

McFarlane, W. R. (2002). *Multifamily groups in the treatment of severe psychiatric disorders.* New York: Guilford Press.

McFarlane, W. R., Link, B., Dushay, R., Marchal, J., & Crilly, J. (1995). Psychoeducational multiple family groups: Four-year relapse outcome in schizophrenia. *Family Process, 34*(2), 127–144.

McGaha, J., & Leoni, E. (1995). Family violence, abuse, and related family issues of incarcerated delinquents with alcoholic parents compared to those with nonalcoholic parents. *Adolescence, 30,* 473–482.

McNabb, T. R. (1983). Family function and depression. *Journal of Family Practice, 16,* 169–170.

McWhirter, J. J., McWhirter, B. T., McWhirter, A. M., & McWhirter, E. H. (1993). *At risk youth: A comprehensive response.* Pacific Grove, CA: Brooks Cole.

Mengel, M. (1987). The use of the family APGAR in screening for family dysfunction in a family practice center. *Journal of Family Practice, 24*(4), 394–398.

Minuchin, S. (1974). *Families and family therapy.* Cambridge, MA: Harvard University Press.

Minuchin, S., & Nichols, M. P. (1993). *Family healing: Tales of hope and renewal from family therapy.* New York: Free Press.

Moffitt, T. E. (1994). Adolescence-limited and life-course-persistent antisocial behavior: A developmental taxonomy. *Psychological Review, 100,* 674–701.

Multisite Violence Prevention Project. The Multisite Violence Prevention Project: Background and Overview (2004). *American Journal of Preventive Medicine, 26,* 3–11.

Murphey, J. M., Kellher, K., Pagano, M. E., Stulp, C., Nutting, P. A., Jellinek, M. S., Gardner, W., & Childs, G. E. (1998). The family APGAR and psychosocial problems in children: A report from ASPN and PROS. *Journal of Family Practice, 46,* 54–64.

Murray, C. A., & Cox, L. A. (1979). *Beyond retribution: Juvenile corrections and the chronic delinquent.* Beverly Hills: Sage.

National Research Council (1993). Commission on Behavioral and Social Sciences Education. *Losing generations: Adolescents in high risk settings.* Washington, DC: National Academy Press.

National School Boards Association (1984). *Toward better and safer schools: A school leader's guide to delinquency prevention.* Alexandria, VA: National School Boards Association.

Nelson, K. (1990). Family based services for juvenile offenders. *Children and Youth Services Review, 12*(3), 193–212.

Nichols, M. P., & Schwartz, R. C. (2004). *Family therapy: Concepts and methods.* Boston: Allyn and Bacon.

Office of Juvenile Justice and Delinquency Prevention (1995). *Delinquency prevention works.* Washington, DC: U.S. Department of Justice.

OJJDP Model Programs 1993 (1994). Washington, DC: Juvenile Justice Bulletin, U.S. Department of Justice.

OJJDP Statistical Briefing Book (2002, January 20). Retrieved from http://ojjdp.ncjrs.org/ojstatbb/html/qa251.html.

Patterson, G. R., & Fleischman, M. J. (1979). Maintenance of treatment effects: Some considerations concerning family systems and follow-up data. *Behavioral Therapy, 10,* 165–185.

Patterson, G. R., Crosby, L., & Vuchinich, S. (1992). Predicting risk for early police arrest. *Journal of Quantitative Criminology, 8*(4), 335–355.

Peeples, F., & Loeber, R. (1994). Do individual factors and neighborhood context explain ethnic differences in juvenile delinquency? *Journal of Quantitative Criminology, 10*(2), 141–157.

Petersilia, J., & Turner, S. (1993). Intensive probation and parole. In M. Tonry (Ed.), *Crime and justice: A review of research* (Vol. 17, pp. 281–336). Chicago: University of Chicago Press.

Pipher, M. (1994). *Reviving Ophelia.* New York: Putnam.

Pomeroy, E. C., Rubin, A., VanLianingham, L., & Walker, R. J. (1997). Straight talk: The effectiveness of a psychoeducational group intervention for heterosexuals with HIV/AIDS. *Research on Social Work Practice, 7,* 149–164.

Poulan, F., Dishion, T. J., & Buyrraston, B. (2001). Three year iatrogenic effects associated with aggregating high-risk adolescents in preventive interventions. *Applied Developmental Science, 5,* 214–224.

Puzzanchera, C., Stahl, A. L., Finnegan, T. A., Tierney, N., & Snyder, H. N. (2002). *Juvenile court statistics 1998.* Washington, DC: Office of Juvenile Justice and Delinquency Prevention (NCJ193696).

Puzzanchera, C., Stahl, A., Finnegan, T., Snyder, H., Poole, R., & Tierney, N. (2002). *Juvenile Court Statistics 1999.* Washington, DC: Office of Juvenile Justice and Delinquency Prevention.

Quinn, W. H. (1995). Expanding the focus of intervention: The importance of family/community relations. In K. Nelson & P. Adams (Eds.), *Reinventing human services: Community and family-centered practice.* New York: Aldine deGruyter.

Quinn, W. H. (1996a). Achieving harmony from tension of family advocacy. *Journal of Family Social Work, 1*(3), 83–98.

Quinn, W. H. (1996b). The client speaks out: Three domains of meaning. *Journal of Family Psychotherapy, 7*(2), 71–93.

Quinn, W. H. (1998). *Family solutions: A program for juvenile offenders, truant students and at-risk youth.* Athens, GA: University of Georgia.

Quinn, W. H. (1999). The family solutions program: A collaboration of the Athens/Clarke County Juveniles Court. In T. R. Chibucos & R. M. Lerner (Eds.), *Serving children and families through community-university partnerships* (pp. 89–101). Boston: Kluwer Academic.

Quinn, W. H. (2003). Multiple family group intervention and assessment: Issues and strategies. In K. Jordan (Ed.), *Handbook of couple and family assessment* (pp. 259–274). Hauppauge, NY: Nova Science Publishers.

Quinn, W. H., & Nagirreddy, C. (2001). Utilizing clients' voices in clinical supervision. The interpersonal process recall method. In R. Lee & S. Emerson (Eds.), *The eclectic supervisor.* Geist and Russell Publishers.

Quinn, W. H., & VanDyke, D. J. (2001). At-risk youth in the United States: Current status, family influences, and the Family Solutions Program. In I. Pervova, *People, Time, and Society* (pp. 60–85). St. Petersburg, Russia: St. Petersburg University Press.

Quinn, W. H., & VanDyke, D. J. (2004). A multiple family group intervention for first-time juvenile offenders: Comparisons with probation and drop-outs on recidivism. *Journal of Community Psychology, 32*(2), 177–200.

Quinn, W. H., Bell, K., & Ward, J. (1987). Family solutions for juvenile first offenders. *The Prevention Researcher, 4,* 10–12.

Quinn, W. H., Dotson, D., & Jordan, K. (1997). Dimensions of therapeutic alliance and their associations with outcome in family therapy. *Psychotherapy Research, 7*(4), 429–438.

Quinn, W. H., Hill, J., Wiley, G., & Dotson, D. (1994). The family–school intervention team: A meta-level and multisystemic approach. In C. Huber (Ed.), *Transitioning: individual to family counseling* (pp. 87–106). Alexandria, VA: American Counseling Association.

Quinn, W. H., Kuehl, B. P., Thomas, F. N., & Joanning, H. (1988). Families of adolescent drug abusers: Systemic interventions to attain drug-free behavior. *American Journal of Alcohol and Drug Abuse, 14,* 65–87.

Quinn, W. H., Sutphen, R., Michaels, M., & Gale, J. (1994). Juvenile offenders: Characteristics of at risk families and strategies for intervention. *Journal of Addictions and Offender Counseling, 15*(1), 2–23.

Quinn, W. H., VanDyke, D. J., & Kurth, S. (2002). A brief multiple family group model for juvenile offenders (pp. 226–251). In C. Figley (Ed.), *Brief therapy for the traumatized.* Westport, CT: Greenwood.

Rankin, J. H., & Kern, R. (1994). Parental attachment and delinquency. *Criminology, 32*(4), 495–515.

Reid, J. B. C. (1993). Prevention of conduct disorder before and after school entry: Relating interventions to development findings. *Development and Psychopathology, 5*, 243–262.

Ring, K. (1967). Experimental social psychology: Some sober questions about frivolous values. *Journal of Experimental Social Psychology, 3*, 113–123.

Rohrman, D. (1993). Combating truancy in our schools: A community effort. NAASP Bull Peeples, F. & Loeber, R. (1994) Do individual factors and neighborhood context explain ethnic differences in juvenile delinquency? *Journal of Quantitative Criminology, 10*(2), 141–157.

Romig, D. A., Cleland, C., & Romig, J. (1989). *Juvenile delinquency: Visionary approaches.* Columbus, OH: Merrill.

Roosa, M. W. (1991). Adolescent pregnancy programs collection: An introduction. *Family Relations, 40*, 370–372.

Rutter, M. (1980). *Changing youth in a changing society: Patterns of adolescent development and disorder.* Cambridge, MA: Harvard University Press.

Sameroff, A., & McDonough, S. (1984). The role of motor activity in human cognitive and social development. In E. Pollitt & P. Amante (Eds.), *Energy intake and activity* (pp. 331–353). New York: Alan R. Liss.

Sampson, R. J., & Lamb, J. H. (1994). Urban poverty and the family context of delinquency: A new look at structure and process in a classic study. *Child Development, 65*, 523–540.

Sanders, M. R. (1999). Triple P—positive parenting program: Towards an empirically validated multilevel parenting and family support strategy for the prevention of behavioral and emotional problems in children. *Clinical Child and Family Psychology Review, 2*(2), 71–90.

Sayger, T. V., Horne, A. M., & Glaser, B. A. (1993). Marital satisfaction and social learning family therapy for child conduct problems: Generalization of treatment effects. *Journal of Marital and Family Therapy, 19*(4), 393–402.

Schneider, B. (1995, August 23). Social capital in the community and schools. Paper presented at the American Sociology Association Annual Conference, Washington, DC.

Scholte, E. M. (1991). Social control theory, educational intervention, and the prevention of delinquency. In J. Junger-Tas & L. Boendermaker (Eds.), *The future of the juvenile justice system* (pp. 167–180). Noordwijkerhout: The Netherlands.

Schorr, L. B. (1988). *Within our reach: Breaking the cycle of disadvantage.* New York: Anchor Press.

Schur, E. (1973). *Radical non-intervention: Re-thinking the best interests of children.* Lexington, MA: D.C. Heath.

Select Committee on Children, Youth, and Families. (1988, March 9). *Youth and violence: The current crisis* (No. 84–898). Washington, DC: U.S. Government Printing Office.

Sexton, R. L. (1996). Tackling juvenile crime. *Journal of Social, Political, and Economic Studies, 1*(2), 191–197.

Shapiro, J., Neinstein, L. S., & Rabinovitz, S. (1987). The family APGAR: Use of a simple family-function screening test with adolescents. *Family Systems Medicine, 5*(2), 220–227.

Shereran, T., Marvin, R. S., & Pianta, R. C. (1997). Mothers' resolution of their child's diagnosis and self-reported measures of parenting stress, marital relations, and social support. *Journal of Pediatric Psychology, 22*(2), 197–212.

Shumaker, A. W. (1997). Preventing juvenile delinquency through early intervention. *Journal of Family Social Work, 2*(3), 73–85.

Simons, R. L., Whitbeck, L. B., Conger, R. D., & Conger, K. J. (1991). Parenting factors, social skills, and value commitments as precursors to school failure, involvement with deviant peers, and delinquent behavior. *Journal of Youth and Adolescence, 20*, 645–664.

Smale, G. (1995). Integrating community and individual practice: A new paradigm for practice (pp. 59–80). In K. Nelson & P. Adams (Eds.), *Reinventing human services: Community and family centered practice.* NY: Aldine de Gruyter.

Smilkstein, G. The family APGAR: A proposal for a family function test and its use by physicians. *Journal of Family Practice, 6*, 1231–1239.

Smilkstein, G., Ashworth, C., & Montalvo, D. (1982) Validity and reliability of the family APGAR as a test of family function. *Journal of Family Practice, 15*, 303–311.

Smith, C., & Krohn, M. D. (1995). Delinquency and family life among male adolescents: The role of ethnicity. *Journal of Youth and Adolescence, 24*(1), 69–93.

Smith, E. P., Gorman-Smith, D., Quinn, W. H., Rabiner, D. L., Tolan, P. H., Winn, D. M., & the Multisite Violence Prevention Project. Community-based multiple family groups to prevent and reduce violent and aggressive behavior: The Great Family program. *American Journal of Preventive Medicine, 26*, 39–48.

Smith, M. B. (1968). School and home: Focus on achievement. In A. H. Passow (Ed.), *Developing programs for the educationally disadvantaged.* New York: Teachers College Press.

Smith, W. A. (1991). *Social structure, family structure, childrearing, and delinquency: Another look.* Research Report 33. Stockholm, Sweden: University of Stockholm Press.

Snyder, H. (2002). *Juvenile arrests 2000.* Washington, DC: Office of Juvenile Justice and Delinquency Prevention.

Snyder, H. N., & Sickmund, M. (1995). *Juvenile offenders and victims: A national report* [Preview]. National Center for Juvenile Justice, Pittsburgh, PA.

Snyder, H. N., & Sickmund, M. (1999). Juvenile offenders and victims: 1999 National Report. Washington, DC: Office of Juvenile Justice and Delinquency Prevention.

Snyder, H. N., Sickmund, M., & Poe-Yamagata, E. (1996). *Juvenile offenders and victims: 1996 update on violence.* Washington, DC: Department of Justice, Office of Juvenile Justice and Delinquency Prevention.

Stattin, H., & Klackenberg-Larsson, I. (1993). Early language and intelligence development and their relationship to future criminal behavior. *Journal of Abnormal Psychology, 102*(3), 369–378.

Steinglass, P. (1995). The clinical power of research. *Family Process, 34*(2), 125–126.

Steinglass, P., Bennett, A., Wolin, S., & Reiss, D. (1987). *The alcoholic family.* NY: Basic Books.

Steinhauer, P. D., Santa-Barbara, J., & Skinner, H. (1984). The process model of family functioning. *Canadian Journal of Psychiatry, 29*, 77–87.

Stouthamer-Loeber, M., Loeber, R., VanKammen, W. B., & Zhang, Q. (1995). Uninterrupted delinquent careers: The timing of parental help-seeking in juvenile court contact. *Studies of Crime and Crime Prevention*, 4, 236–251.

Stouthamer-Loeber, M., Loeber, R., Wei, E., Farrington, D. P., & Wikstrom, P. H. (2002). Risk and promotive effects in the explanation of persistent serious delinquency in boys. *Journal of Consulting and Clinical Psychology, 70*(1), 111–123.

Tagiuri, R. (1968). The concept of organizational climate. In R. Tagiuri & G. H. Litwin (Eds.), *Organizational climate: Exploration of a concept* (pp. 10–32). Cambridge, MA: Harvard University Press.

Tarolla, S. M., Wagner, E. F., Rabinowitz, J., & Tubman, J. G. (2002). Understanding and treating juvenile offenders: A review of current knowledge and future directions. *Aggression and Violent Behavior, 7*(2), 125–143.

Taylor, B. K. (1990). *Imagine no possessions: Towards a sociology of poverty.* New York: Harvester Wheatsheaf.

Thornberry, T. P., Smith, C. A., Rivera, C., Huizinga, D., & Stouthamer-Loeber, M. (1999). *Family disruption and delinquency* [Bulletin]. Washington, DC: Department of Justice, Office of Justice Programs, Office of Juvenile Justice and Delinquency Prevention.

Todd, T. C., & Selekman, M. D. (1991). *Family therapy approaches with adolescent substance abusers.* Boston, MA: Allyn and Bacon.

Tremblay, R. E., Masse, B., Perron, D., Leblanc, M., Schwartzman, A. E., & Ledingham, J. E. (1992). Early disruptive behavior, poor school achievement, delinquent behavior, and delinquent personality: Longitudinal analyses. *Journal of Consulting and Clinical Psychology, 60*, 64–72.

Trojanowicz, R. C., & Morash, M. (1992). *Juvenile delinquency concepts and control.* Englewood Cliffs, NJ: Prentice Hall.

VanDyke, D. J. (2000). Effectiveness of a multiple family group therapy in reducing recidivism for first-time juvenile offenders. Unpublished doctoral dissertation, University of Georgia.

Vgotsky, L. S. (1962). *Thought and language* (E. Hanfmann and G. Vakar, Trans.). Cambridge, MA: MIT Press.

Walker, H., & Silvester, R. (1991). Where is school along the path to prison? *Educational Leadership, 49*(1), 14–16.

Wasserman, G. A., Miller, L. S., & Cothern, L. (2000). *Prevention of serious and violent juvenile offending.* Washington, DC: U.S. Department of Justice, Office of Juvenile Justice and Delinquency Prevention.

Watzlawick, P., Weakland, J., & Fisch, R. (1967). *Pragmatics of human communication.* New York: Norton.

Wells, L. E., & Rankin, J. H. (1991). Families and delinquency: A meta-analysis of the impact of broken homes. *Social Problems, 38*, 71–83.

Widom, C. W. (1992). *The cycle of violence* (National Institute of Justice: Research in Brief). Washington, DC: Department of Justice.

Williams, S., Anderson, J., McGee, R., & Silva, P. A. (1990). Risk factors for behavioral and emotional disorder in preadolescent children. *Journal of the American Academy of Child and Adolescent Psychiatry, 29*(3), 413–419.

Williams, T., & Kornblum, W. (1985). *Growing up poor.* Lexington, MA: Lexington Books.

Yalom, I. D. (1975). *The theory and practice of group psychotherapy* (2nd ed.). New York: Basic Books.

Yamamoto, J., et al. (1967, May). Racial factors in patient selection. *American Journal of Psychiatry, 124,* 630–636.

Yoshikawa, H. (1995). Long-term effects of early childhood programs on social outcomes and delinquency. *The Future of Childhood, 5*(3), 51–75.

Zigler, E. (1990). Preface. In S. J. Meisels & J. P. Shonkoff (Eds.), *Handbook of early childhood intervention* (pp. ix–xiv). New York: Cambridge University Press.

Zigler, E., Taussig, C., & Black, K. (1992). Early childhood prevention: A promising preventative for juvenile delinquency. *American Psychologist, 47,* 997–1006.

Zingraff, M. T., Leiter, J., Johnsen, M. C, & Myers, K. A. (1994). Mediating effect of good school performance on the maltreatment-delinquency relationship. *Journal of Research in Crime and Delinquency, 31*(1), 62–91.

Zingraff, M. T., Leiter, J., Myers, K. A., & Johnsen, M. C. (1993). Child maltreatment and youthful problem behavior. *Criminology, 31,* 173–202.

Index

**Indianapolis
Marion County
Public Library**

Renew by Phone
269-5222

Renew on the Web
www.imcpl.org

For general Library information
please call 269-1700.